STEPHEN CURRY PRESENTS!
SPORTS SUPERHEROES VOL. #2
WILMA RUDOLPH
THE GRAPHIC NOVEL

To Megan, Zach, and Max . . . you are my superheroes (sorry, it was right there!)—JB

For Ella, Oscar, and Kim—my favorite superheroes, villains, and jokers!—RK

PENGUIN WORKSHOP
An imprint of Penguin Random House LLC
1745 Broadway, New York, New York 10019

First published in the United States of America by Penguin Workshop,
an imprint of Penguin Random House LLC, 2025

Text and illustrations copyright © 2025 by Joshua Bycel, Richard Korson, and Unanimous Media Holdings, LLC.
Creative Direction by Erick Peyton
Content Editor Kalyna Maria Kutny
Design by Mary Claire Cruz

Penguin Random House values and supports copyright. Copyright fuels creativity, encourages diverse voices, promotes free speech, and creates a vibrant culture. Thank you for buying an authorized edition of this book and for complying with copyright laws by not reproducing, scanning, or distributing any part of it in any form without permission. You are supporting writers and allowing Penguin Random House to continue to publish books for every reader. Please note that no part of this book may be used or reproduced in any manner for the purpose of training artificial intelligence technologies or systems.

PENGUIN is a registered trademark and PENGUIN WORKSHOP is a trademark of Penguin Books Ltd, and the W colophon is a registered trademark of Penguin Random House LLC.

Visit us online at penguinrandomhouse.com.

Library of Congress Cataloging-in-Publication Data is available.

Manufactured in China

ISBN 9780593382493 (pbk)   10 9 8 7 6 5 4 3 2 1 TOPL
ISBN 9780593382516 (hc)   10 9 8 7 6 5 4 3 2 1 TOPL

The text is set in Victory Speech.
The art in this book is human made.
The art was sketched on paper with pencil, then inked digitally in Clip Studio Paint. Colors were added digitally.

This is a work of nonfiction narrated by fictional characters. The events that unfold in the narrative are rooted in historical fact. Some characters have been created and the dialogue of some historical figures has been fictionalized in service of the narrative.

The authorized representative in the EU for product safety and compliance is Penguin Random House Ireland, Morrison Chambers, 32 Nassau Street, Dublin D02 YH68, Ireland, https://eu-contact.penguin.ie.

STEPHEN CURRY PRESENTS!

SPORTS SUPERHEROES

VOL. #2

WILMA RUDOLPH

THE GRAPHIC NOVEL

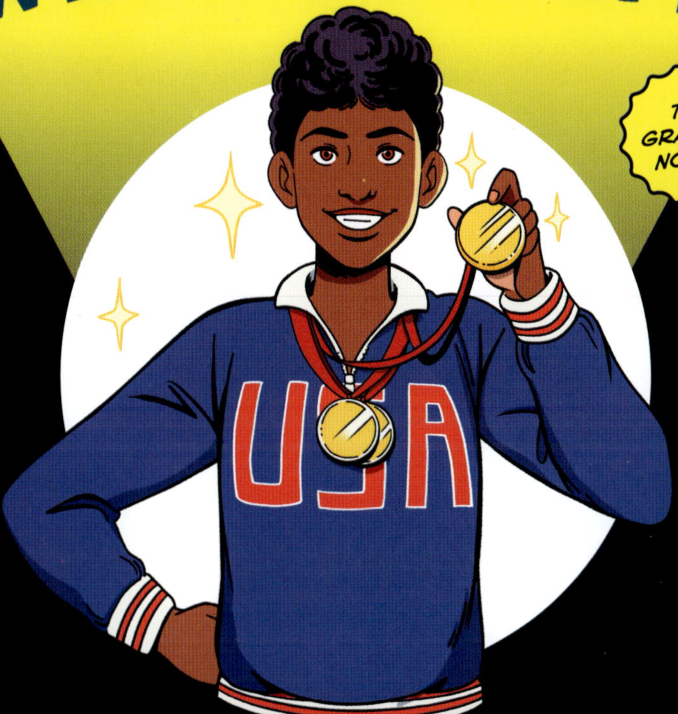

USA

BY JOSH BYCEL AND RICH KORSON

ILLUSTRATED BY BRITTNEY WILLIAMS

COLORS BY RICO RENZI

LETTERING BY HASSAN OTSMANE-ELHAOU

Unanimous Publishing

Penguin Workshop

CHAPTER ONE

THE SUPER RECAP!

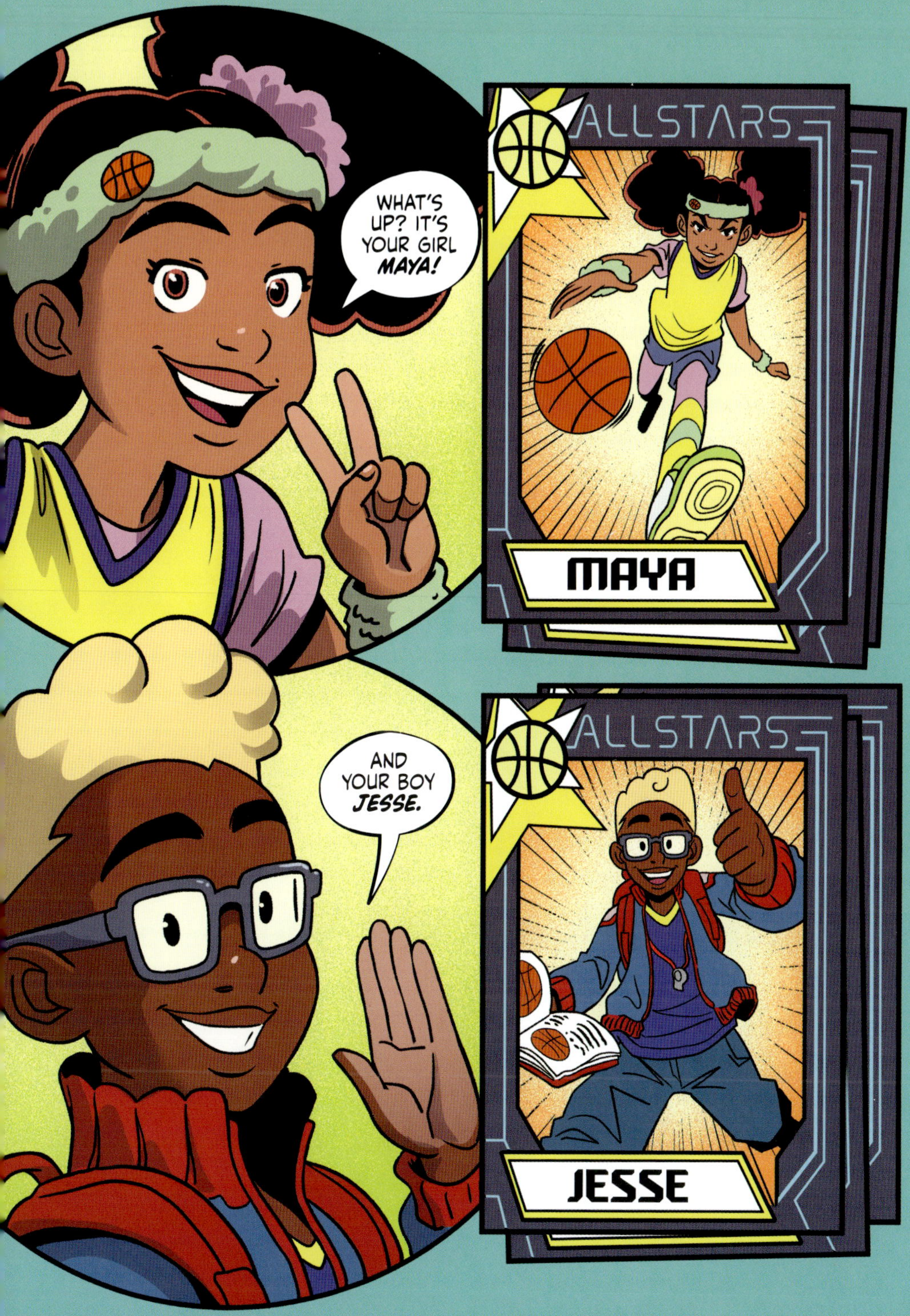
WHAT'S UP? IT'S YOUR GIRL MAYA!
ALLSTARS
MAYA
AND YOUR BOY JESSE.
ALLSTARS
JESSE

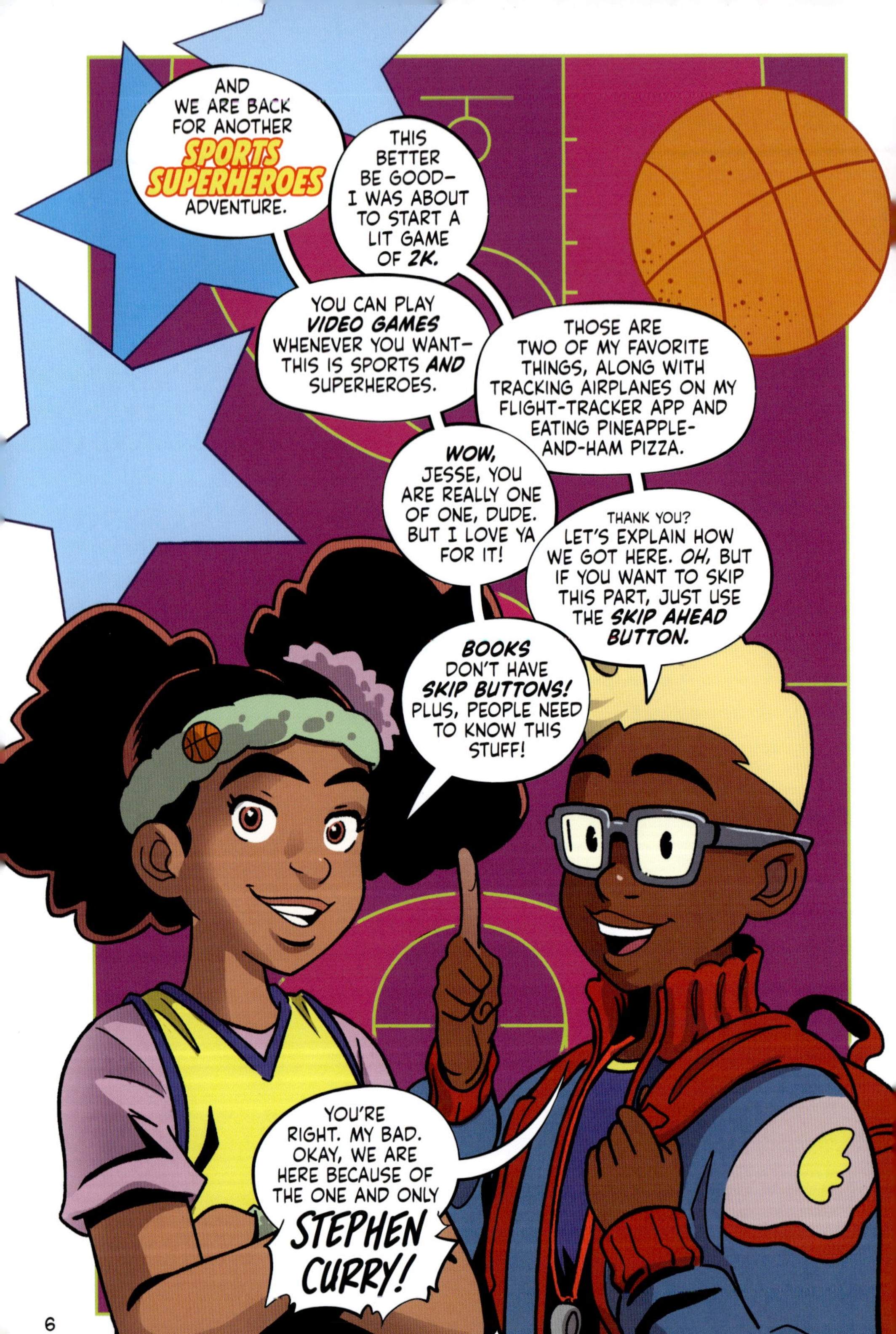
AND WE ARE BACK FOR ANOTHER SPORTS SUPERHEROES ADVENTURE.
THIS BETTER BE GOOD— I WAS ABOUT TO START A LIT GAME OF 2K.
YOU CAN PLAY VIDEO GAMES WHENEVER YOU WANT— THIS IS SPORTS AND SUPERHEROES.
THOSE ARE TWO OF MY FAVORITE THINGS, ALONG WITH TRACKING AIRPLANES ON MY FLIGHT-TRACKER APP AND EATING PINEAPPLE-AND-HAM PIZZA.
WOW, JESSE, YOU ARE REALLY ONE OF ONE, DUDE. BUT I LOVE YA FOR IT!
THANK YOU? LET'S EXPLAIN HOW WE GOT HERE. OH, BUT IF YOU WANT TO SKIP THIS PART, JUST USE THE SKIP AHEAD BUTTON.
BOOKS DON'T HAVE SKIP BUTTONS! PLUS, PEOPLE NEED TO KNOW THIS STUFF!
YOU'RE RIGHT. MY BAD. OKAY, WE ARE HERE BECAUSE OF THE ONE AND ONLY STEPHEN CURRY!

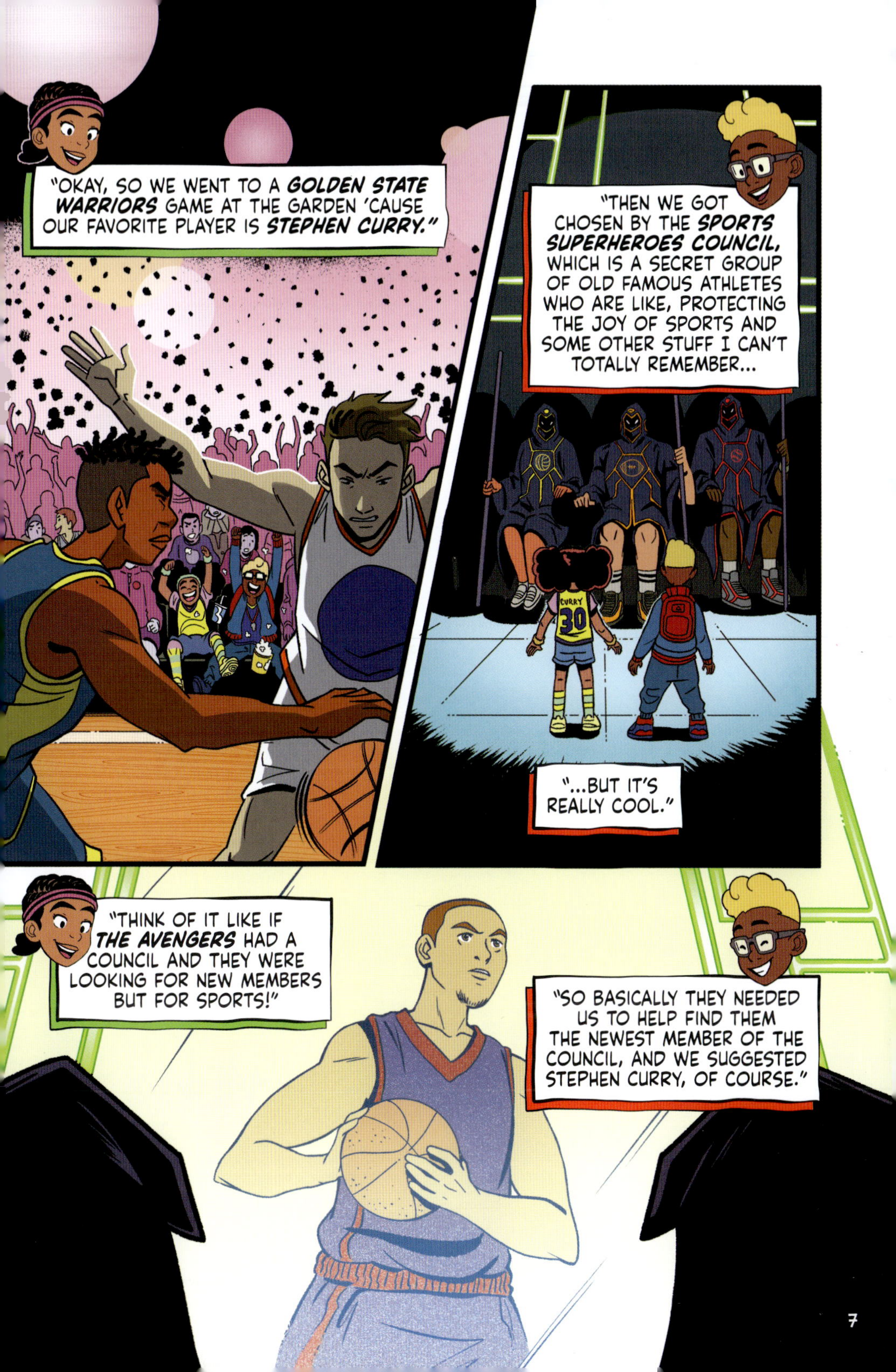
"OKAY, SO WE WENT TO A GOLDEN STATE WARRIORS GAME AT THE GARDEN 'CAUSE OUR FAVORITE PLAYER IS STEPHEN CURRY."
"THEN WE GOT CHOSEN BY THE SPORTS SUPERHEROES COUNCIL, WHICH IS A SECRET GROUP OF OLD FAMOUS ATHLETES WHO ARE LIKE, PROTECTING THE JOY OF SPORTS AND SOME OTHER STUFF I CAN'T TOTALLY REMEMBER...
CURRY
30
"...BUT IT'S REALLY COOL."
"THINK OF IT LIKE IF THE AVENGERS HAD A COUNCIL AND THEY WERE LOOKING FOR NEW MEMBERS BUT FOR SPORTS!"
"SO BASICALLY THEY NEEDED US TO HELP FIND THEM THE NEWEST MEMBER OF THE COUNCIL, AND WE SUGGESTED STEPHEN CURRY, OF COURSE."

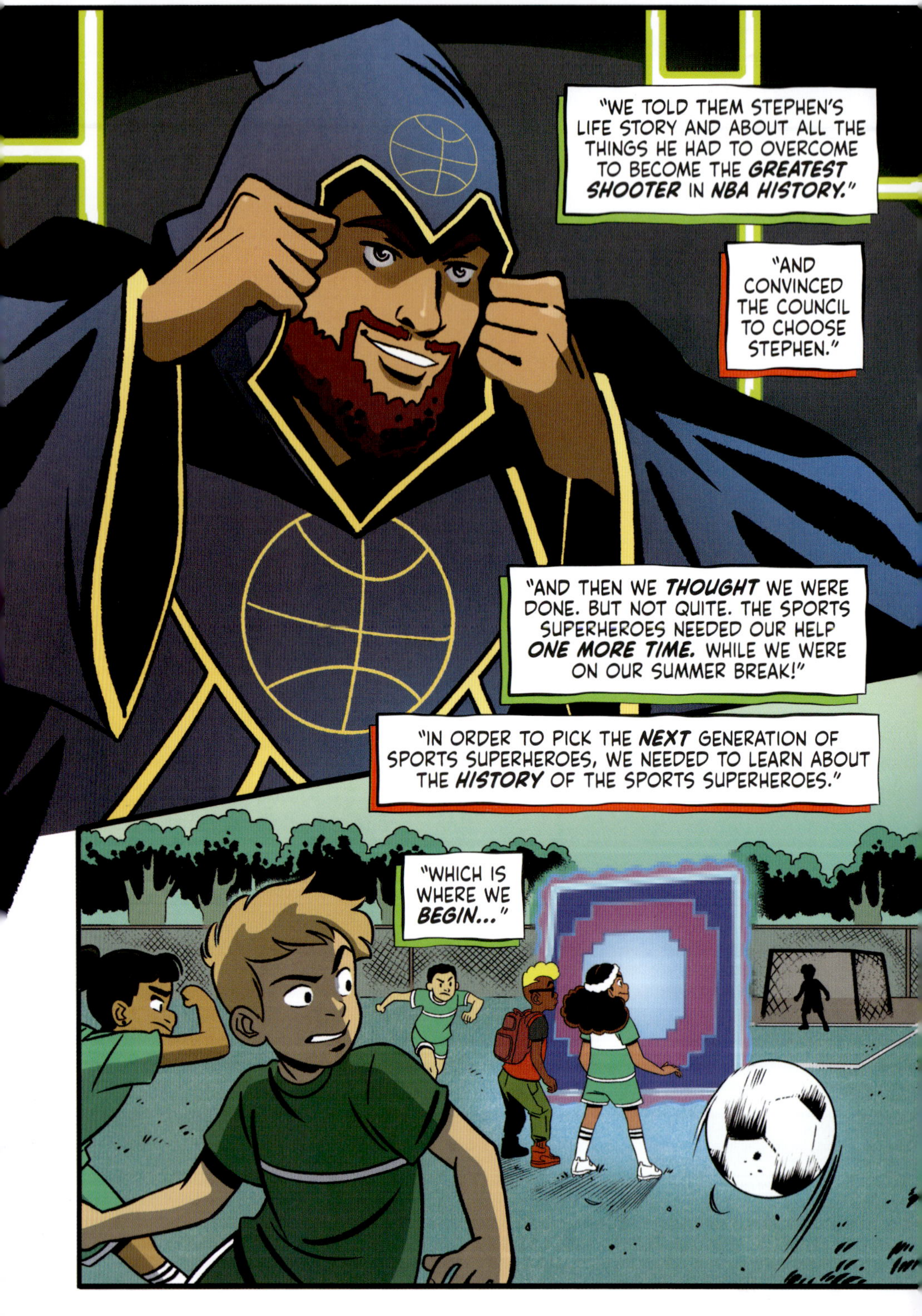
"WE TOLD THEM STEPHEN'S LIFE STORY AND ABOUT ALL THE THINGS HE HAD TO OVERCOME TO BECOME THE ***GREATEST SHOOTER*** IN ***NBA HISTORY.***"
"AND CONVINCED THE COUNCIL TO CHOOSE STEPHEN."
"AND THEN WE ***THOUGHT*** WE WERE DONE. BUT NOT QUITE. THE SPORTS SUPERHEROES NEEDED OUR HELP ***ONE MORE TIME.*** WHILE WE WERE ON OUR SUMMER BREAK!"
"IN ORDER TO PICK THE ***NEXT*** GENERATION OF SPORTS SUPERHEROES, WE NEEDED TO LEARN ABOUT THE ***HISTORY*** OF THE SPORTS SUPERHEROES."
"WHICH IS WHERE WE ***BEGIN...***"

CHAPTER TWO

BACK TO THE PAST

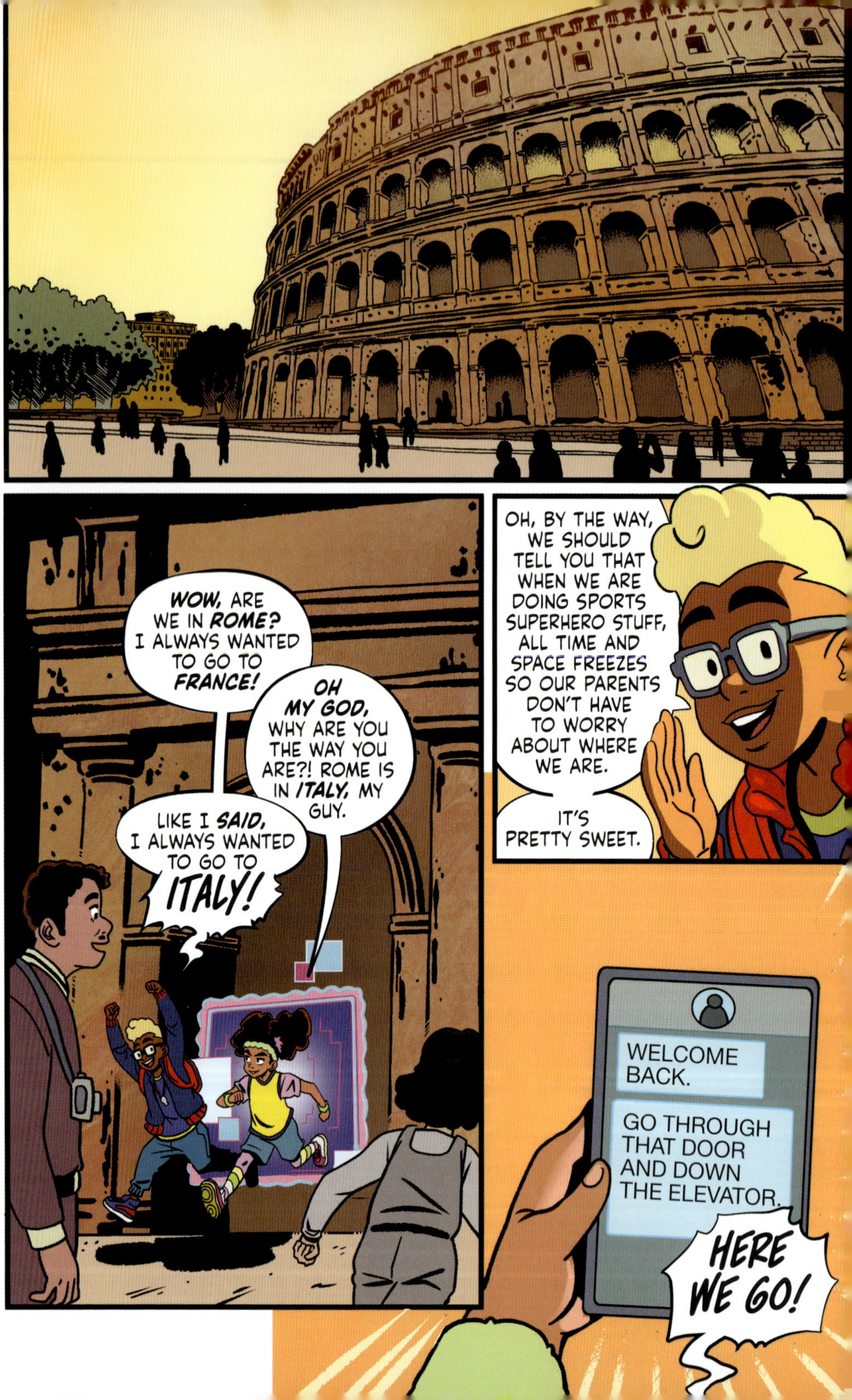
WOW, ARE WE IN ROME? I ALWAYS WANTED TO GO TO FRANCE!
OH MY GOD, WHY ARE YOU THE WAY YOU ARE?! ROME IS IN ITALY, MY GUY.
LIKE I SAID, I ALWAYS WANTED TO GO TO ITALY!
OH, BY THE WAY, WE SHOULD TELL YOU THAT WHEN WE ARE DOING SPORTS SUPERHERO STUFF, ALL TIME AND SPACE FREEZES SO OUR PARENTS DON'T HAVE TO WORRY ABOUT WHERE WE ARE.
IT'S PRETTY SWEET.
WELCOME BACK.
GO THROUGH THAT DOOR AND DOWN THE ELEVATOR.
HERE WE GO!

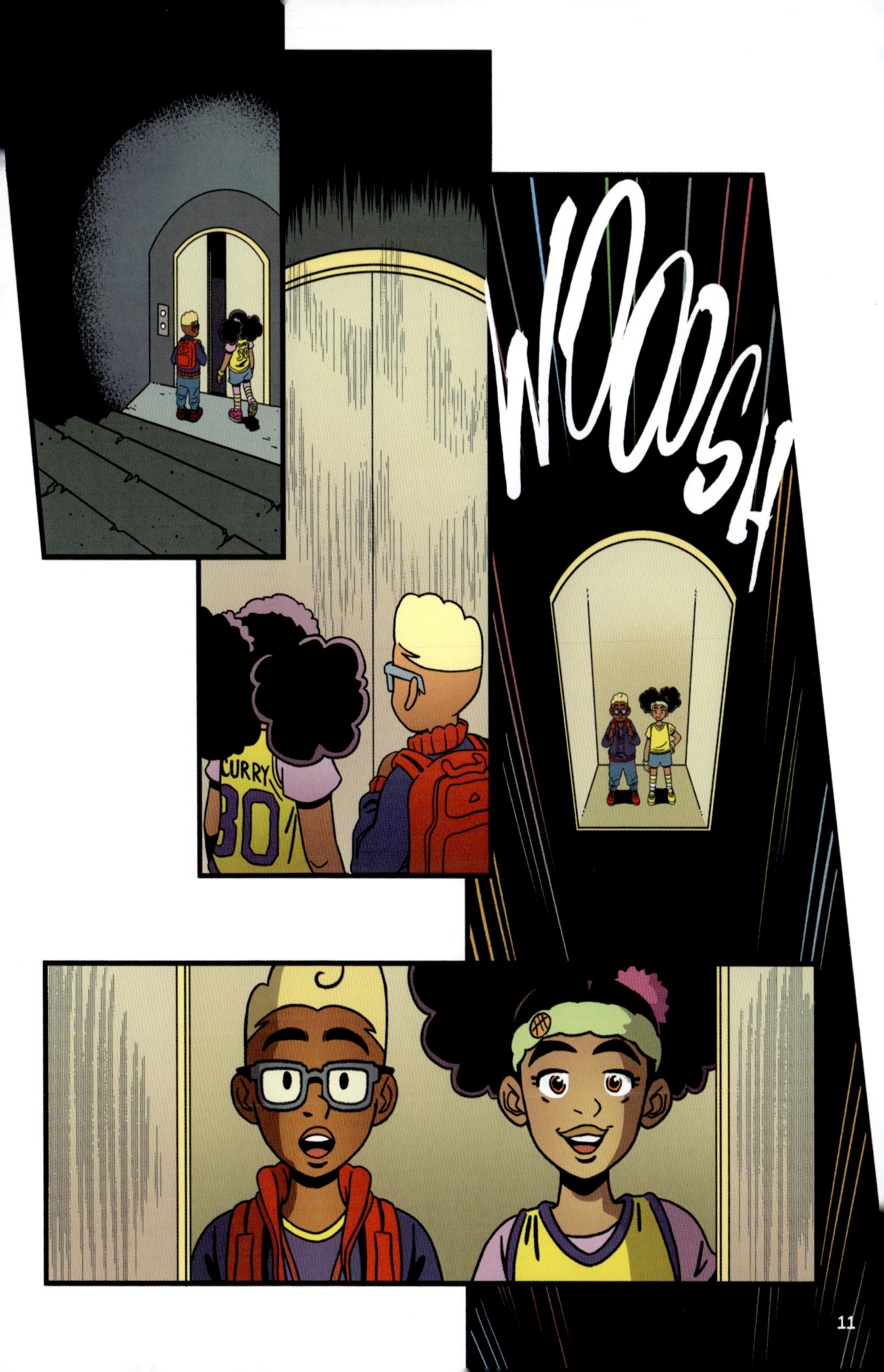
CURRY
30
WOOOSH

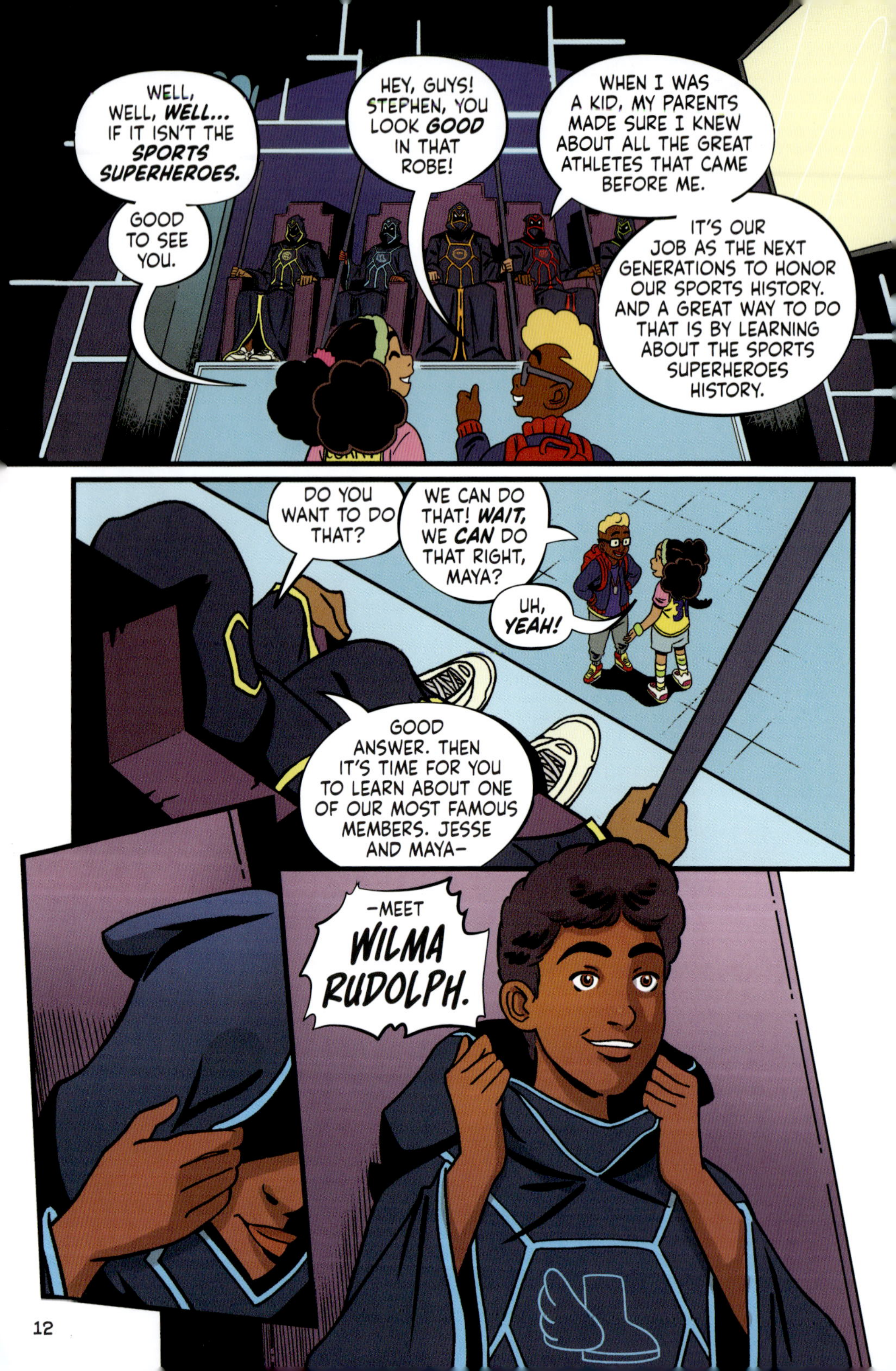
WELL, WELL, WELL... IF IT ISN'T THE SPORTS SUPERHEROES.
GOOD TO SEE YOU.
HEY, GUYS! STEPHEN, YOU LOOK GOOD IN THAT ROBE!
WHEN I WAS A KID, MY PARENTS MADE SURE I KNEW ABOUT ALL THE GREAT ATHLETES THAT CAME BEFORE ME.
IT'S OUR JOB AS THE NEXT GENERATIONS TO HONOR OUR SPORTS HISTORY. AND A GREAT WAY TO DO THAT IS BY LEARNING ABOUT THE SPORTS SUPERHEROES HISTORY.
DO YOU WANT TO DO THAT?
WE CAN DO THAT! WAIT, WE CAN DO THAT RIGHT, MAYA?
UH, YEAH!
GOOD ANSWER. THEN IT'S TIME FOR YOU TO LEARN ABOUT ONE OF OUR MOST FAMOUS MEMBERS. JESSE AND MAYA–
–MEET WILMA RUDOLPH.

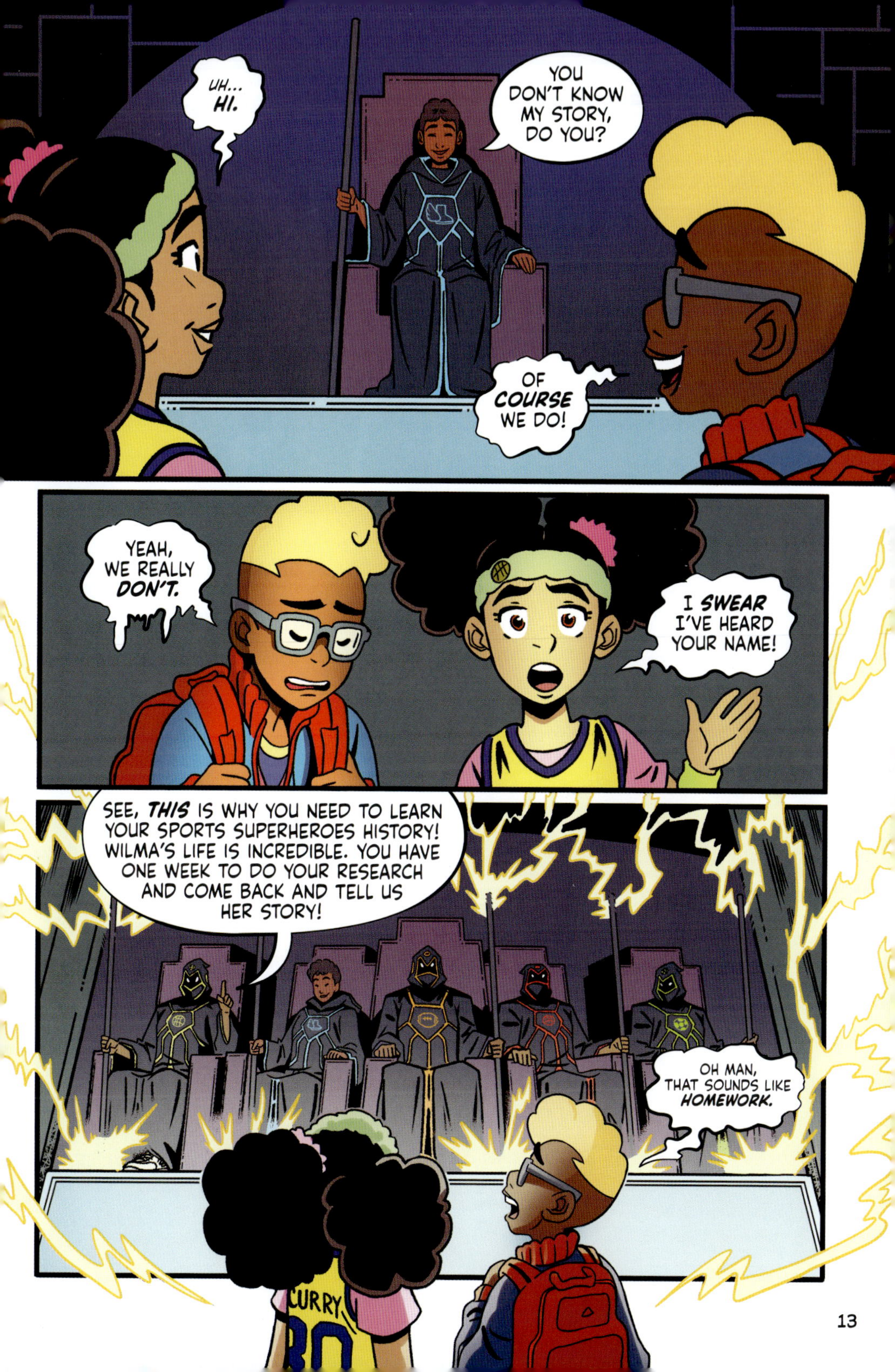
UH... HI.
YOU DON'T KNOW MY STORY, DO YOU?
OF COURSE WE DO!
YEAH, WE REALLY DON'T.
I SWEAR I'VE HEARD YOUR NAME!
SEE, THIS IS WHY YOU NEED TO LEARN YOUR SPORTS SUPERHEROES HISTORY! WILMA'S LIFE IS INCREDIBLE. YOU HAVE ONE WEEK TO DO YOUR RESEARCH AND COME BACK AND TELL US HER STORY!
OH MAN, THAT SOUNDS LIKE HOMEWORK.
CURRY
30

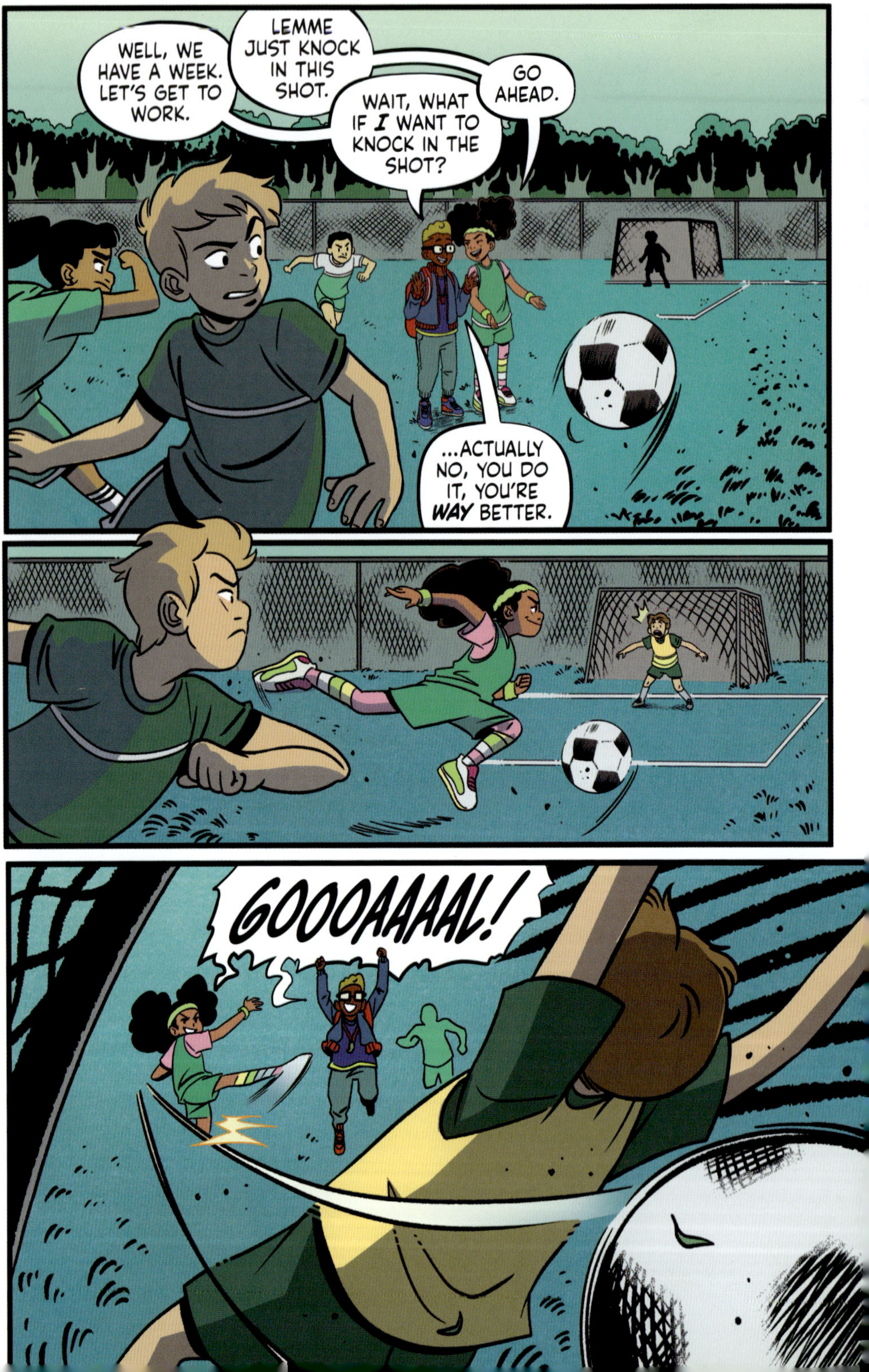
WELL, WE HAVE A WEEK. LET'S GET TO WORK.
LEMME JUST KNOCK IN THIS SHOT.
WAIT, WHAT IF *I* WANT TO KNOCK IN THE SHOT?
GO AHEAD.
...ACTUALLY NO, YOU DO IT, YOU'RE *WAY* BETTER.
GOOOAAAAL!

CHAPTER THREE

ONE WEEK LATER

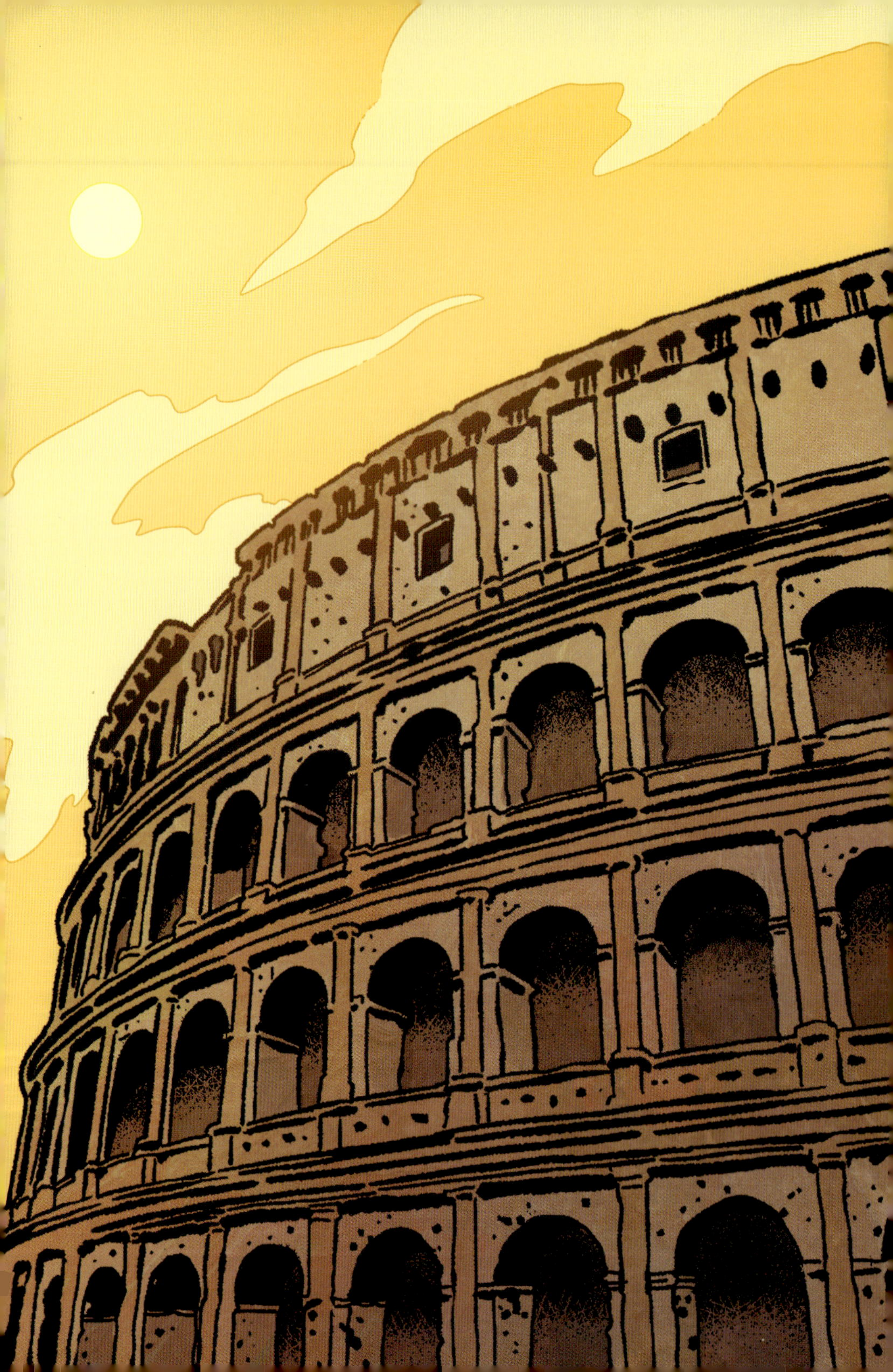

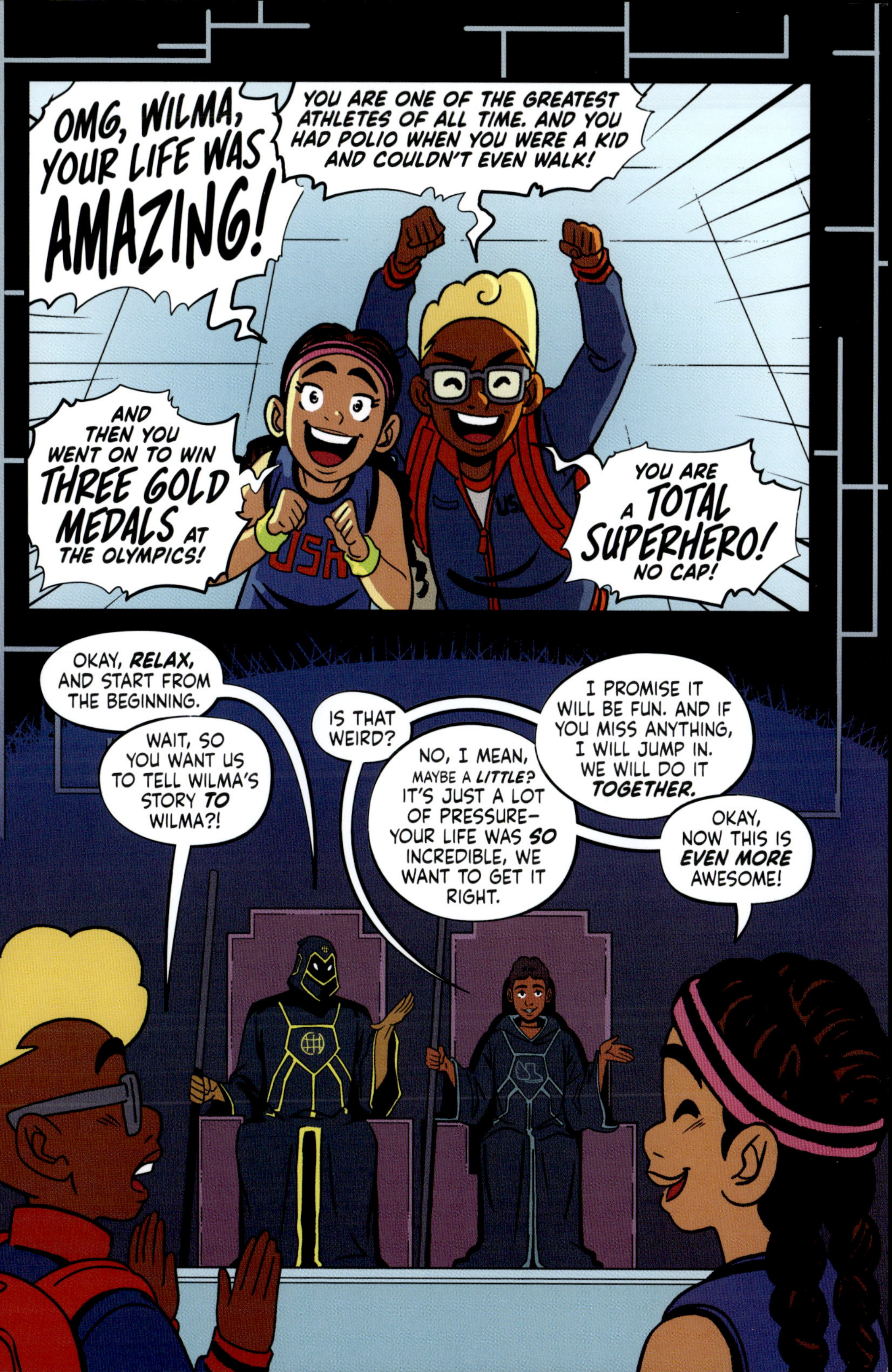

OMG, WILMA, YOUR LIFE WAS AMAZING!
YOU ARE ONE OF THE GREATEST ATHLETES OF ALL TIME. AND YOU HAD POLIO WHEN YOU WERE A KID AND COULDN'T EVEN WALK!
AND THEN YOU WENT ON TO WIN THREE GOLD MEDALS AT THE OLYMPICS!
YOU ARE A TOTAL SUPERHERO! NO CAP!
OKAY, RELAX, AND START FROM THE BEGINNING.
WAIT, SO YOU WANT US TO TELL WILMA'S STORY TO WILMA?!
IS THAT WEIRD?
NO, I MEAN, MAYBE A LITTLE? IT'S JUST A LOT OF PRESSURE—YOUR LIFE WAS SO INCREDIBLE, WE WANT TO GET IT RIGHT.
I PROMISE IT WILL BE FUN. AND IF YOU MISS ANYTHING, I WILL JUMP IN. WE WILL DO IT TOGETHER.
OKAY, NOW THIS IS EVEN MORE AWESOME!

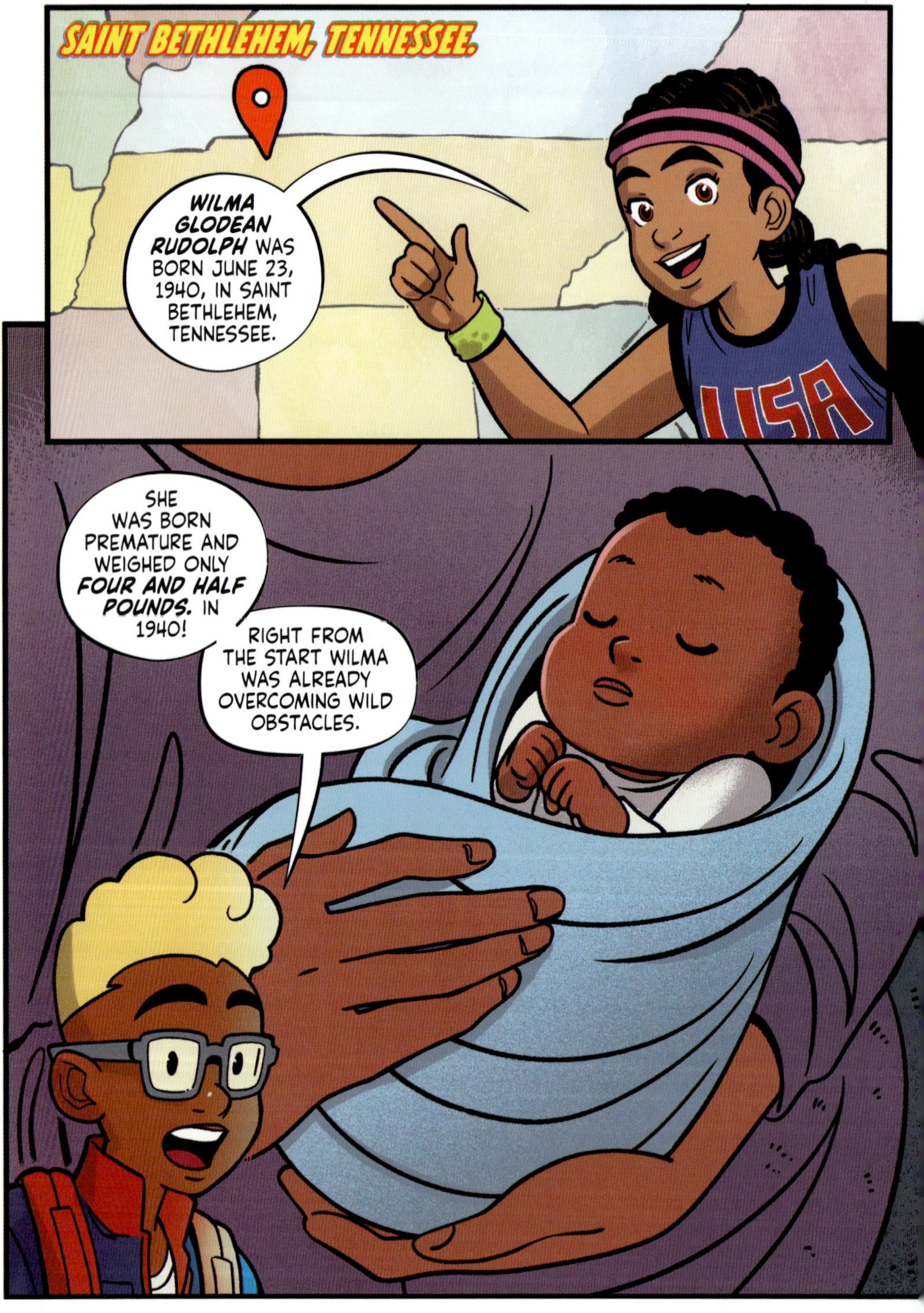
SAINT BETHLEHEM, TENNESSEE.
WILMA GLODEAN RUDOLPH WAS BORN JUNE 23, 1940, IN SAINT BETHLEHEM, TENNESSEE.
SHE WAS BORN PREMATURE AND WEIGHED ONLY FOUR AND HALF POUNDS. IN 1940!
RIGHT FROM THE START WILMA WAS ALREADY OVERCOMING WILD OBSTACLES.
USA

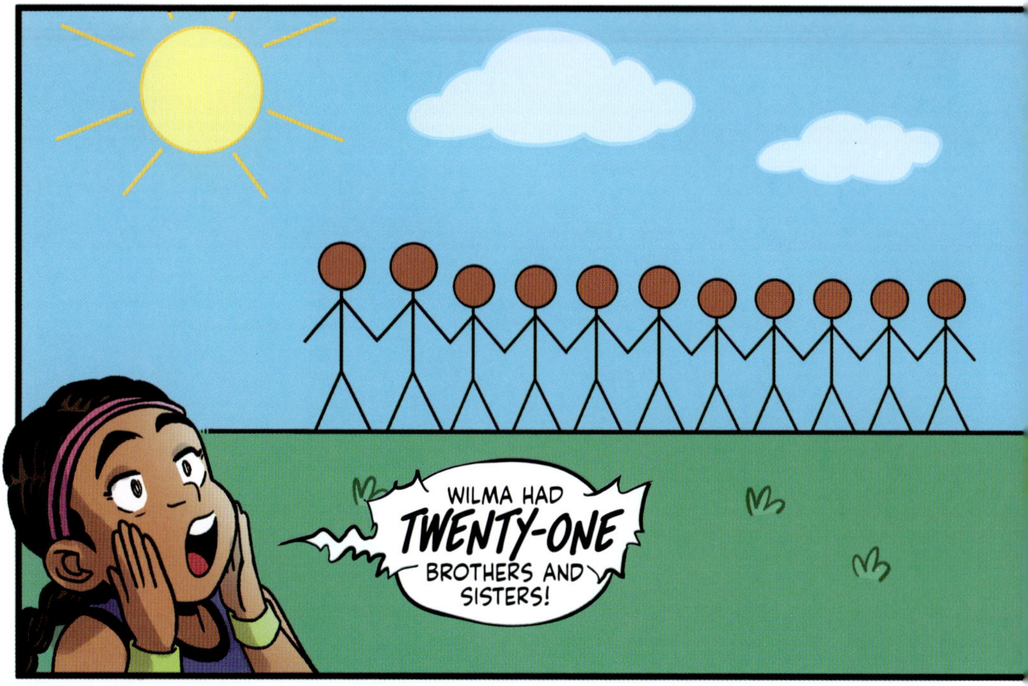
WILMA HAD TWENTY-ONE BROTHERS AND SISTERS!

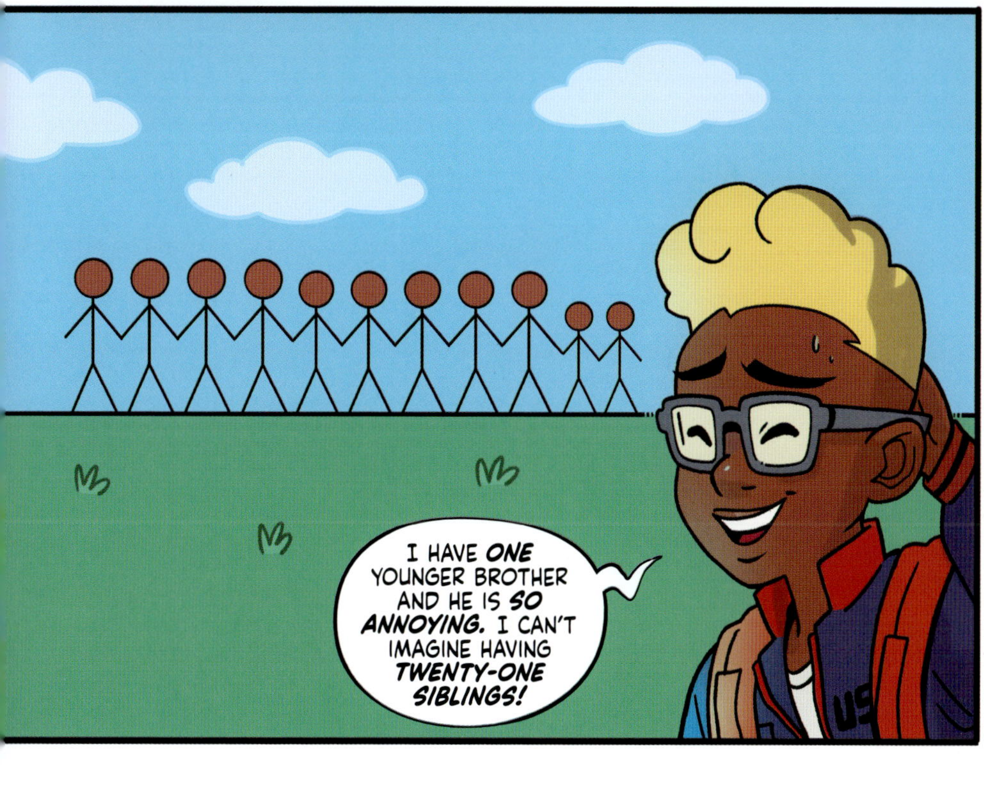
I HAVE ONE YOUNGER BROTHER AND HE IS SO ANNOYING. I CAN'T IMAGINE HAVING TWENTY-ONE SIBLINGS!

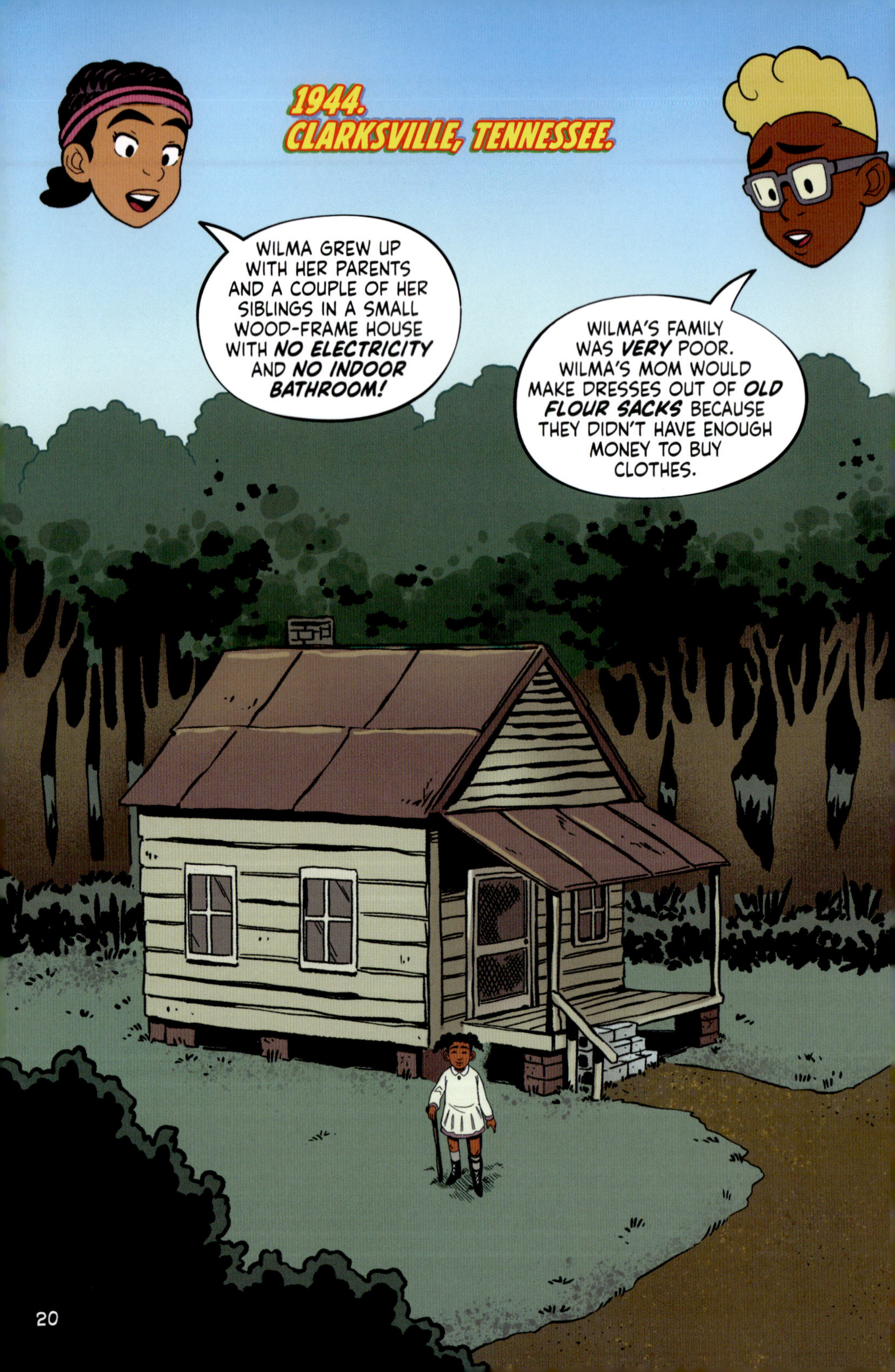
1944. CLARKSVILLE, TENNESSEE.
WILMA GREW UP WITH HER PARENTS AND A COUPLE OF HER SIBLINGS IN A SMALL WOOD-FRAME HOUSE WITH **NO ELECTRICITY** AND **NO INDOOR BATHROOM!**
WILMA'S FAMILY WAS **VERY** POOR. WILMA'S MOM WOULD MAKE DRESSES OUT OF **OLD FLOUR SACKS** BECAUSE THEY DIDN'T HAVE ENOUGH MONEY TO BUY CLOTHES.

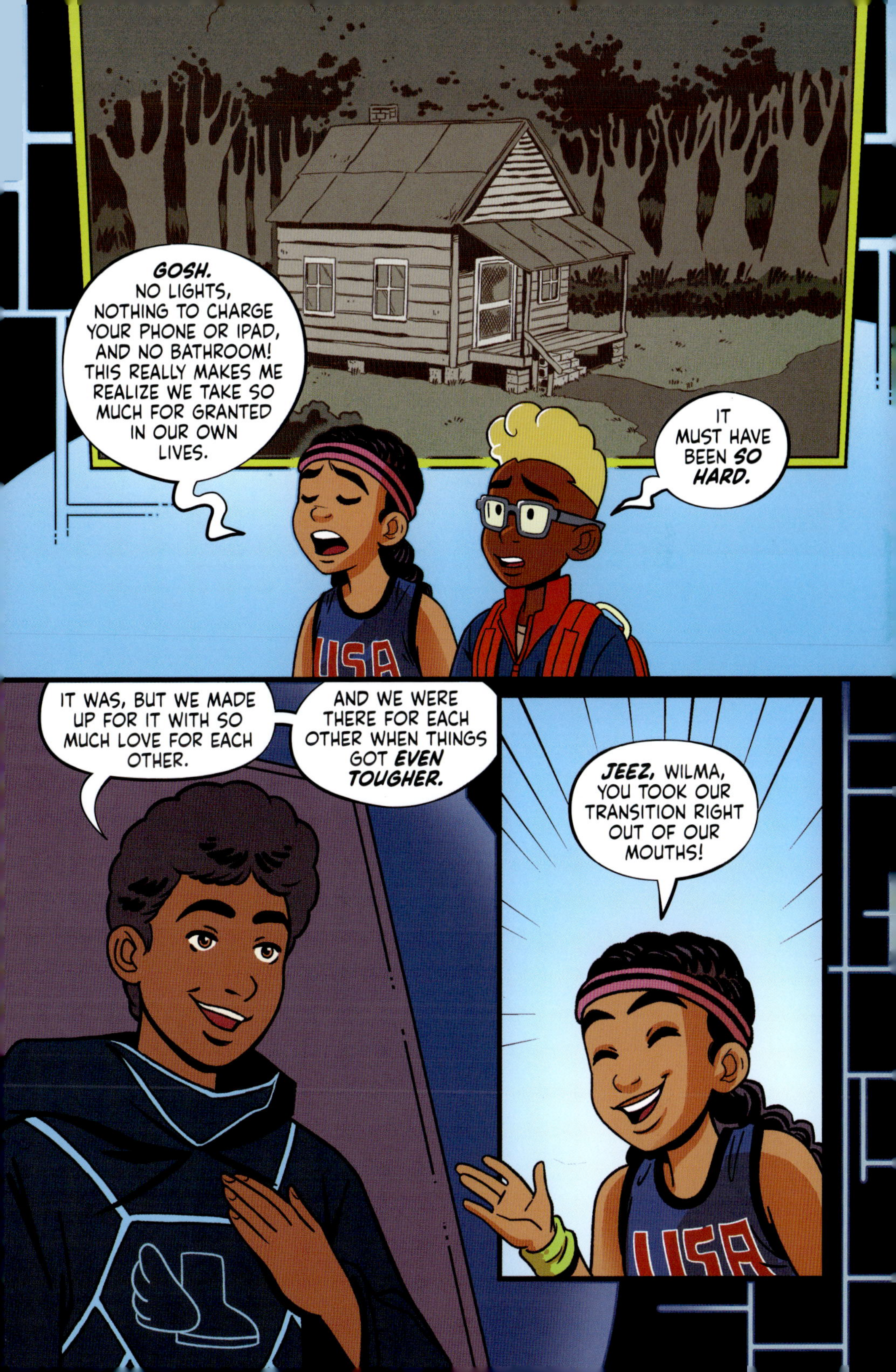
GOSH. NO LIGHTS, NOTHING TO CHARGE YOUR PHONE OR IPAD, AND NO BATHROOM! THIS REALLY MAKES ME REALIZE WE TAKE SO MUCH FOR GRANTED IN OUR OWN LIVES.
IT MUST HAVE BEEN SO HARD.
USA
IT WAS, BUT WE MADE UP FOR IT WITH SO MUCH LOVE FOR EACH OTHER.
AND WE WERE THERE FOR EACH OTHER WHEN THINGS GOT EVEN TOUGHER.
JEEZ, WILMA, YOU TOOK OUR TRANSITION RIGHT OUT OF OUR MOUTHS!
USA

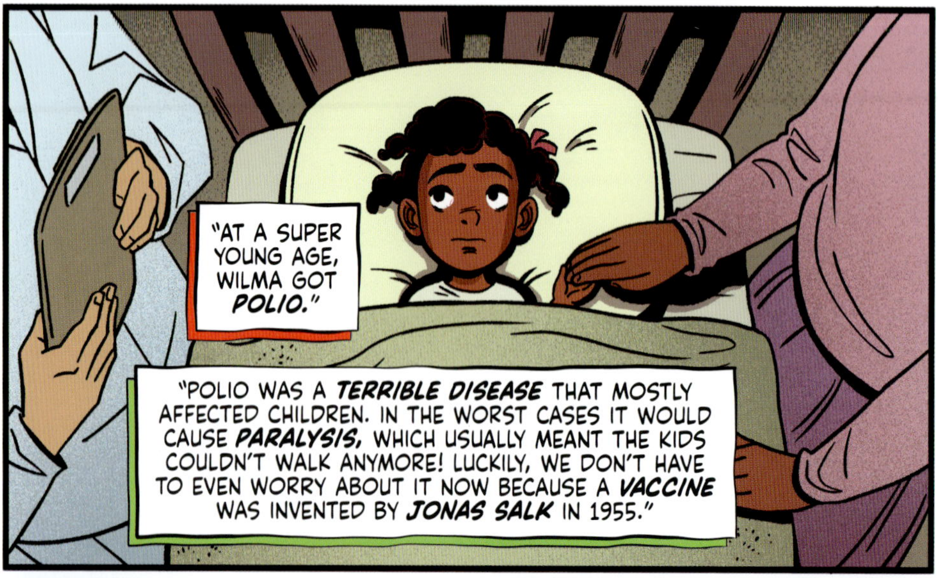
"AT A SUPER YOUNG AGE, WILMA GOT ***POLIO.***"
"POLIO WAS A ***TERRIBLE DISEASE*** THAT MOSTLY AFFECTED CHILDREN. IN THE WORST CASES IT WOULD CAUSE ***PARALYSIS,*** WHICH USUALLY MEANT THE KIDS COULDN'T WALK ANYMORE! LUCKILY, WE DON'T HAVE TO EVEN WORRY ABOUT IT NOW BECAUSE A ***VACCINE*** WAS INVENTED BY ***JONAS SALK*** IN 1955."

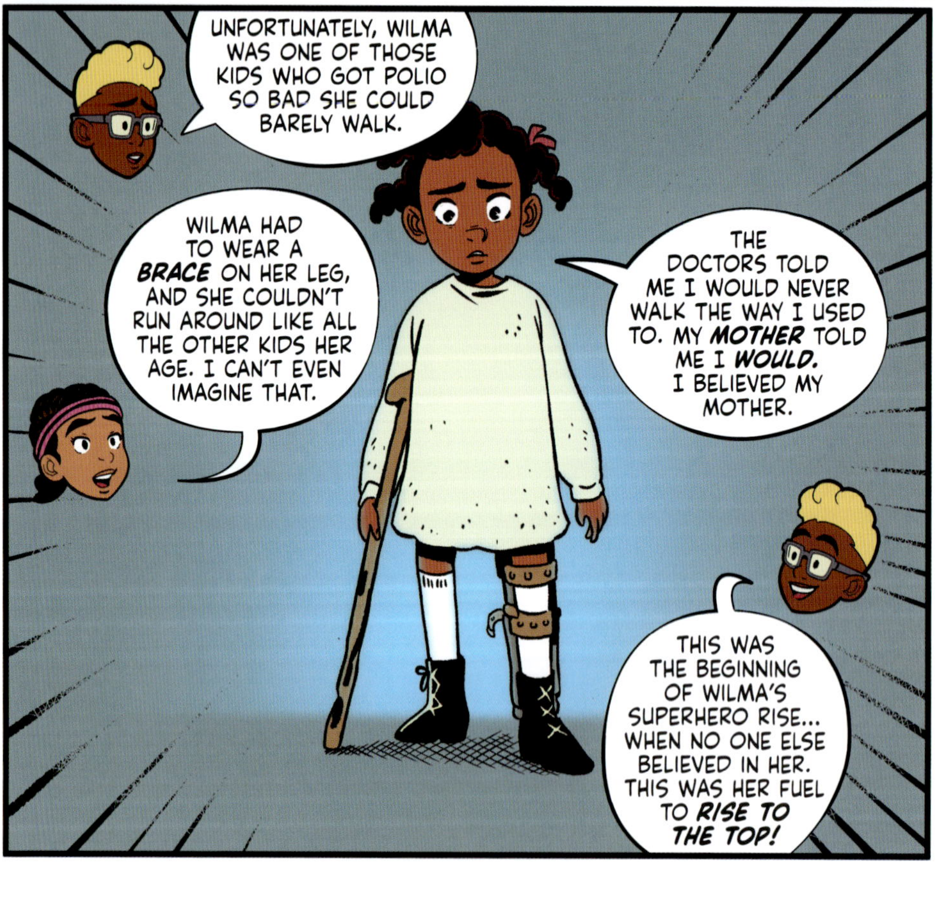
UNFORTUNATELY, WILMA WAS ONE OF THOSE KIDS WHO GOT POLIO SO BAD SHE COULD BARELY WALK.
WILMA HAD TO WEAR A ***BRACE*** ON HER LEG, AND SHE COULDN'T RUN AROUND LIKE ALL THE OTHER KIDS HER AGE. I CAN'T EVEN IMAGINE THAT.
THE DOCTORS TOLD ME I WOULD NEVER WALK THE WAY I USED TO. MY ***MOTHER*** TOLD ME I ***WOULD.*** I BELIEVED MY MOTHER.
THIS WAS THE BEGINNING OF WILMA'S SUPERHERO RISE... WHEN NO ONE ELSE BELIEVED IN HER. THIS WAS HER FUEL TO ***RISE TO THE TOP!***

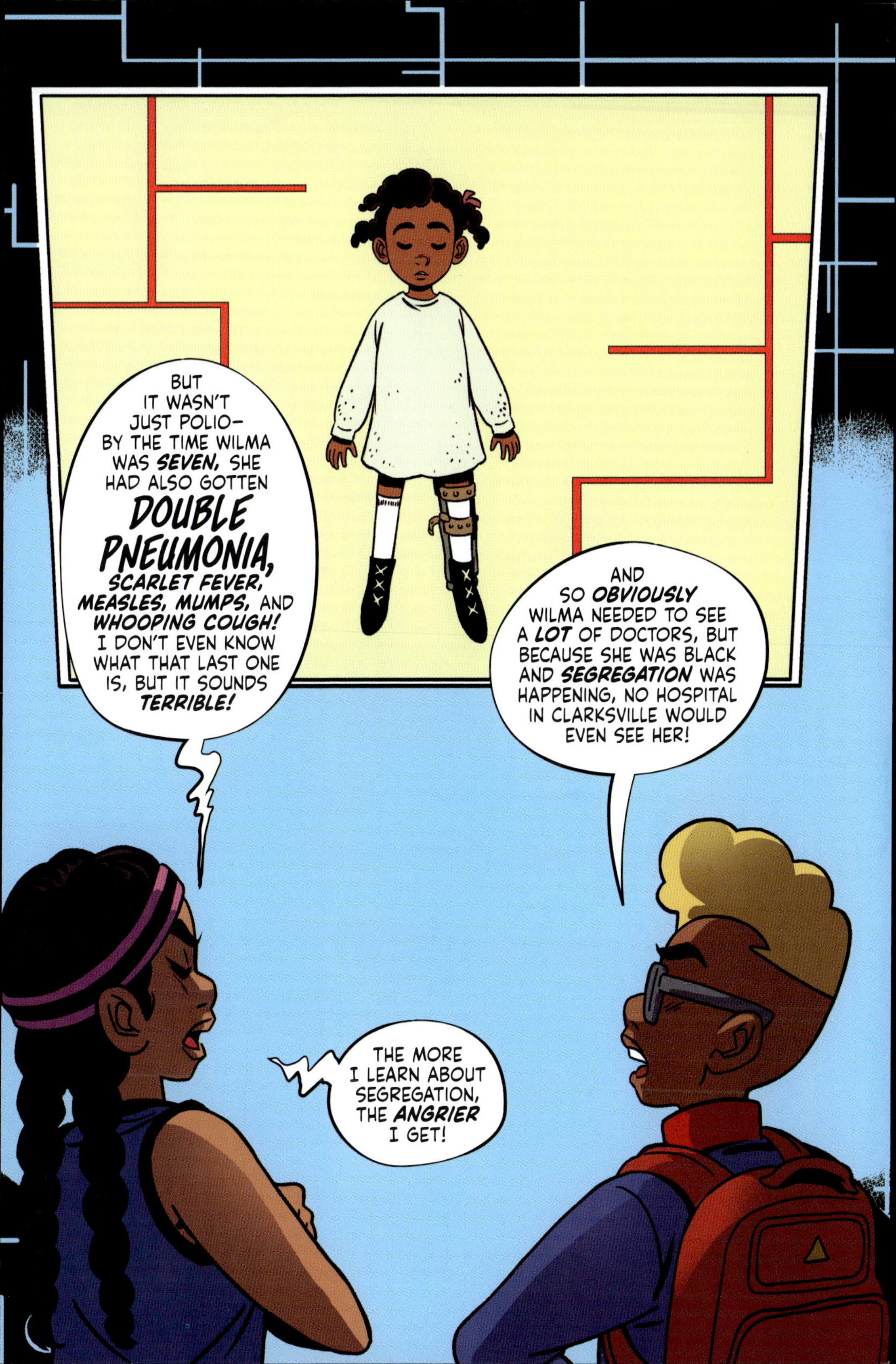
BUT IT WASN'T JUST POLIO— BY THE TIME WILMA WAS SEVEN, SHE HAD ALSO GOTTEN DOUBLE PNEUMONIA, SCARLET FEVER, MEASLES, MUMPS, AND WHOOPING COUGH! I DON'T EVEN KNOW WHAT THAT LAST ONE IS, BUT IT SOUNDS TERRIBLE!
AND SO OBVIOUSLY WILMA NEEDED TO SEE A LOT OF DOCTORS, BUT BECAUSE SHE WAS BLACK AND SEGREGATION WAS HAPPENING, NO HOSPITAL IN CLARKSVILLE WOULD EVEN SEE HER!
THE MORE I LEARN ABOUT SEGREGATION, THE ANGRIER I GET!

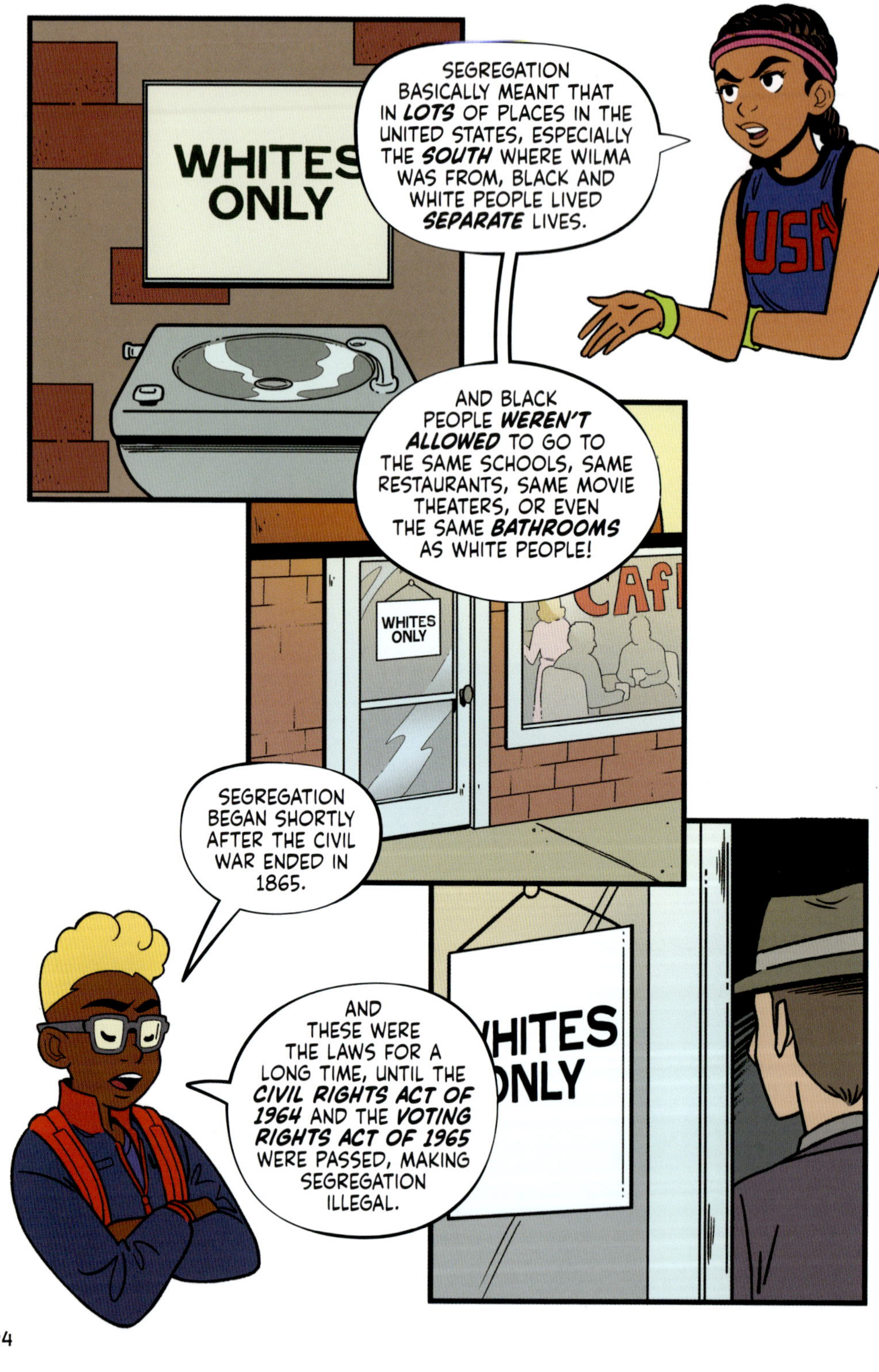
WHITES ONLY
SEGREGATION BASICALLY MEANT THAT IN *LOTS* OF PLACES IN THE UNITED STATES, ESPECIALLY THE *SOUTH* WHERE WILMA WAS FROM, BLACK AND WHITE PEOPLE LIVED *SEPARATE* LIVES.
USA
AND BLACK PEOPLE *WEREN'T ALLOWED* TO GO TO THE SAME SCHOOLS, SAME RESTAURANTS, SAME MOVIE THEATERS, OR EVEN THE SAME *BATHROOMS* AS WHITE PEOPLE!
WHITES ONLY
SEGREGATION BEGAN SHORTLY AFTER THE CIVIL WAR ENDED IN 1865.
AND THESE WERE THE LAWS FOR A LONG TIME, UNTIL THE *CIVIL RIGHTS ACT OF 1964* AND THE *VOTING RIGHTS ACT OF 1965* WERE PASSED, MAKING SEGREGATION ILLEGAL.

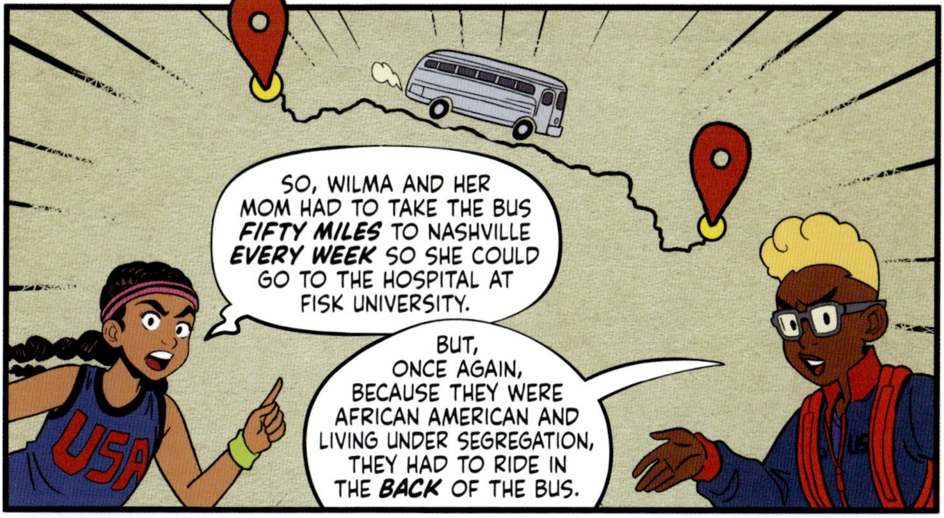
SO, WILMA AND HER MOM HAD TO TAKE THE BUS **FIFTY MILES** TO NASHVILLE **EVERY WEEK** SO SHE COULD GO TO THE HOSPITAL AT FISK UNIVERSITY.
BUT, ONCE AGAIN, BECAUSE THEY WERE AFRICAN AMERICAN AND LIVING UNDER SEGREGATION, THEY HAD TO RIDE IN THE **BACK** OF THE BUS.

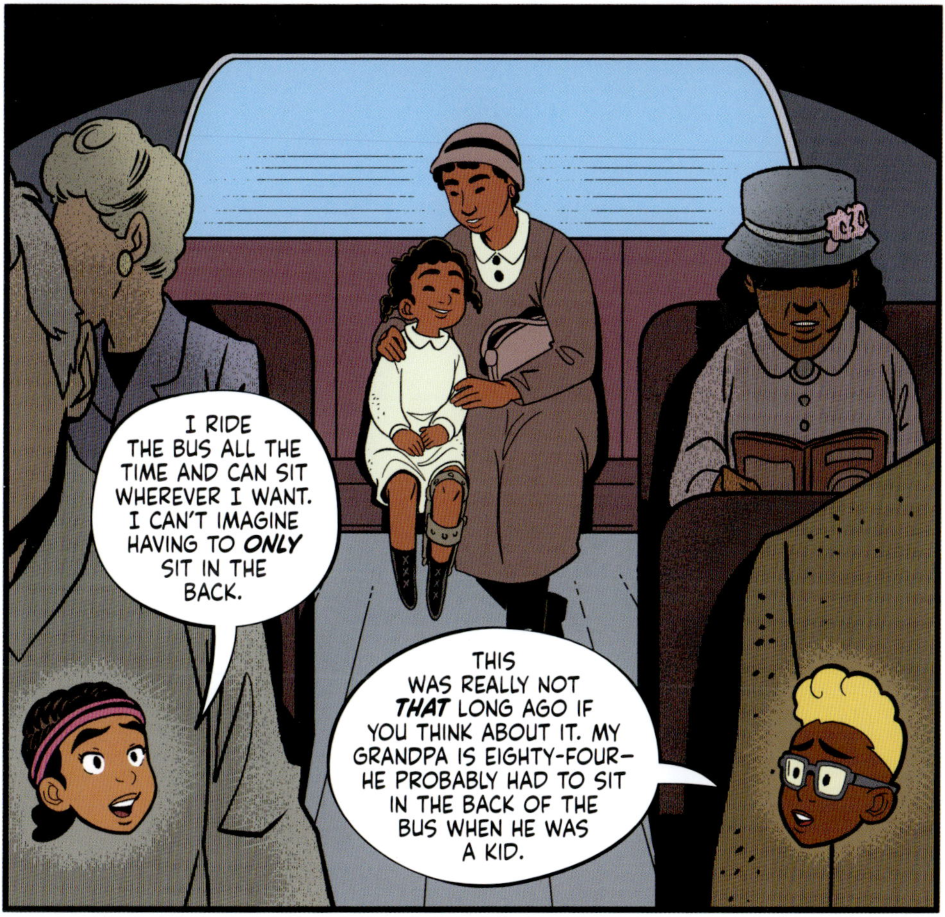
I RIDE THE BUS ALL THE TIME AND CAN SIT WHEREVER I WANT. I CAN'T IMAGINE HAVING TO **ONLY** SIT IN THE BACK.
THIS WAS REALLY NOT **THAT** LONG AGO IF YOU THINK ABOUT IT. MY GRANDPA IS EIGHTY-FOUR—HE PROBABLY HAD TO SIT IN THE BACK OF THE BUS WHEN HE WAS A KID.

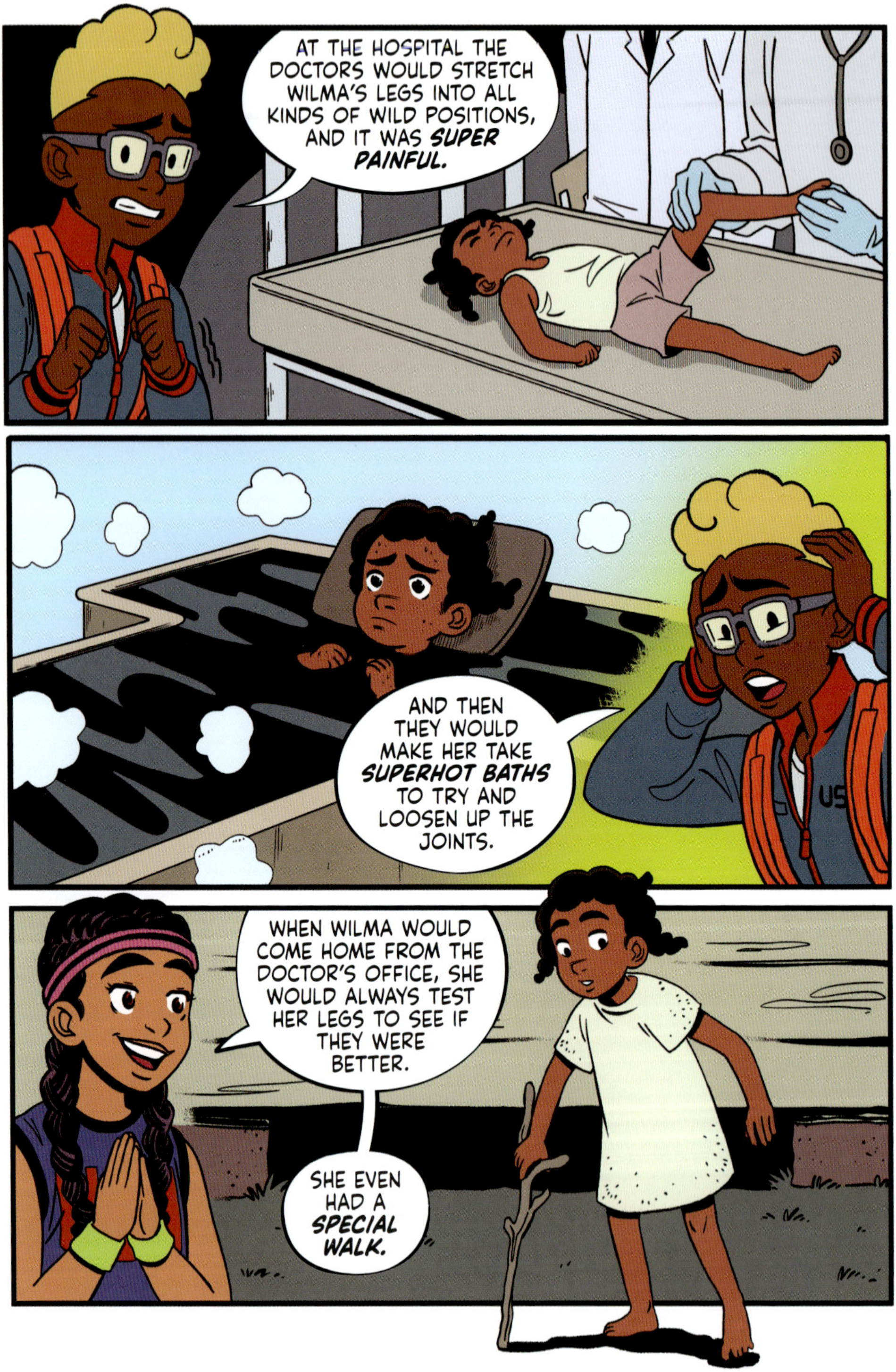
AT THE HOSPITAL THE DOCTORS WOULD STRETCH WILMA'S LEGS INTO ALL KINDS OF WILD POSITIONS, AND IT WAS ***SUPER PAINFUL.***
AND THEN THEY WOULD MAKE HER TAKE ***SUPERHOT BATHS*** TO TRY AND LOOSEN UP THE JOINTS.
US
WHEN WILMA WOULD COME HOME FROM THE DOCTOR'S OFFICE, SHE WOULD ALWAYS TEST HER LEGS TO SEE IF THEY WERE BETTER.
SHE EVEN HAD A ***SPECIAL WALK.***

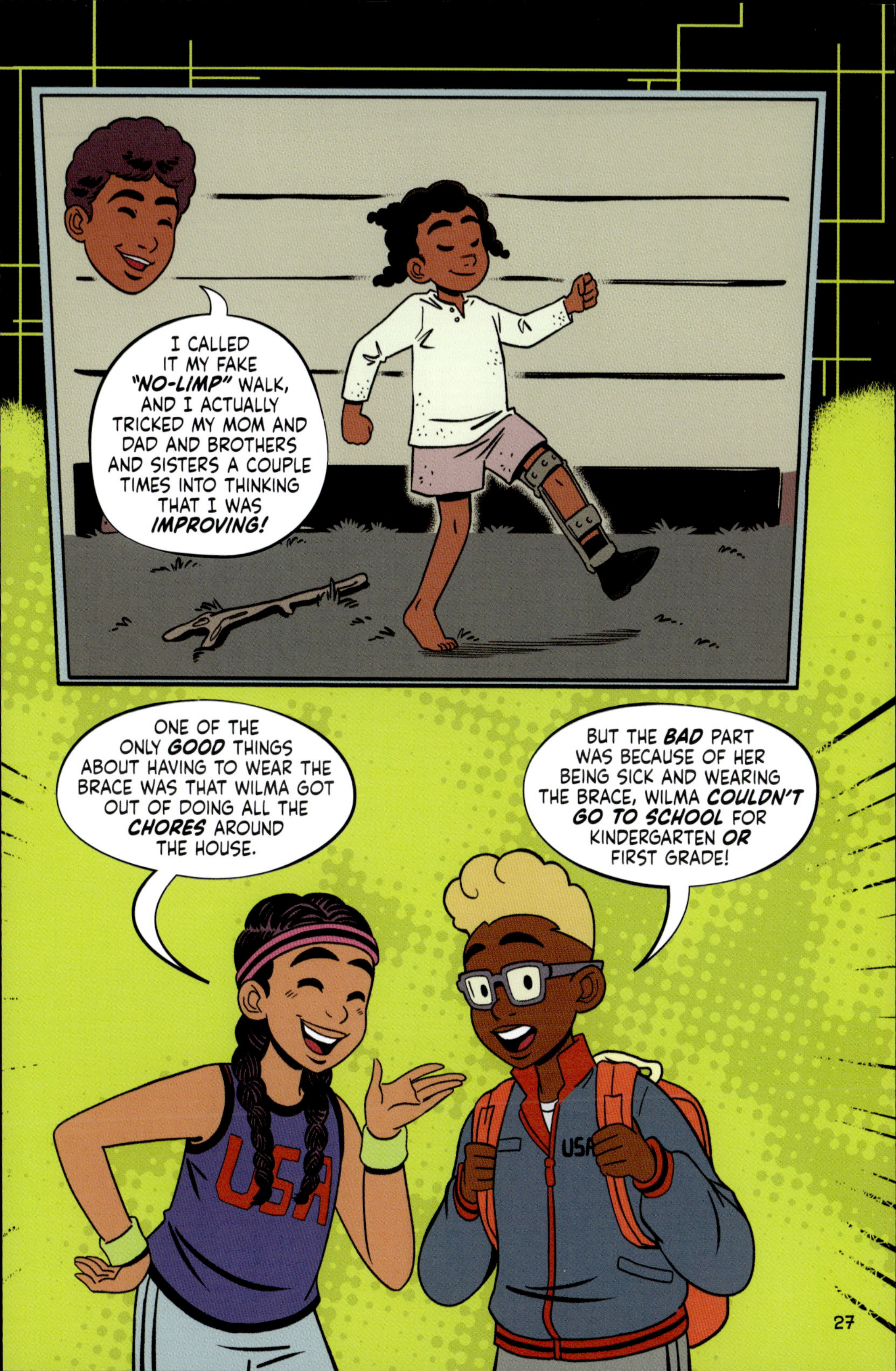

I CALLED IT MY FAKE *"NO-LIMP"* WALK, AND I ACTUALLY TRICKED MY MOM AND DAD AND BROTHERS AND SISTERS A COUPLE TIMES INTO THINKING THAT I WAS *IMPROVING!*
ONE OF THE ONLY *GOOD* THINGS ABOUT HAVING TO WEAR THE BRACE WAS THAT WILMA GOT OUT OF DOING ALL THE *CHORES* AROUND THE HOUSE.
BUT THE *BAD* PART WAS BECAUSE OF HER BEING SICK AND WEARING THE BRACE, WILMA *COULDN'T GO TO SCHOOL* FOR KINDERGARTEN *OR* FIRST GRADE!
USA
USA

CHAPTER FOUR

FINALLY, SCHOOL!

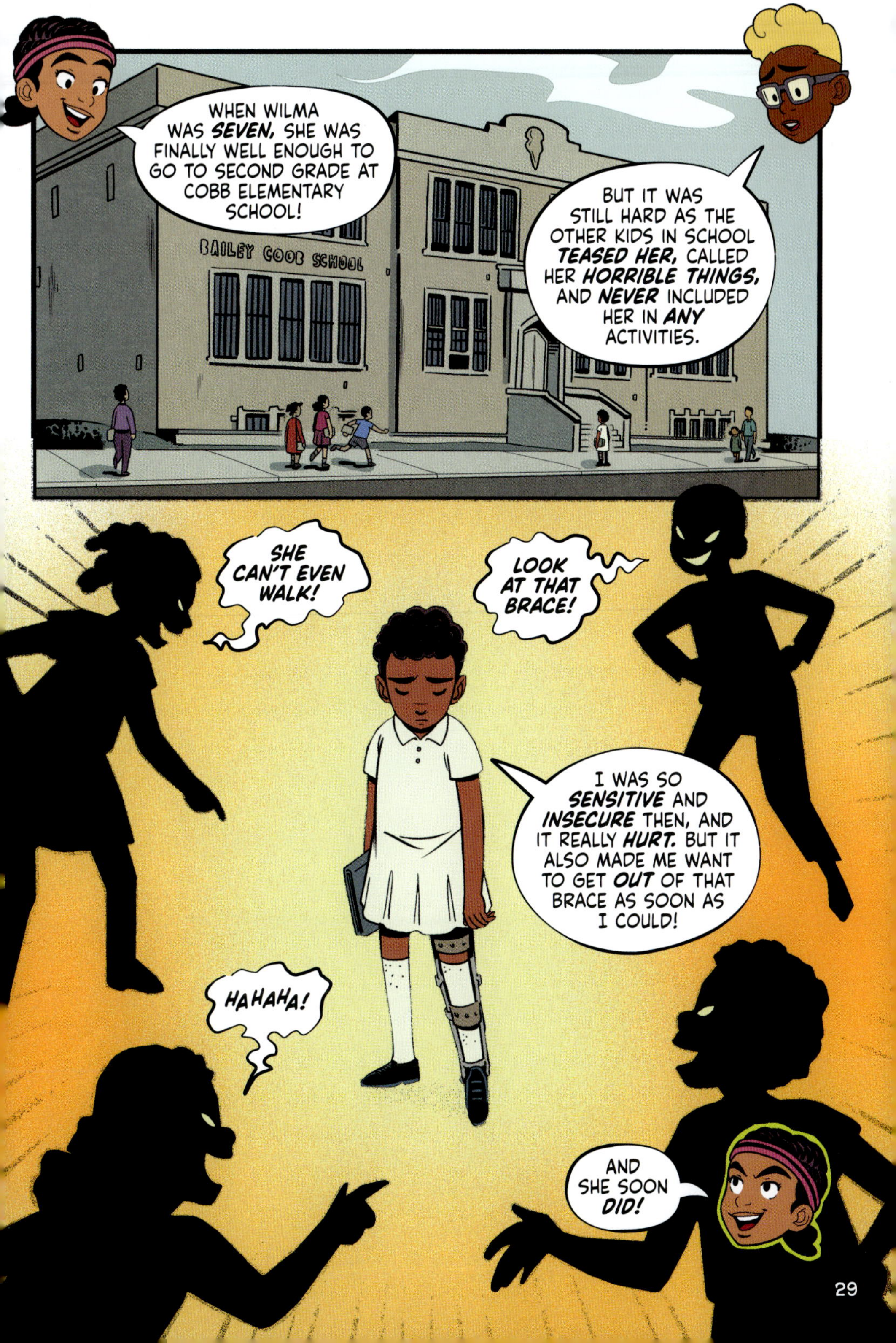

WHEN WILMA WAS SEVEN, SHE WAS FINALLY WELL ENOUGH TO GO TO SECOND GRADE AT COBB ELEMENTARY SCHOOL!
BAILEY COOB SCHOOL
BUT IT WAS STILL HARD AS THE OTHER KIDS IN SCHOOL TEASED HER, CALLED HER HORRIBLE THINGS, AND NEVER INCLUDED HER IN ANY ACTIVITIES.
SHE CAN'T EVEN WALK!
LOOK AT THAT BRACE!
I WAS SO SENSITIVE AND INSECURE THEN, AND IT REALLY HURT. BUT IT ALSO MADE ME WANT TO GET OUT OF THAT BRACE AS SOON AS I COULD!
HAHAHA!
AND SHE SOON DID!

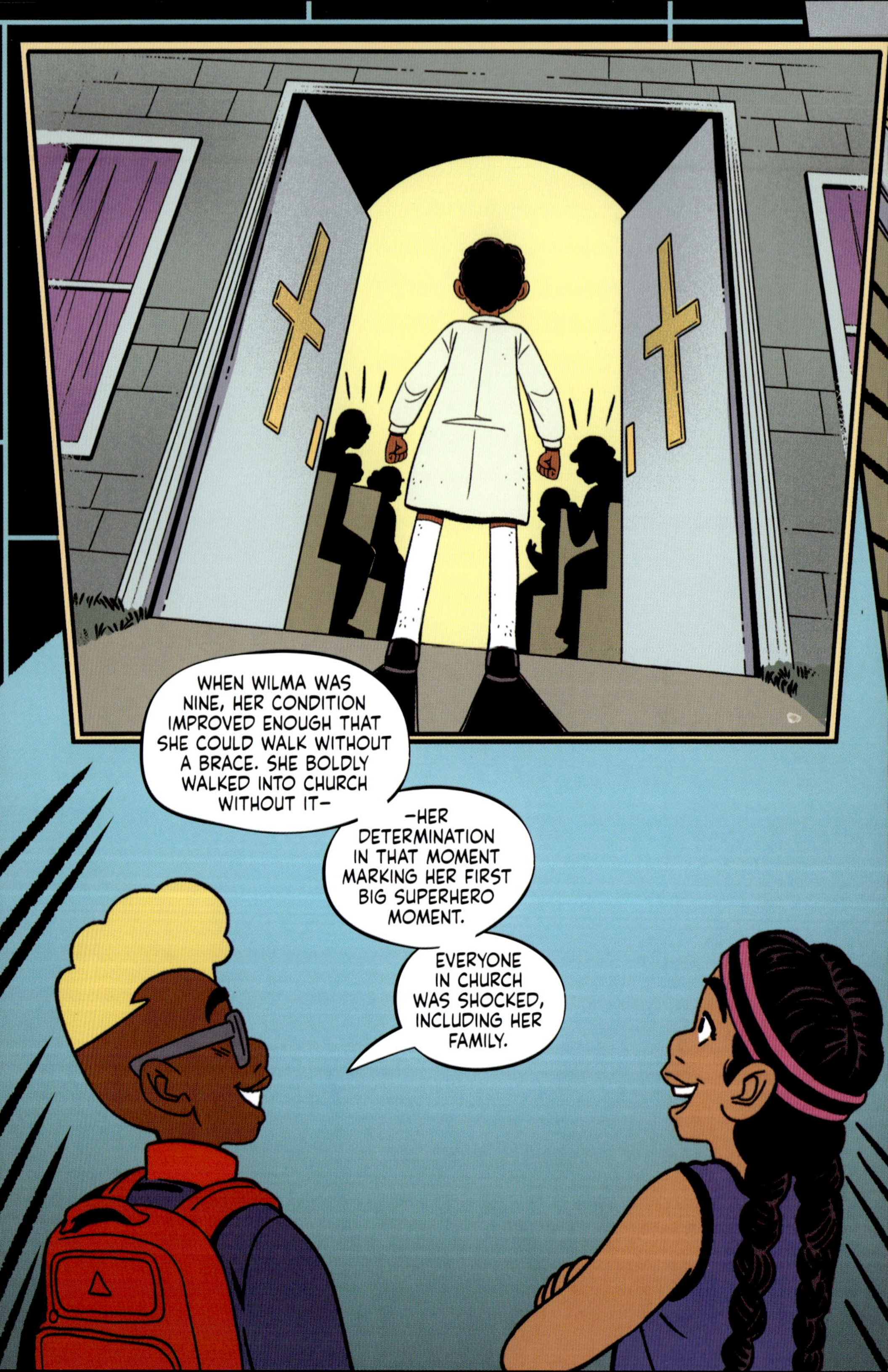
WHEN WILMA WAS NINE, HER CONDITION IMPROVED ENOUGH THAT SHE COULD WALK WITHOUT A BRACE. SHE BOLDLY WALKED INTO CHURCH WITHOUT IT—
—HER DETERMINATION IN THAT MOMENT MARKING HER FIRST BIG SUPERHERO MOMENT.
EVERYONE IN CHURCH WAS SHOCKED, INCLUDING HER FAMILY.

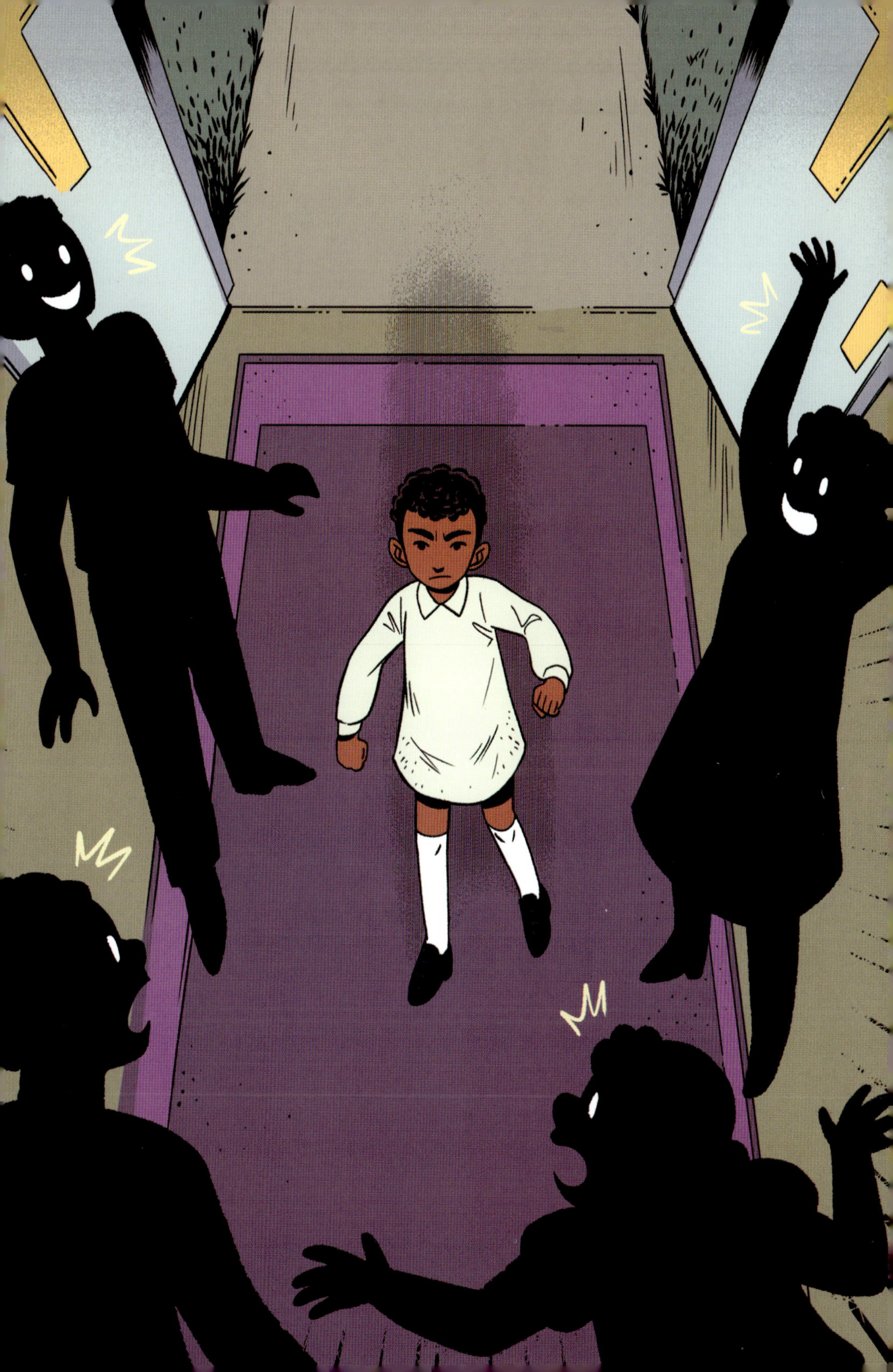

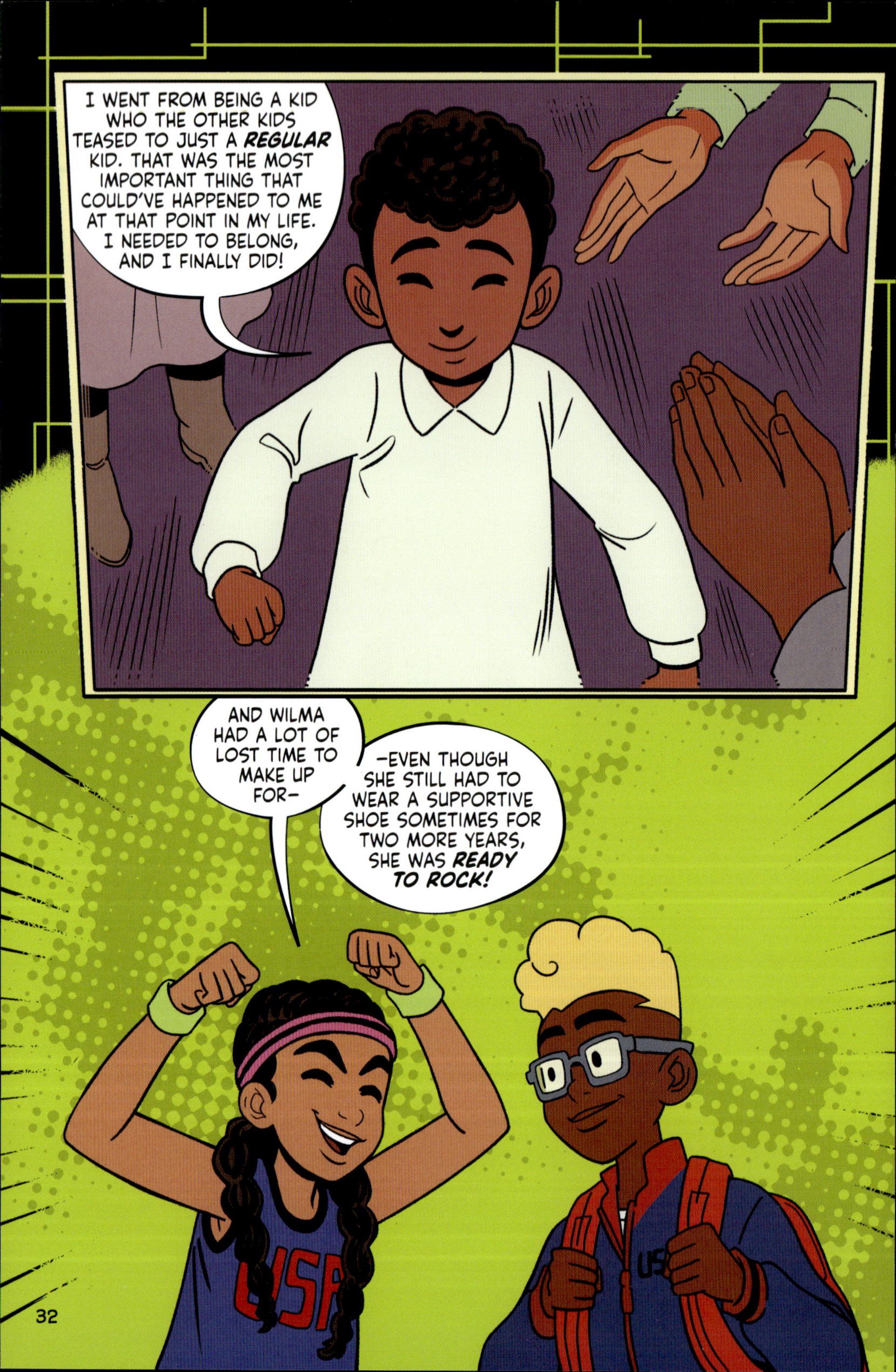
I WENT FROM BEING A KID WHO THE OTHER KIDS TEASED TO JUST A ***REGULAR*** KID. THAT WAS THE MOST IMPORTANT THING THAT COULD'VE HAPPENED TO ME AT THAT POINT IN MY LIFE. I NEEDED TO BELONG, AND I FINALLY DID!
AND WILMA HAD A LOT OF LOST TIME TO MAKE UP FOR—
—EVEN THOUGH SHE STILL HAD TO WEAR A SUPPORTIVE SHOE SOMETIMES FOR TWO MORE YEARS, SHE WAS ***READY TO ROCK!***
USA
USA

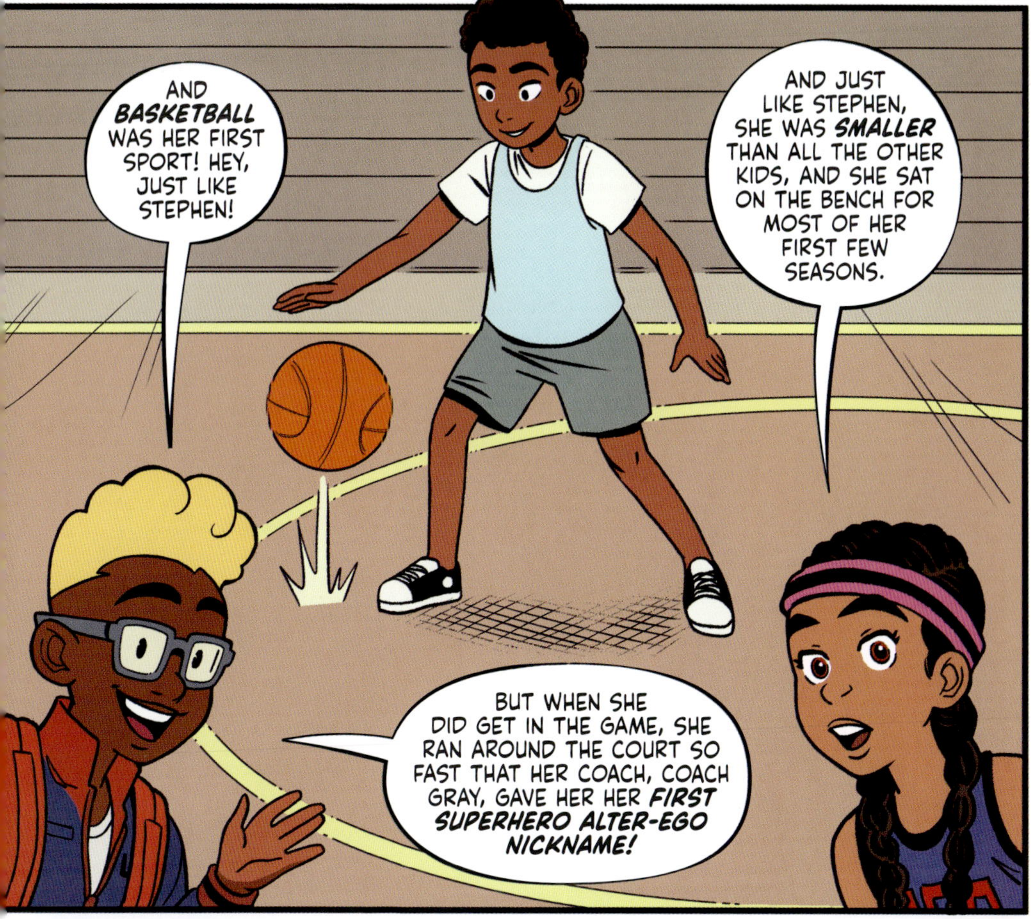
AND BASKETBALL WAS HER FIRST SPORT! HEY, JUST LIKE STEPHEN!
AND JUST LIKE STEPHEN, SHE WAS SMALLER THAN ALL THE OTHER KIDS, AND SHE SAT ON THE BENCH FOR MOST OF HER FIRST FEW SEASONS.
BUT WHEN SHE DID GET IN THE GAME, SHE RAN AROUND THE COURT SO FAST THAT HER COACH, COACH GRAY, GAVE HER HER FIRST SUPERHERO ALTER-EGO NICKNAME!

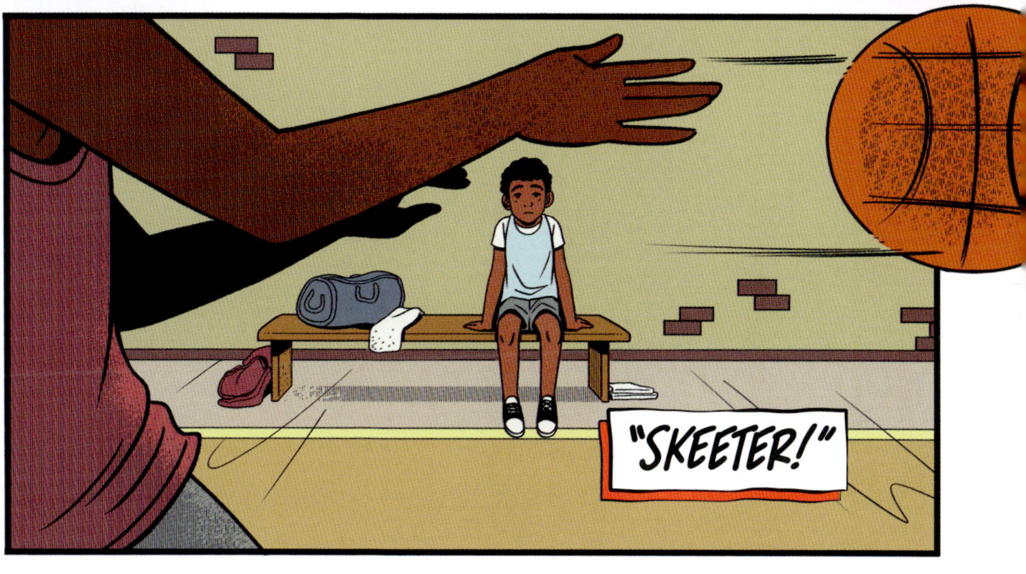
"SKEETER!"

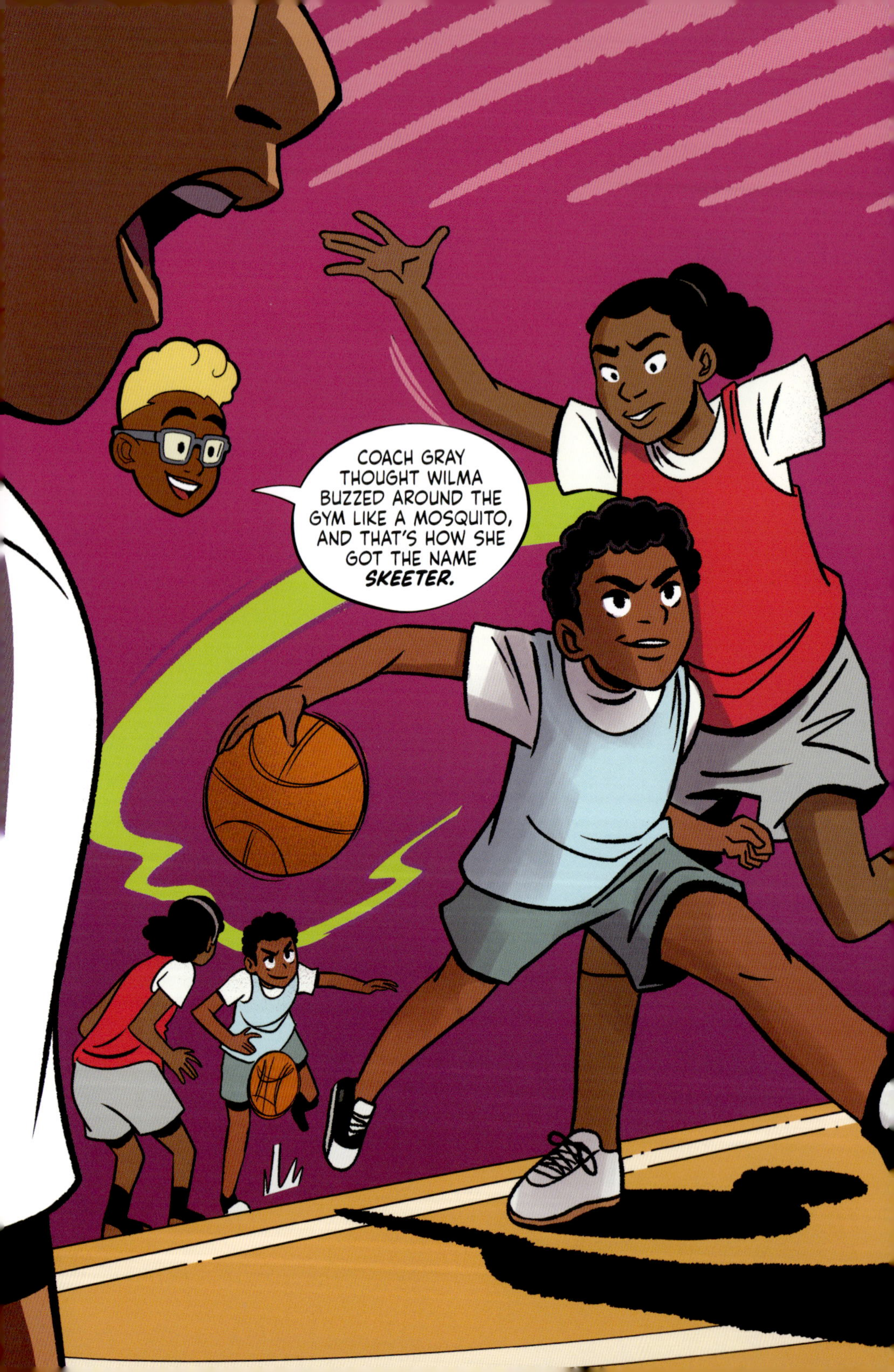
COACH GRAY THOUGHT WILMA BUZZED AROUND THE GYM LIKE A MOSQUITO, AND THAT'S HOW SHE GOT THE NAME SKEETER.

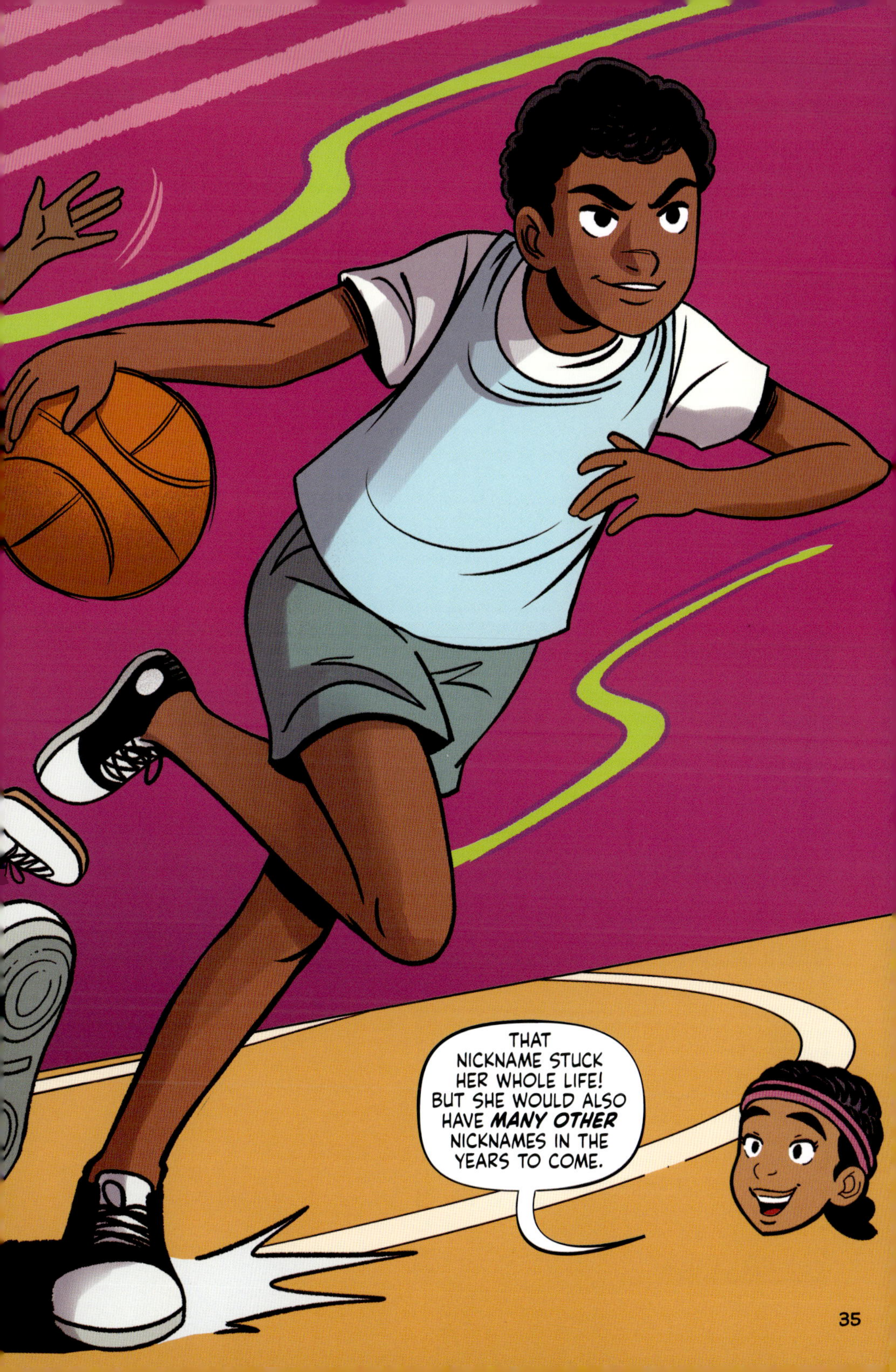
THAT NICKNAME STUCK HER WHOLE LIFE! BUT SHE WOULD ALSO HAVE **MANY OTHER** NICKNAMES IN THE YEARS TO COME.

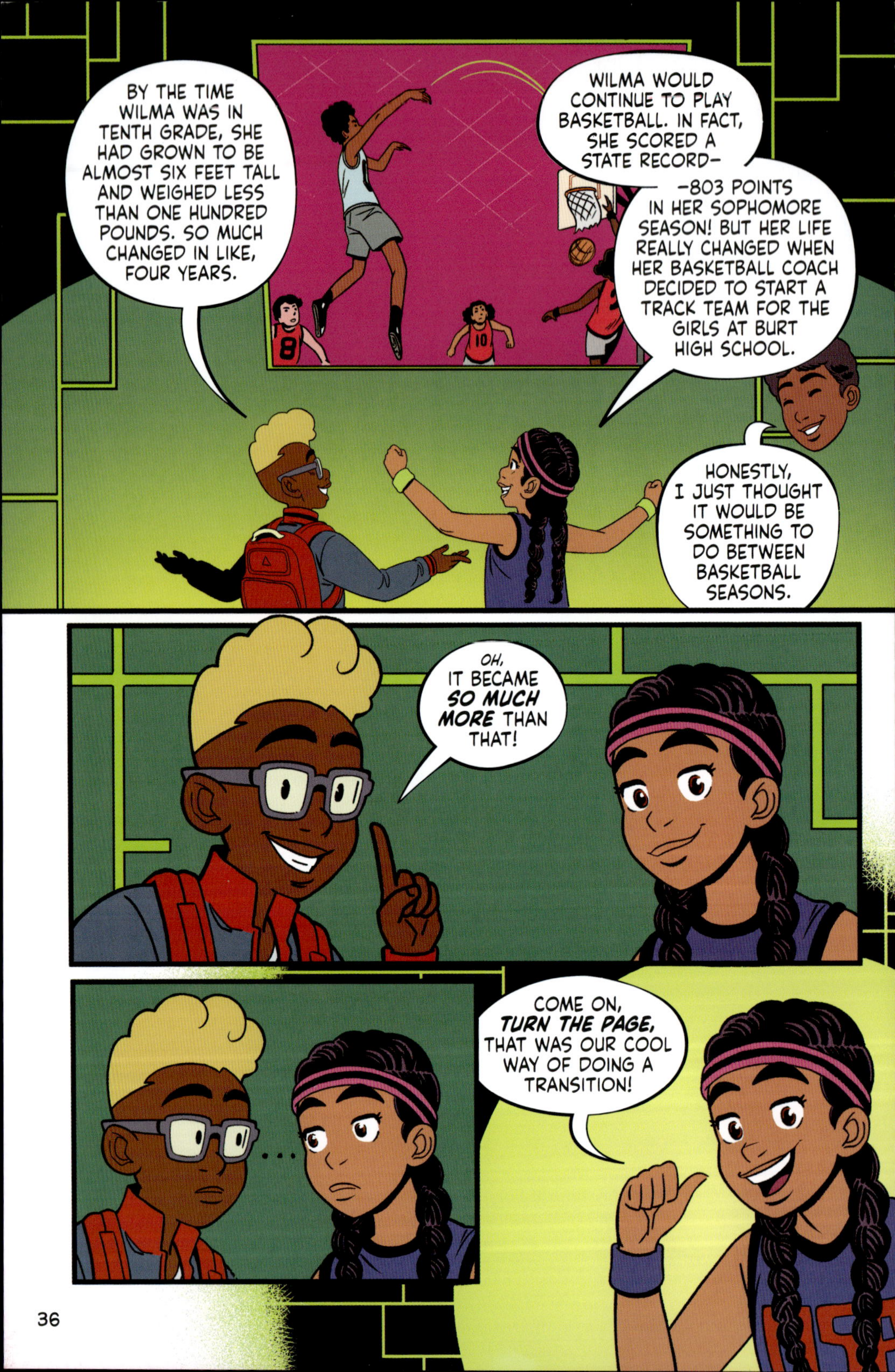

BY THE TIME WILMA WAS IN TENTH GRADE, SHE HAD GROWN TO BE ALMOST SIX FEET TALL AND WEIGHED LESS THAN ONE HUNDRED POUNDS. SO MUCH CHANGED IN LIKE, FOUR YEARS.
WILMA WOULD CONTINUE TO PLAY BASKETBALL. IN FACT, SHE SCORED A STATE RECORD–
–803 POINTS IN HER SOPHOMORE SEASON! BUT HER LIFE REALLY CHANGED WHEN HER BASKETBALL COACH DECIDED TO START A TRACK TEAM FOR THE GIRLS AT BURT HIGH SCHOOL.
HONESTLY, I JUST THOUGHT IT WOULD BE SOMETHING TO DO BETWEEN BASKETBALL SEASONS.
OH, IT BECAME ***SO MUCH MORE*** THAN THAT!
...
COME ON, ***TURN THE PAGE,*** THAT WAS OUR COOL WAY OF DOING A TRANSITION!

CHAPTER FIVE

SKEETER TAKES OFF!

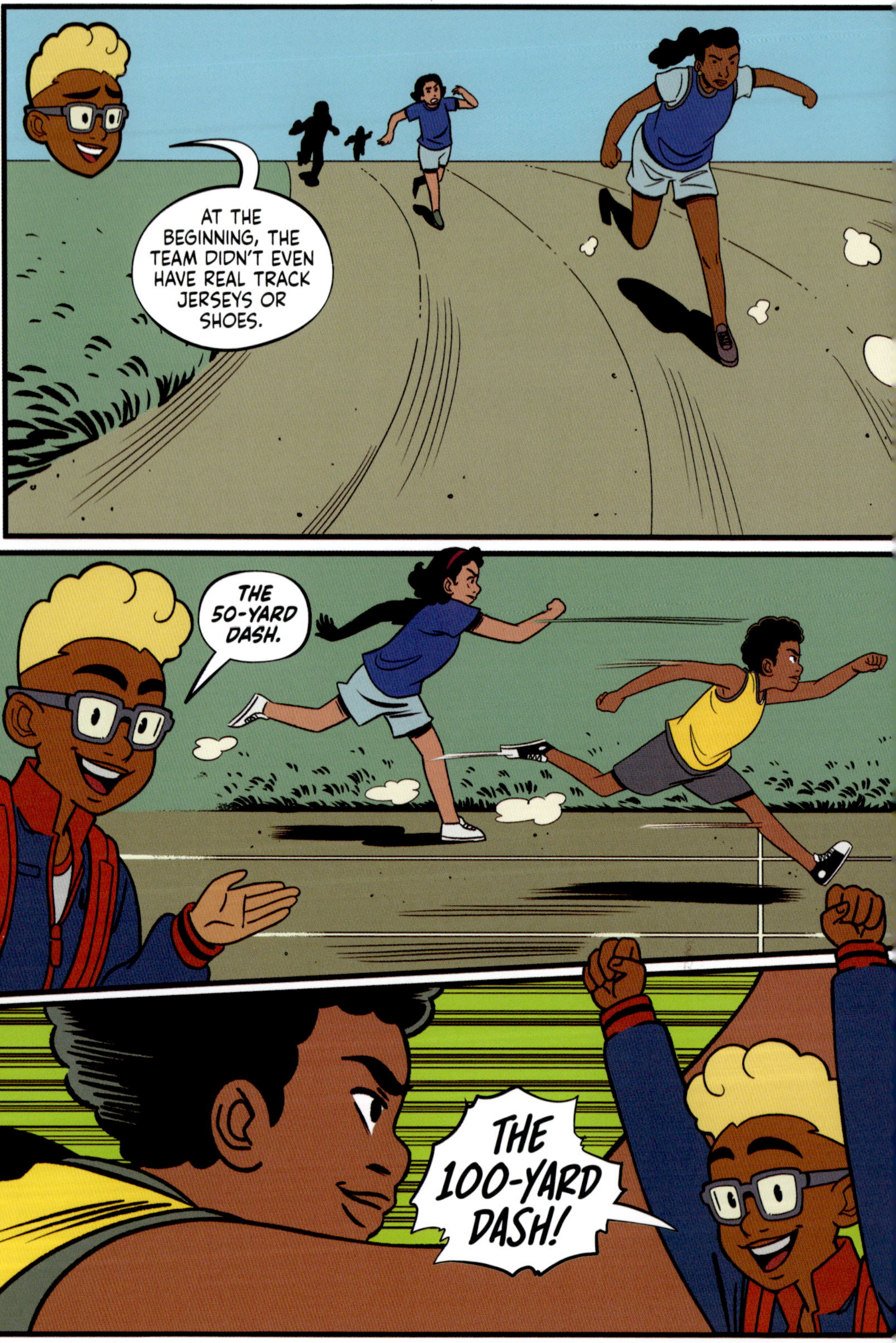
AT THE BEGINNING, THE TEAM DIDN'T EVEN HAVE REAL TRACK JERSEYS OR SHOES.
THE 50-YARD DASH.
THE 100-YARD DASH!

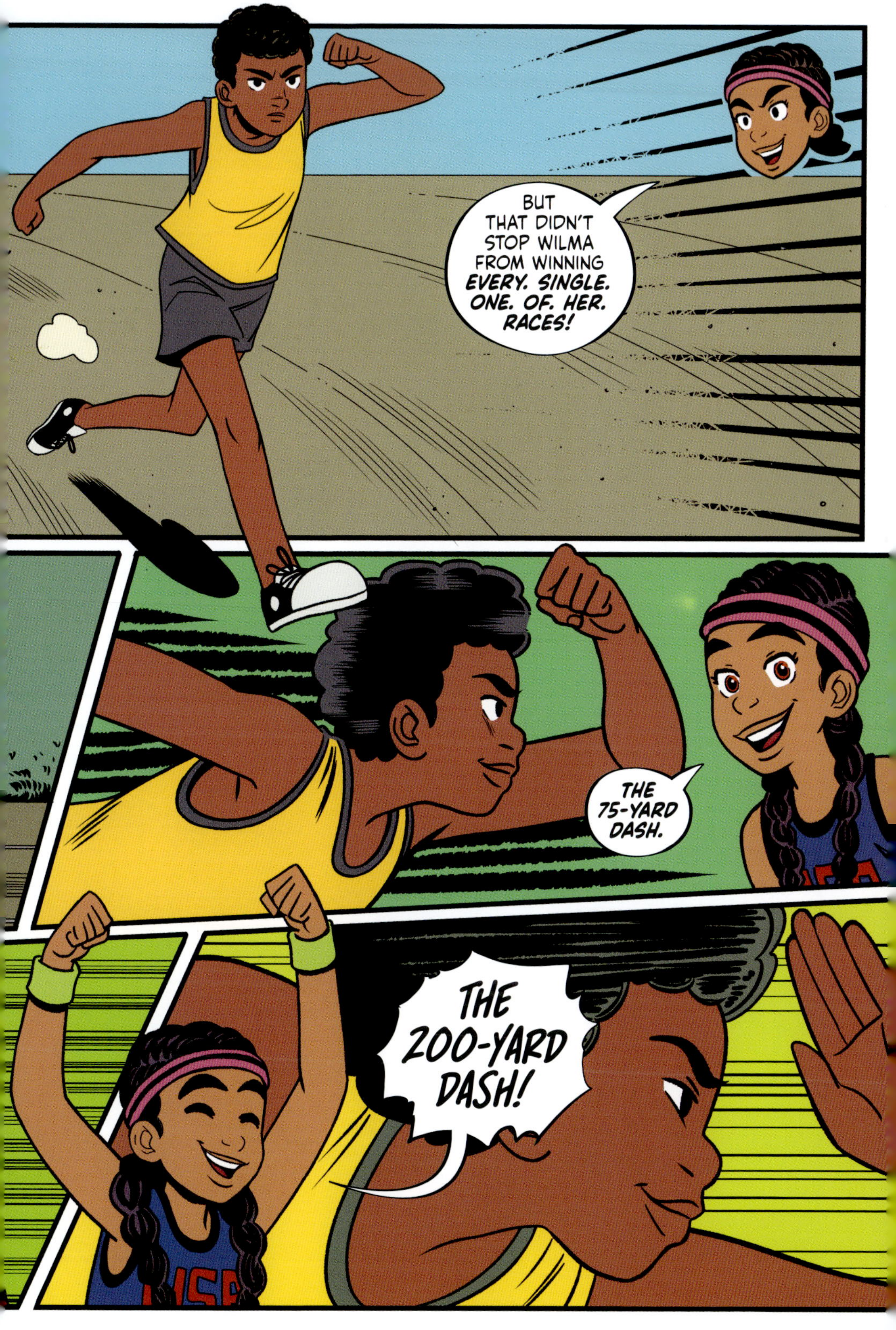
BUT THAT DIDN'T STOP WILMA FROM WINNING EVERY. SINGLE. ONE. OF. HER. RACES!
THE 75-YARD DASH.
THE 200-YARD DASH!

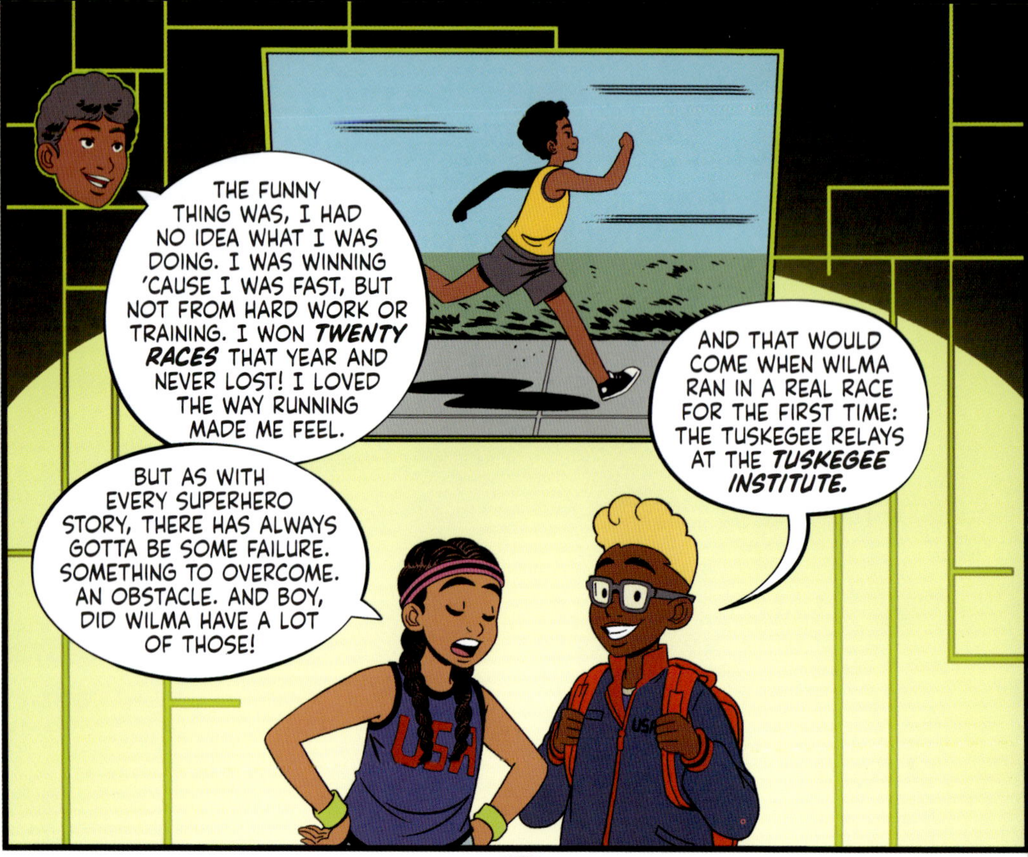
THE FUNNY THING WAS, I HAD NO IDEA WHAT I WAS DOING. I WAS WINNING 'CAUSE I WAS FAST, BUT NOT FROM HARD WORK OR TRAINING. I WON ***TWENTY RACES*** THAT YEAR AND NEVER LOST! I LOVED THE WAY RUNNING MADE ME FEEL.
AND THAT WOULD COME WHEN WILMA RAN IN A REAL RACE FOR THE FIRST TIME: THE TUSKEGEE RELAYS AT THE ***TUSKEGEE INSTITUTE.***
BUT AS WITH EVERY SUPERHERO STORY, THERE HAS ALWAYS GOTTA BE SOME FAILURE. SOMETHING TO OVERCOME. AN OBSTACLE. AND BOY, DID WILMA HAVE A LOT OF THOSE!
USA

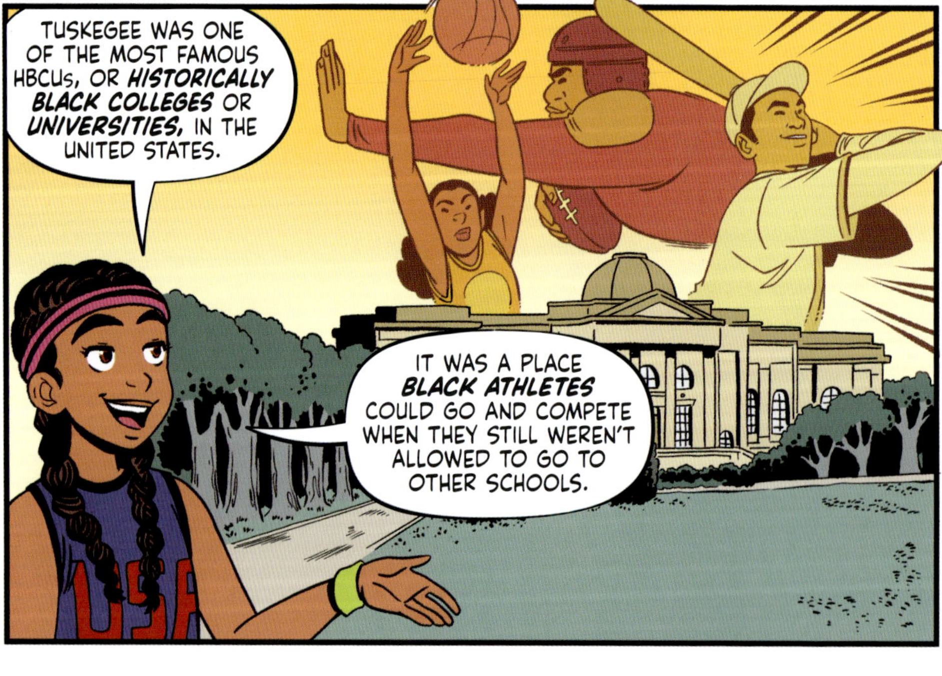
TUSKEGEE WAS ONE OF THE MOST FAMOUS HBCUs, OR ***HISTORICALLY BLACK COLLEGES*** OR ***UNIVERSITIES,*** IN THE UNITED STATES.
IT WAS A PLACE ***BLACK ATHLETES*** COULD GO AND COMPETE WHEN THEY STILL WEREN'T ALLOWED TO GO TO OTHER SCHOOLS.
USA

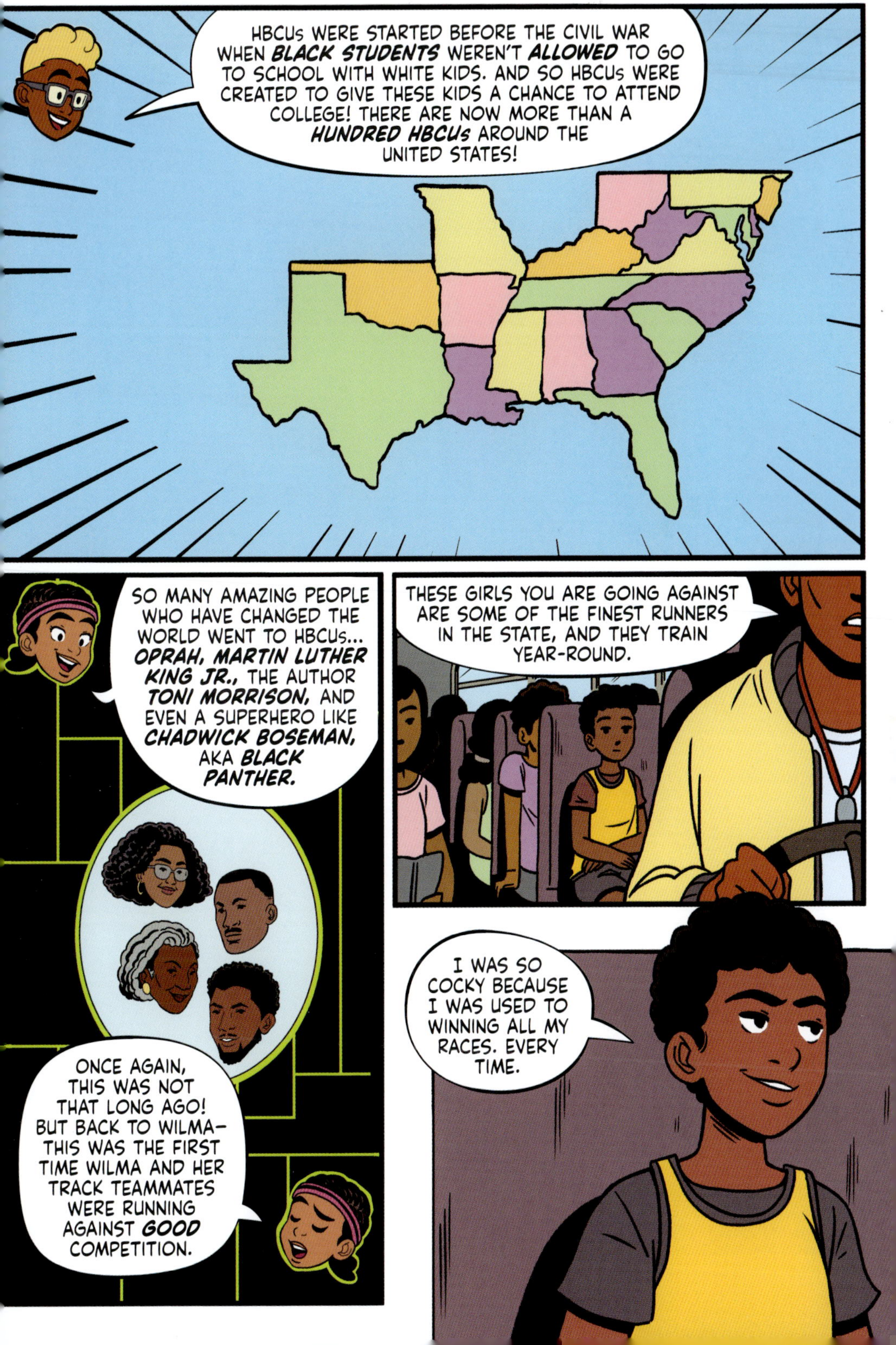
HBCUs WERE STARTED BEFORE THE CIVIL WAR WHEN ***BLACK STUDENTS*** WEREN'T ***ALLOWED*** TO GO TO SCHOOL WITH WHITE KIDS. AND SO HBCUs WERE CREATED TO GIVE THESE KIDS A CHANCE TO ATTEND COLLEGE! THERE ARE NOW MORE THAN A ***HUNDRED HBCUs*** AROUND THE UNITED STATES!
SO MANY AMAZING PEOPLE WHO HAVE CHANGED THE WORLD WENT TO HBCUs... ***OPRAH, MARTIN LUTHER KING JR.,*** THE AUTHOR ***TONI MORRISON,*** AND EVEN A SUPERHERO LIKE ***CHADWICK BOSEMAN,*** AKA ***BLACK PANTHER.***
ONCE AGAIN, THIS WAS NOT THAT LONG AGO! BUT BACK TO WILMA— THIS WAS THE FIRST TIME WILMA AND HER TRACK TEAMMATES WERE RUNNING AGAINST ***GOOD*** COMPETITION.
THESE GIRLS YOU ARE GOING AGAINST ARE SOME OF THE FINEST RUNNERS IN THE STATE, AND THEY TRAIN YEAR-ROUND.
I WAS SO COCKY BECAUSE I WAS USED TO WINNING ALL MY RACES. EVERY TIME.

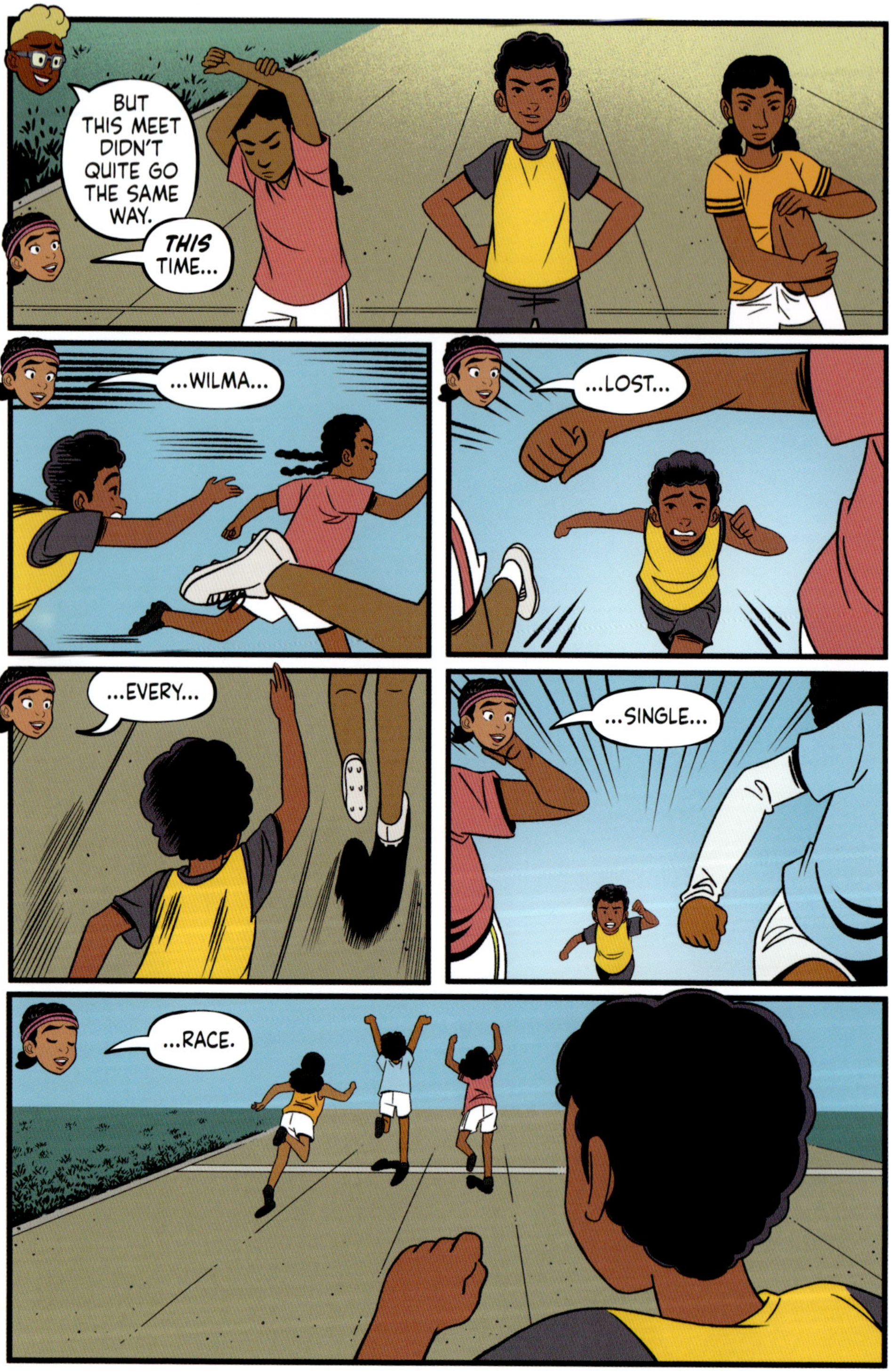
BUT THIS MEET DIDN'T QUITE GO THE SAME WAY.
THIS TIME...
...WILMA...
...LOST...
...EVERY...
...SINGLE...
...RACE.

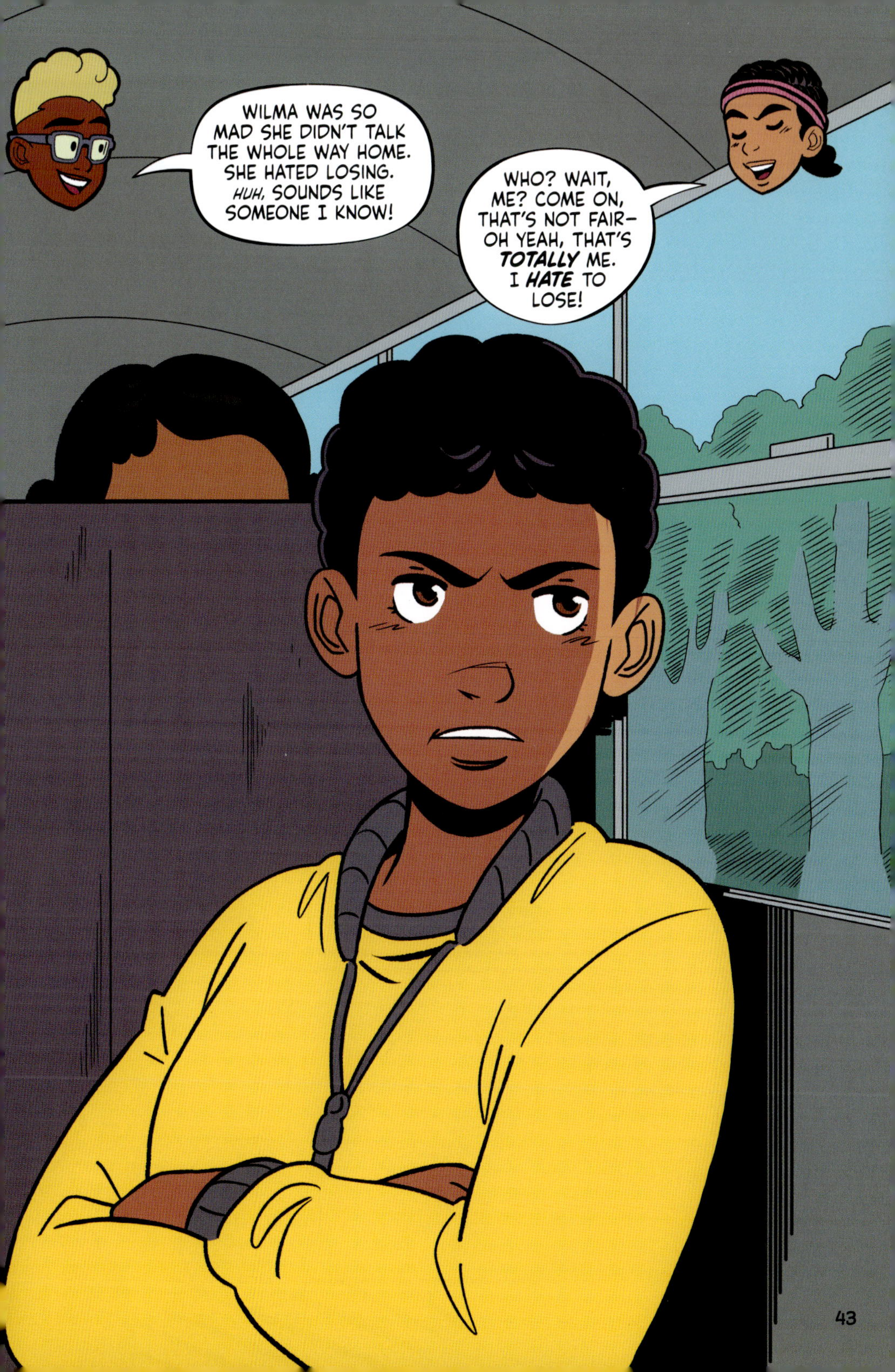
WILMA WAS SO MAD SHE DIDN'T TALK THE WHOLE WAY HOME. SHE HATED LOSING. *HUH,* SOUNDS LIKE SOMEONE I KNOW!
WHO? WAIT, ME? COME ON, THAT'S NOT FAIR– OH YEAH, THAT'S ***TOTALLY*** ME. I ***HATE*** TO LOSE!

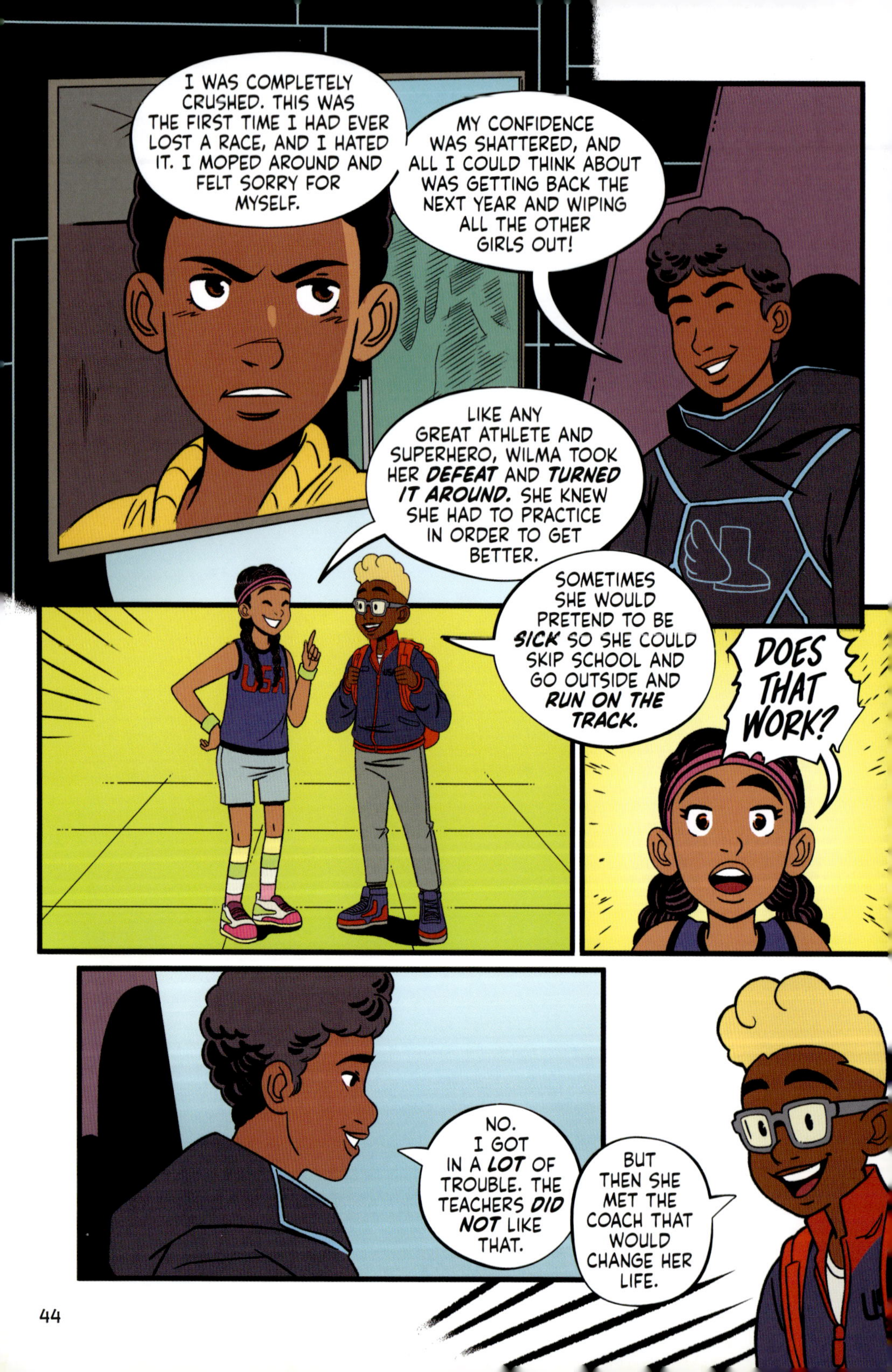
I WAS COMPLETELY CRUSHED. THIS WAS THE FIRST TIME I HAD EVER LOST A RACE, AND I HATED IT. I MOPED AROUND AND FELT SORRY FOR MYSELF.
MY CONFIDENCE WAS SHATTERED, AND ALL I COULD THINK ABOUT WAS GETTING BACK THE NEXT YEAR AND WIPING ALL THE OTHER GIRLS OUT!
LIKE ANY GREAT ATHLETE AND SUPERHERO, WILMA TOOK HER *DEFEAT* AND *TURNED IT AROUND.* SHE KNEW SHE HAD TO PRACTICE IN ORDER TO GET BETTER.
SOMETIMES SHE WOULD PRETEND TO BE *SICK* SO SHE COULD SKIP SCHOOL AND GO OUTSIDE AND *RUN ON THE TRACK.*
DOES THAT WORK?
NO. I GOT IN A *LOT* OF TROUBLE. THE TEACHERS *DID NOT* LIKE THAT.
BUT THEN SHE MET THE COACH THAT WOULD CHANGE HER LIFE.

CHAPTER SIX

COACH ED

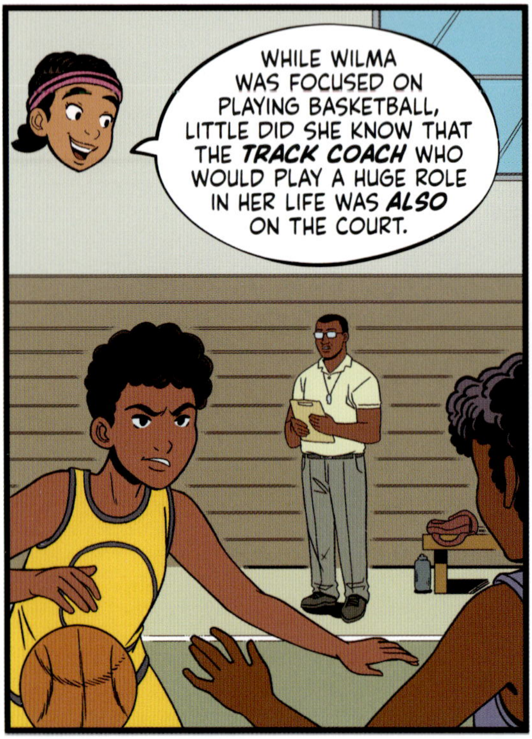
WHILE WILMA WAS FOCUSED ON PLAYING BASKETBALL, LITTLE DID SHE KNOW THAT THE ***TRACK COACH*** WHO WOULD PLAY A HUGE ROLE IN HER LIFE WAS ***ALSO*** ON THE COURT.

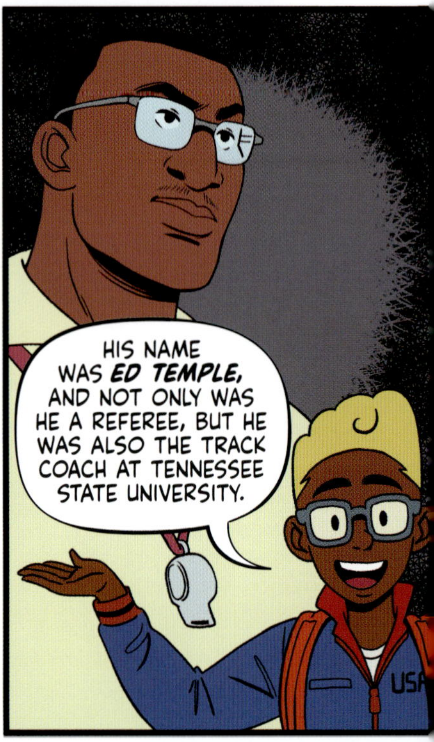
HIS NAME WAS ***ED TEMPLE,*** AND NOT ONLY WAS HE A REFEREE, BUT HE WAS ALSO THE TRACK COACH AT TENNESSEE STATE UNIVERSITY.
USA

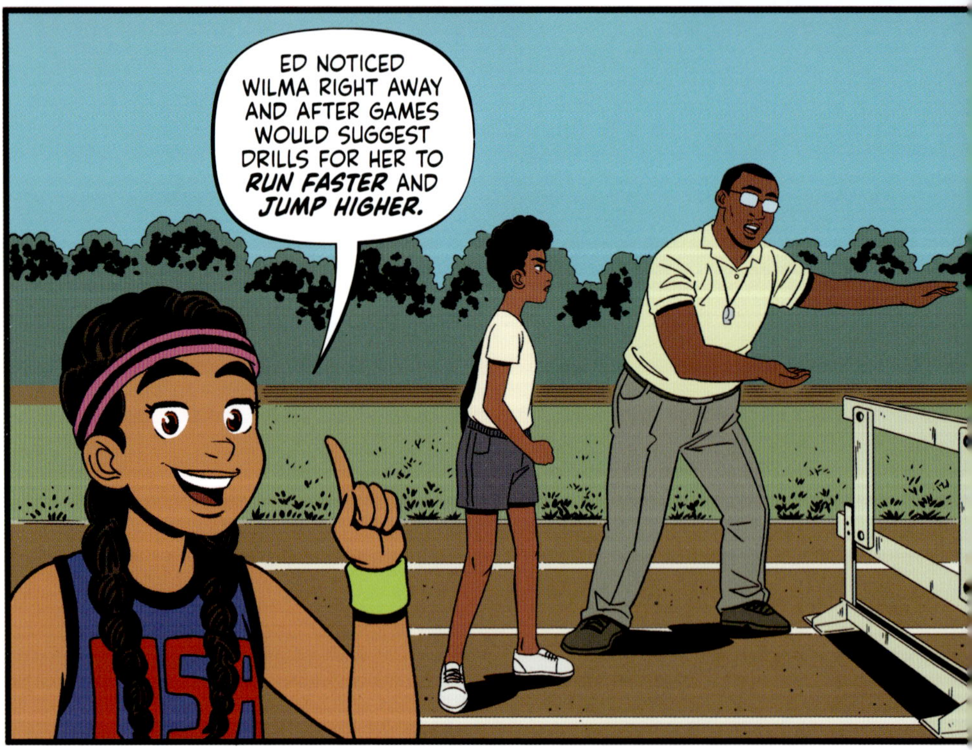
ED NOTICED WILMA RIGHT AWAY AND AFTER GAMES WOULD SUGGEST DRILLS FOR HER TO ***RUN FASTER*** AND ***JUMP HIGHER.***
USA

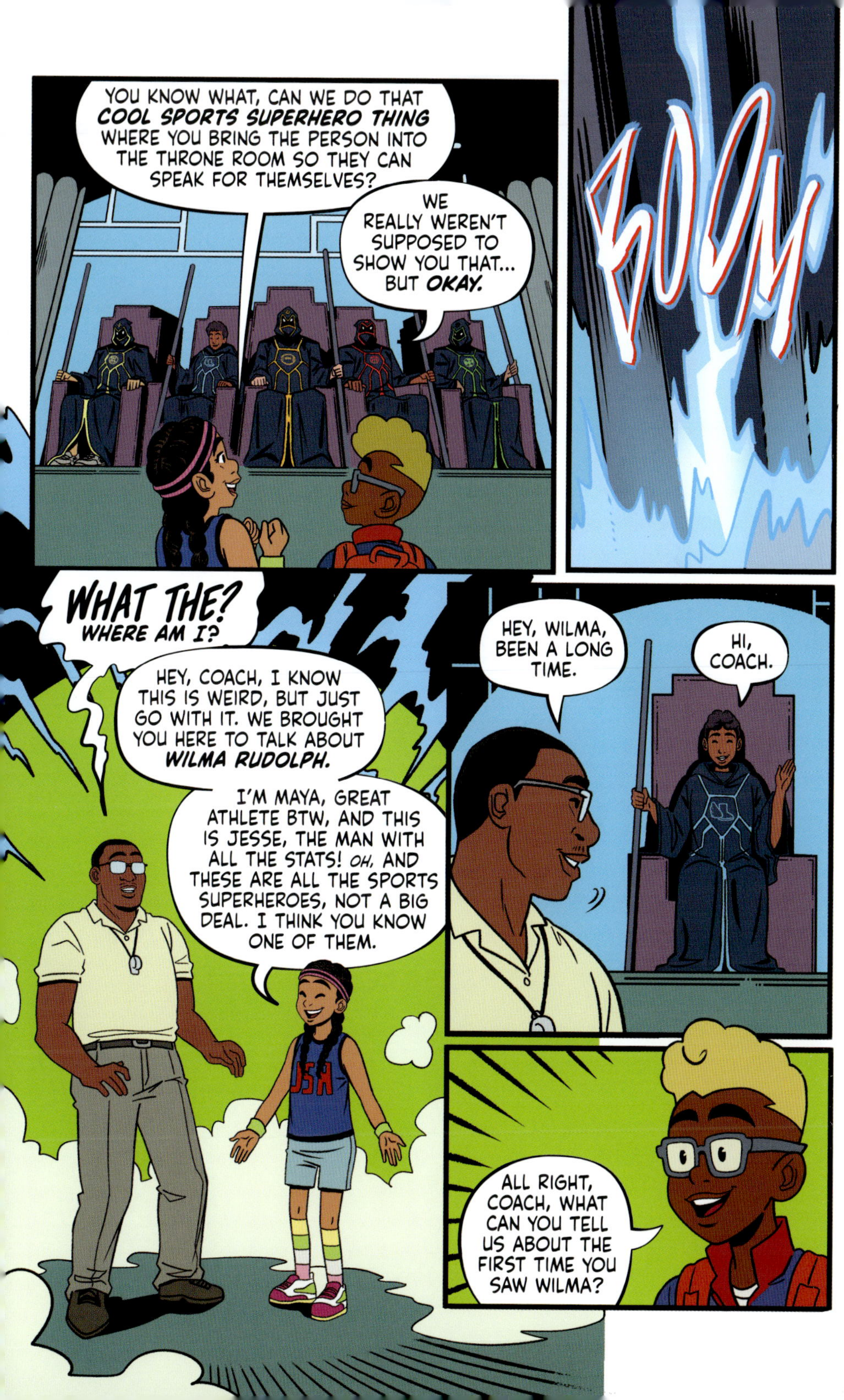
YOU KNOW WHAT, CAN WE DO THAT COOL SPORTS SUPERHERO THING WHERE YOU BRING THE PERSON INTO THE THRONE ROOM SO THEY CAN SPEAK FOR THEMSELVES?
WE REALLY WEREN'T SUPPOSED TO SHOW YOU THAT... BUT OKAY.
BOOM
WHAT THE? WHERE AM I?
HEY, COACH, I KNOW THIS IS WEIRD, BUT JUST GO WITH IT. WE BROUGHT YOU HERE TO TALK ABOUT WILMA RUDOLPH.
I'M MAYA, GREAT ATHLETE BTW, AND THIS IS JESSE, THE MAN WITH ALL THE STATS! OH, AND THESE ARE ALL THE SPORTS SUPERHEROES, NOT A BIG DEAL. I THINK YOU KNOW ONE OF THEM.
USA
HEY, WILMA, BEEN A LONG TIME.
HI, COACH.
ALL RIGHT, COACH, WHAT CAN YOU TELL US ABOUT THE FIRST TIME YOU SAW WILMA?

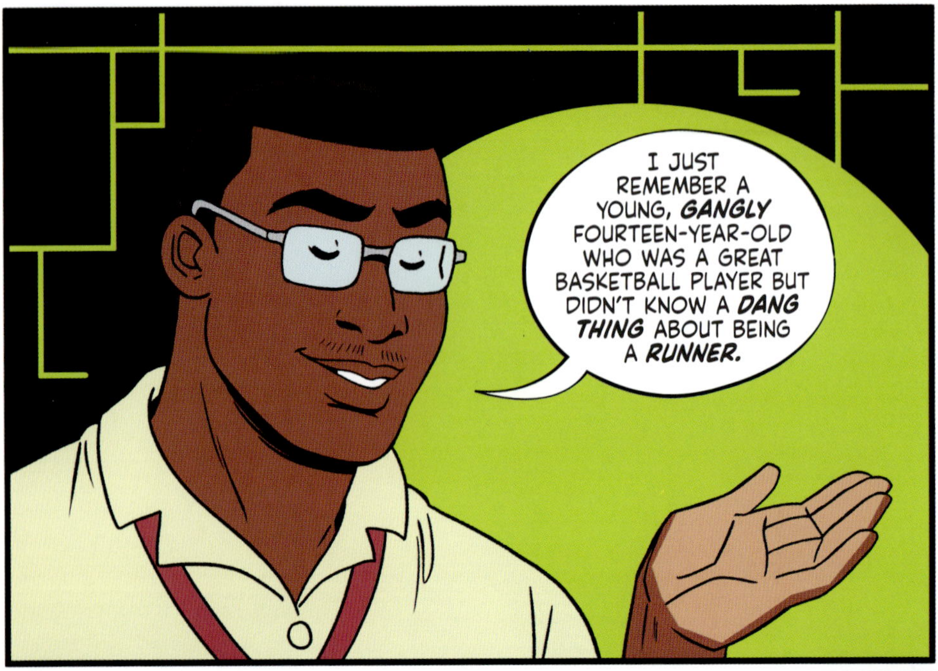
I JUST REMEMBER A YOUNG, ***GANGLY*** FOURTEEN-YEAR-OLD WHO WAS A GREAT BASKETBALL PLAYER BUT DIDN'T KNOW A ***DANG THING*** ABOUT BEING A ***RUNNER.***

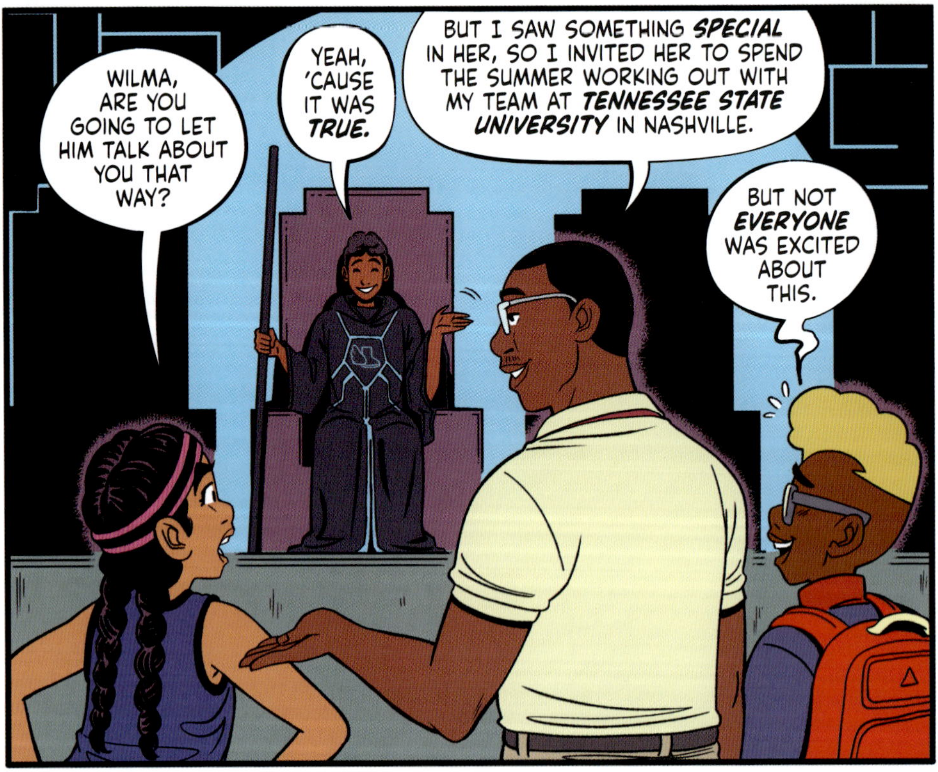
BUT I SAW SOMETHING ***SPECIAL*** IN HER, SO I INVITED HER TO SPEND THE SUMMER WORKING OUT WITH MY TEAM AT ***TENNESSEE STATE UNIVERSITY*** IN NASHVILLE.
YEAH, 'CAUSE IT WAS ***TRUE.***
WILMA, ARE YOU GOING TO LET HIM TALK ABOUT YOU THAT WAY?
BUT NOT ***EVERYONE*** WAS EXCITED ABOUT THIS.

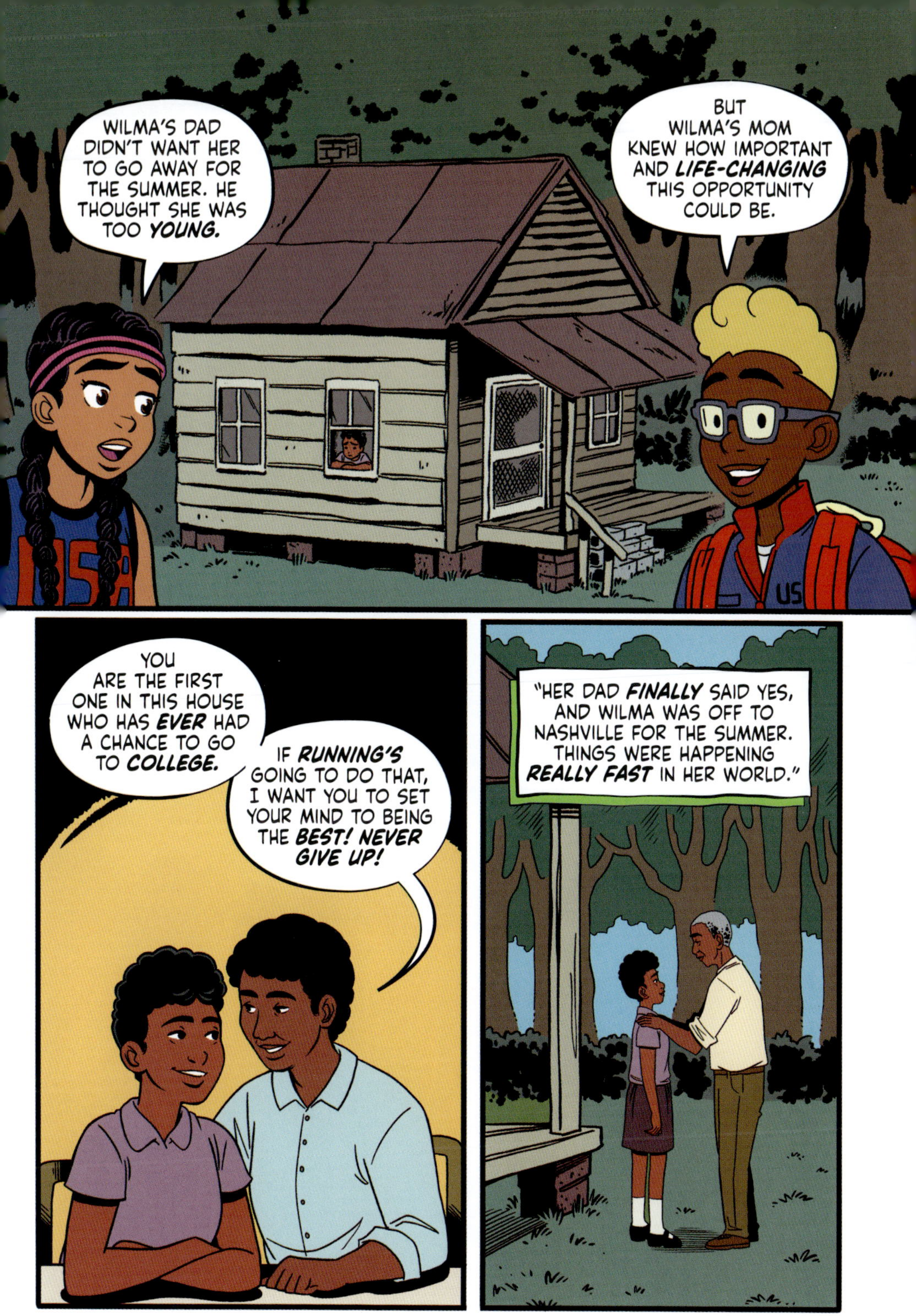

WILMA'S DAD DIDN'T WANT HER TO GO AWAY FOR THE SUMMER. HE THOUGHT SHE WAS TOO *YOUNG.*
BUT WILMA'S MOM KNEW HOW IMPORTANT AND *LIFE-CHANGING* THIS OPPORTUNITY COULD BE.
YOU ARE THE FIRST ONE IN THIS HOUSE WHO HAS *EVER* HAD A CHANCE TO GO TO *COLLEGE.*
IF *RUNNING'S* GOING TO DO THAT, I WANT YOU TO SET YOUR MIND TO BEING THE *BEST! NEVER GIVE UP!*
"HER DAD *FINALLY* SAID YES, AND WILMA WAS OFF TO NASHVILLE FOR THE SUMMER. THINGS WERE HAPPENING *REALLY FAST* IN HER WORLD."

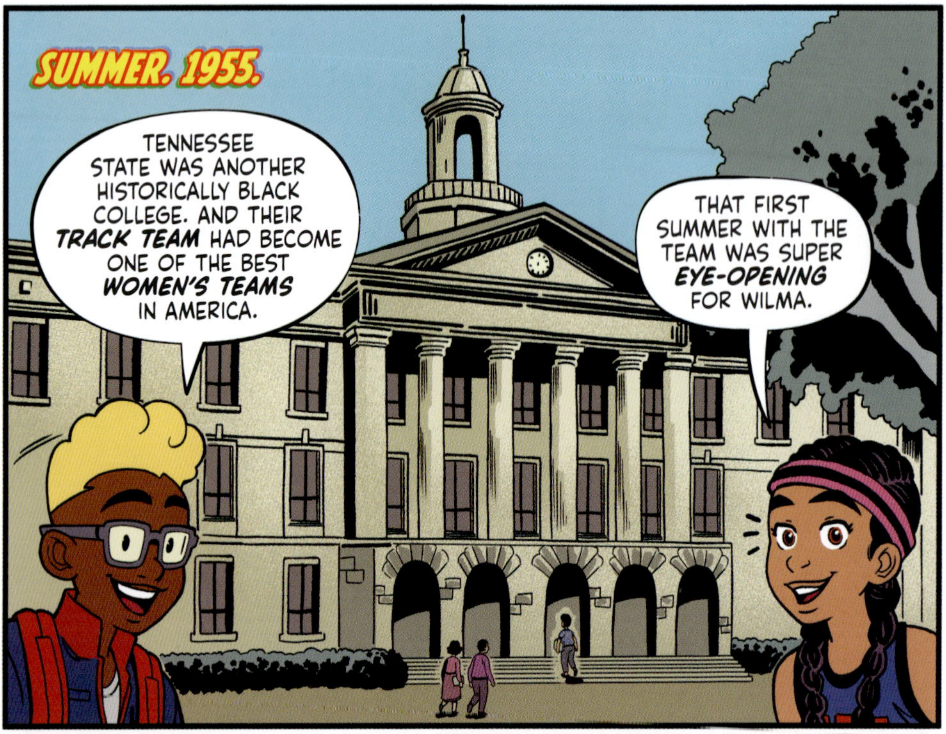
SUMMER. 1955.
TENNESSEE STATE WAS ANOTHER HISTORICALLY BLACK COLLEGE. AND THEIR TRACK TEAM HAD BECOME ONE OF THE BEST WOMEN'S TEAMS IN AMERICA.
THAT FIRST SUMMER WITH THE TEAM WAS SUPER EYE-OPENING FOR WILMA.

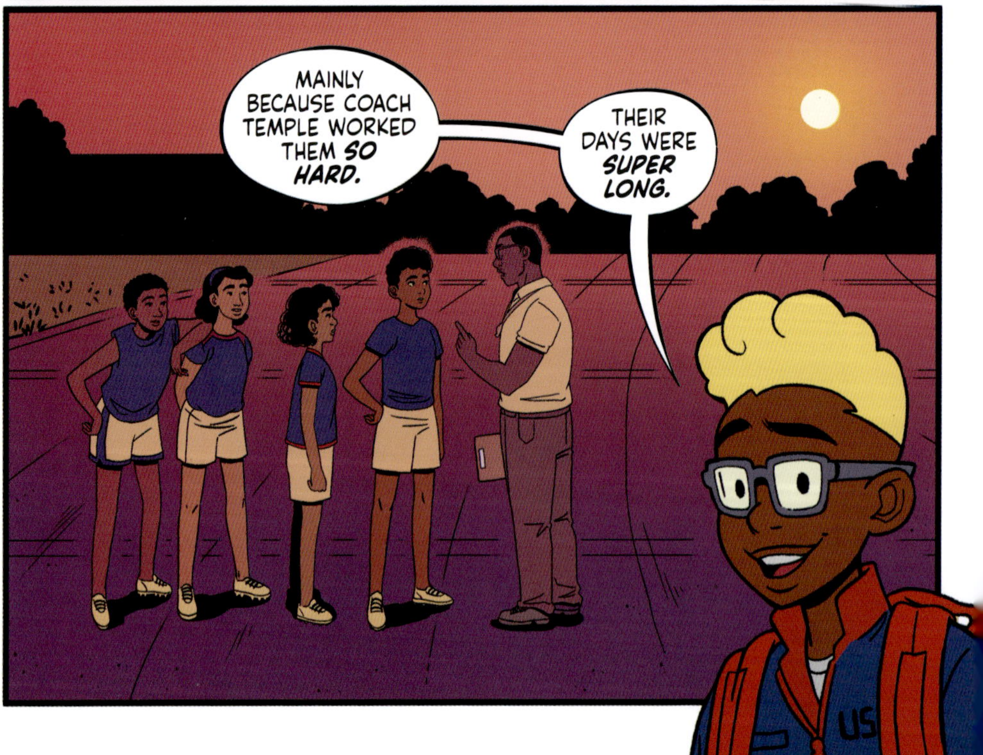
MAINLY BECAUSE COACH TEMPLE WORKED THEM SO HARD.
THEIR DAYS WERE SUPER LONG.
US

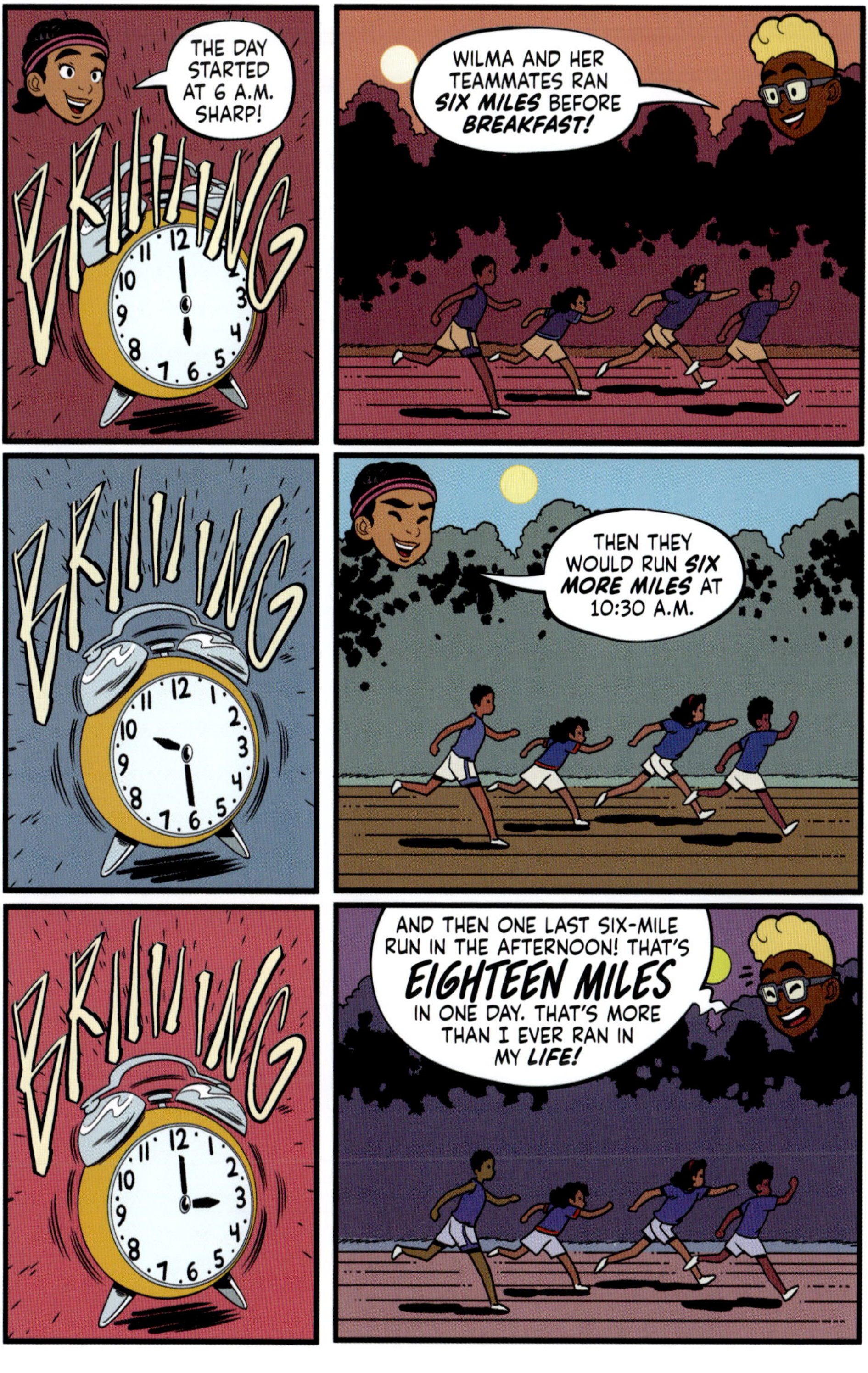
THE DAY STARTED AT 6 A.M. SHARP!
BRIIIING
WILMA AND HER TEAMMATES RAN SIX MILES BEFORE BREAKFAST!
BRIIIING
THEN THEY WOULD RUN SIX MORE MILES AT 10:30 A.M.
BRIIIING
AND THEN ONE LAST SIX-MILE RUN IN THE AFTERNOON! THAT'S EIGHTEEN MILES IN ONE DAY. THAT'S MORE THAN I EVER RAN IN MY LIFE!

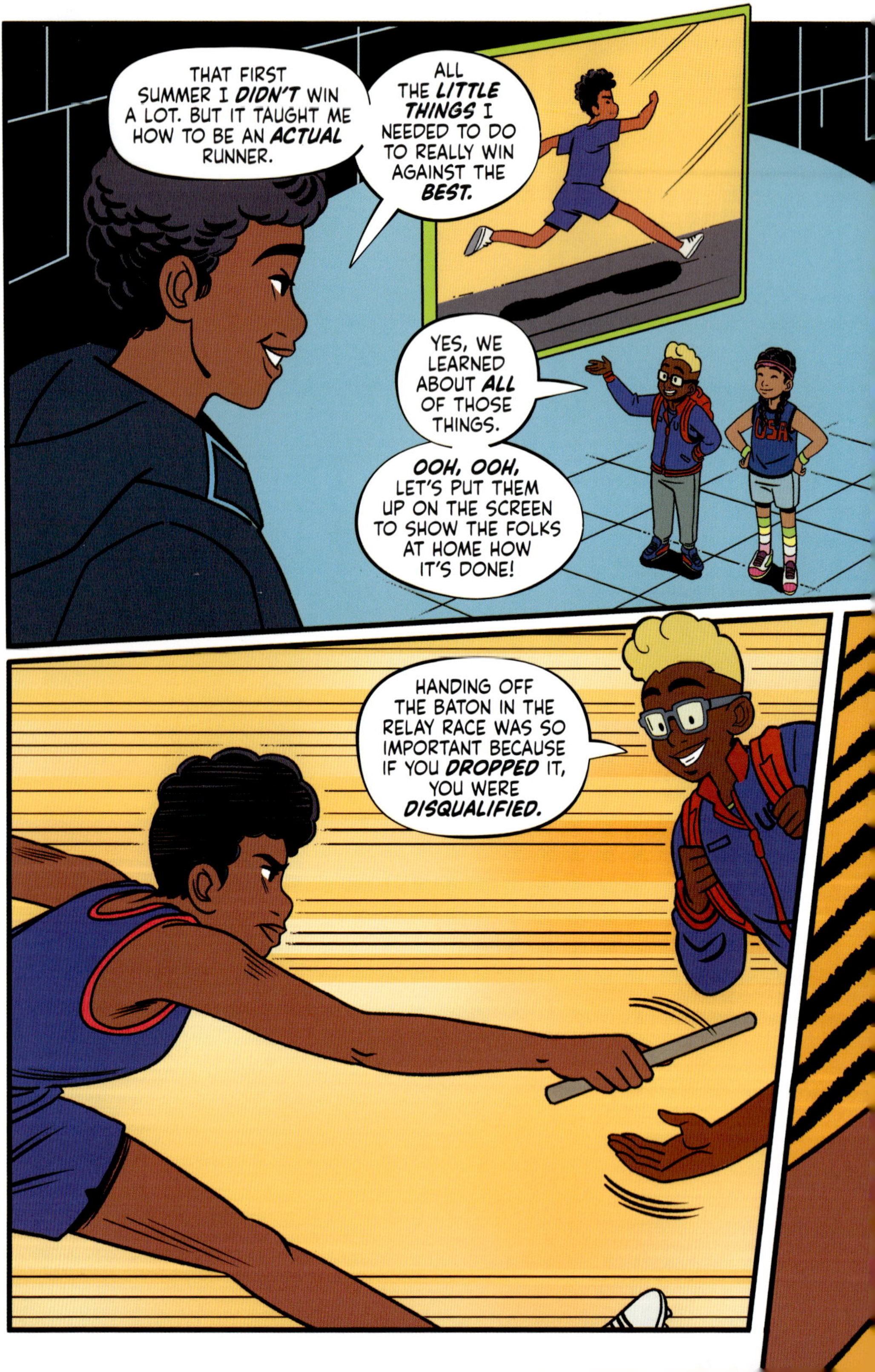
THAT FIRST SUMMER I DIDN'T WIN A LOT. BUT IT TAUGHT ME HOW TO BE AN ACTUAL RUNNER.
ALL THE LITTLE THINGS I NEEDED TO DO TO REALLY WIN AGAINST THE BEST.
YES, WE LEARNED ABOUT ALL OF THOSE THINGS.
OOH, OOH, LET'S PUT THEM UP ON THE SCREEN TO SHOW THE FOLKS AT HOME HOW IT'S DONE!
USA
HANDING OFF THE BATON IN THE RELAY RACE WAS SO IMPORTANT BECAUSE IF YOU DROPPED IT, YOU WERE DISQUALIFIED.

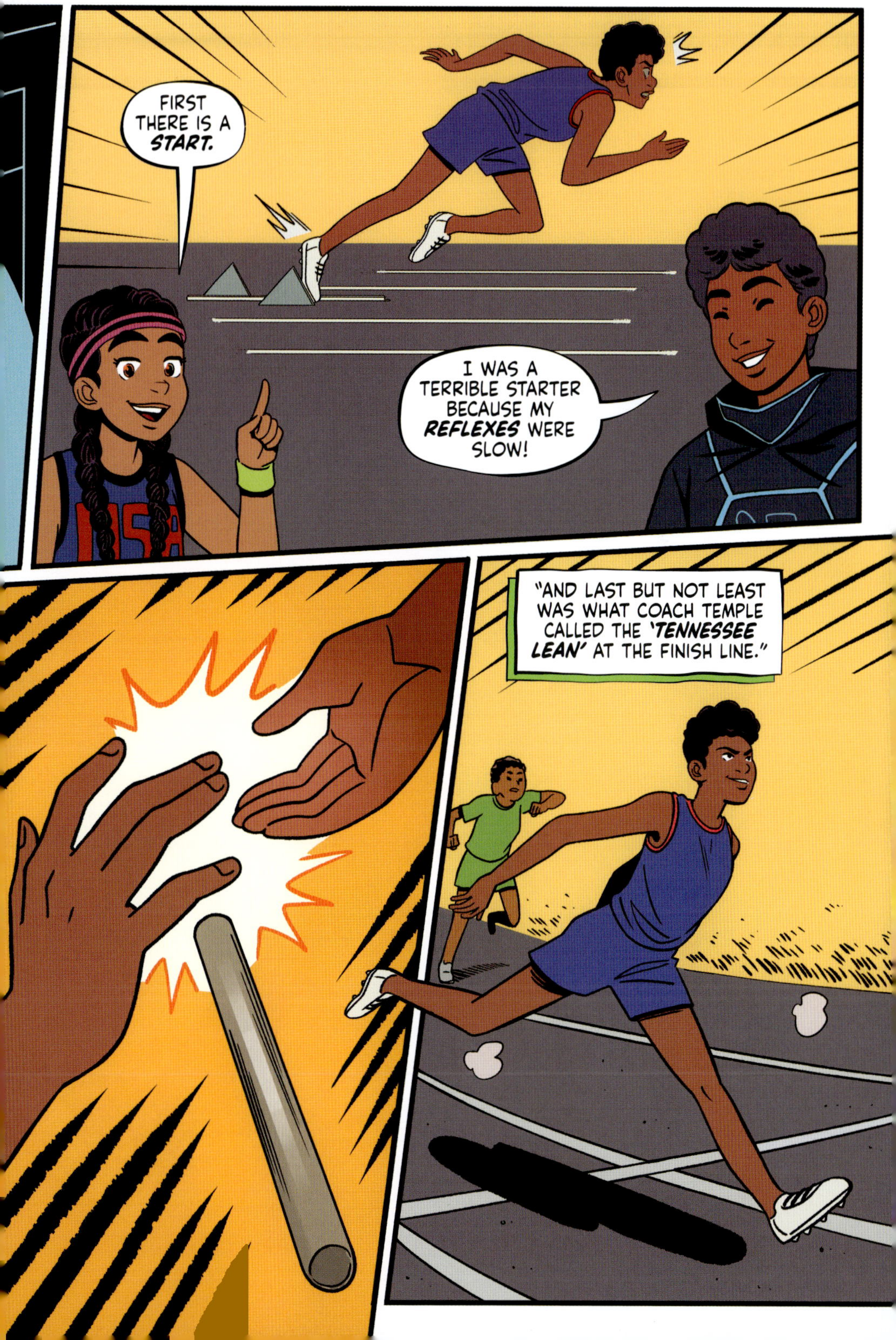
FIRST THERE IS A *START.*
I WAS A TERRIBLE STARTER BECAUSE MY *REFLEXES* WERE SLOW!
"AND LAST BUT NOT LEAST WAS WHAT COACH TEMPLE CALLED THE *'TENNESSEE LEAN'* AT THE FINISH LINE."

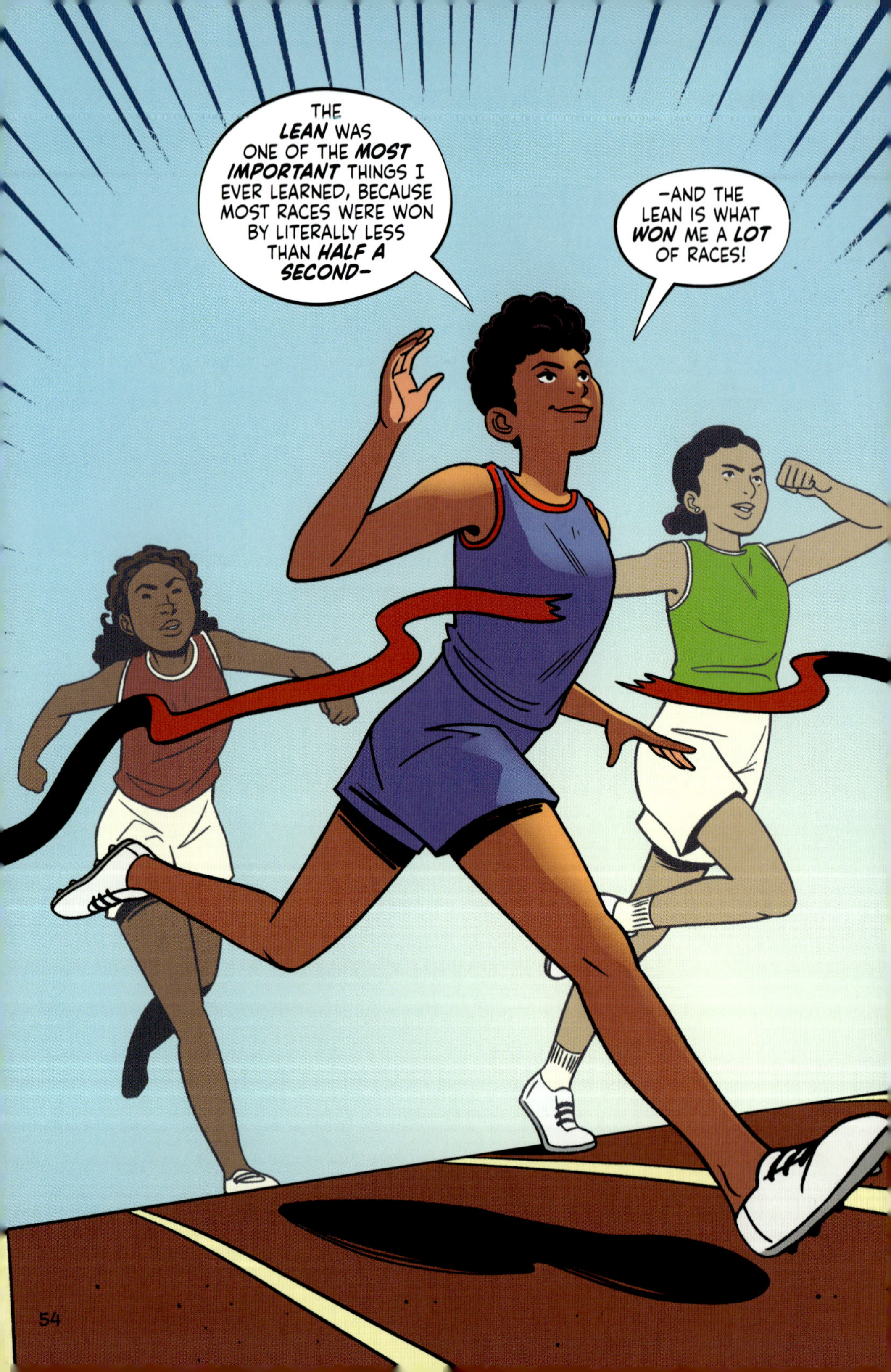
THE LEAN WAS ONE OF THE MOST IMPORTANT THINGS I EVER LEARNED, BECAUSE MOST RACES WERE WON BY LITERALLY LESS THAN HALF A SECOND-
-AND THE LEAN IS WHAT WON ME A LOT OF RACES!

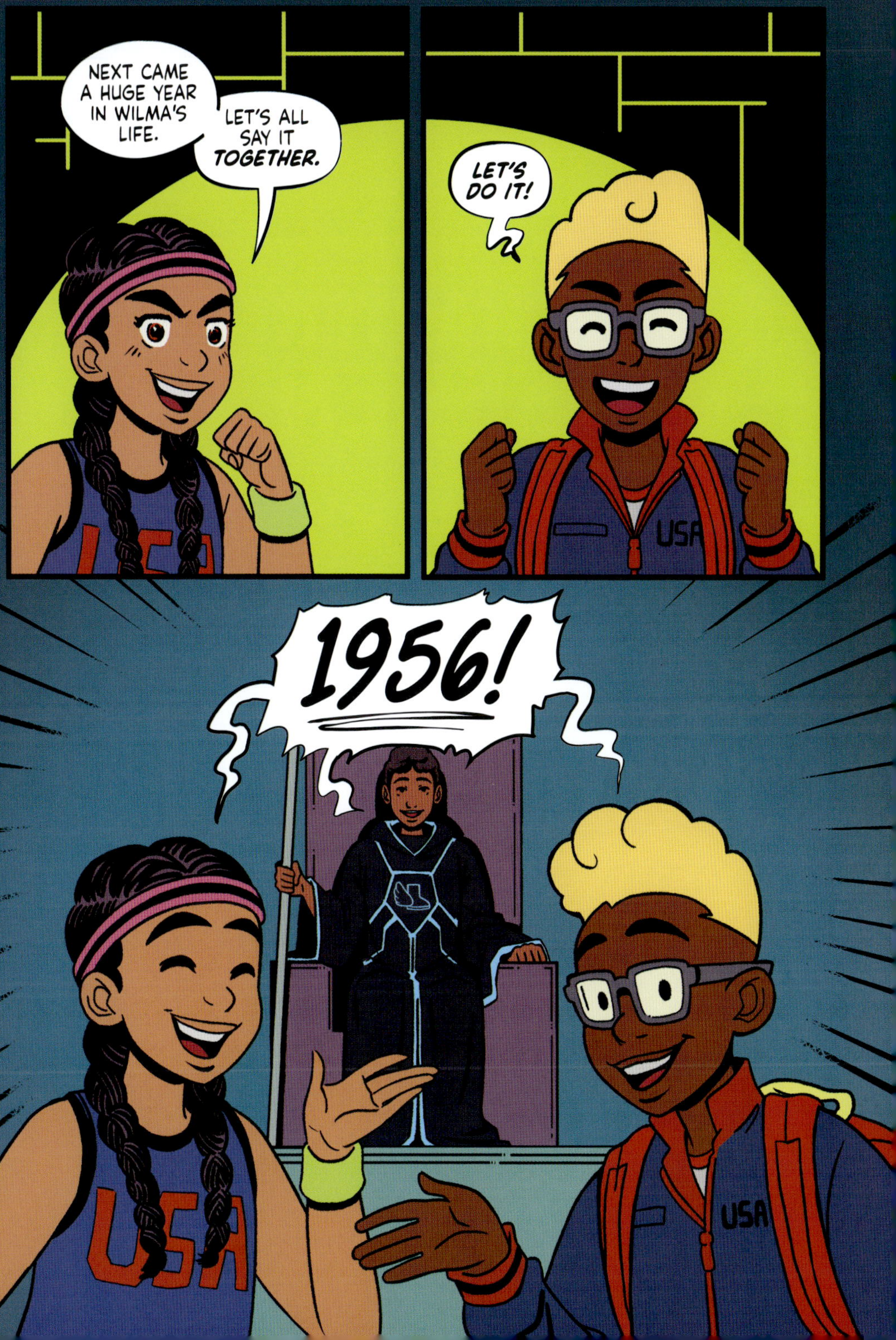
NEXT CAME A HUGE YEAR IN WILMA'S LIFE.
LET'S ALL SAY IT TOGETHER.
LET'S DO IT!
1956!

CHAPTER SEVEN

1956

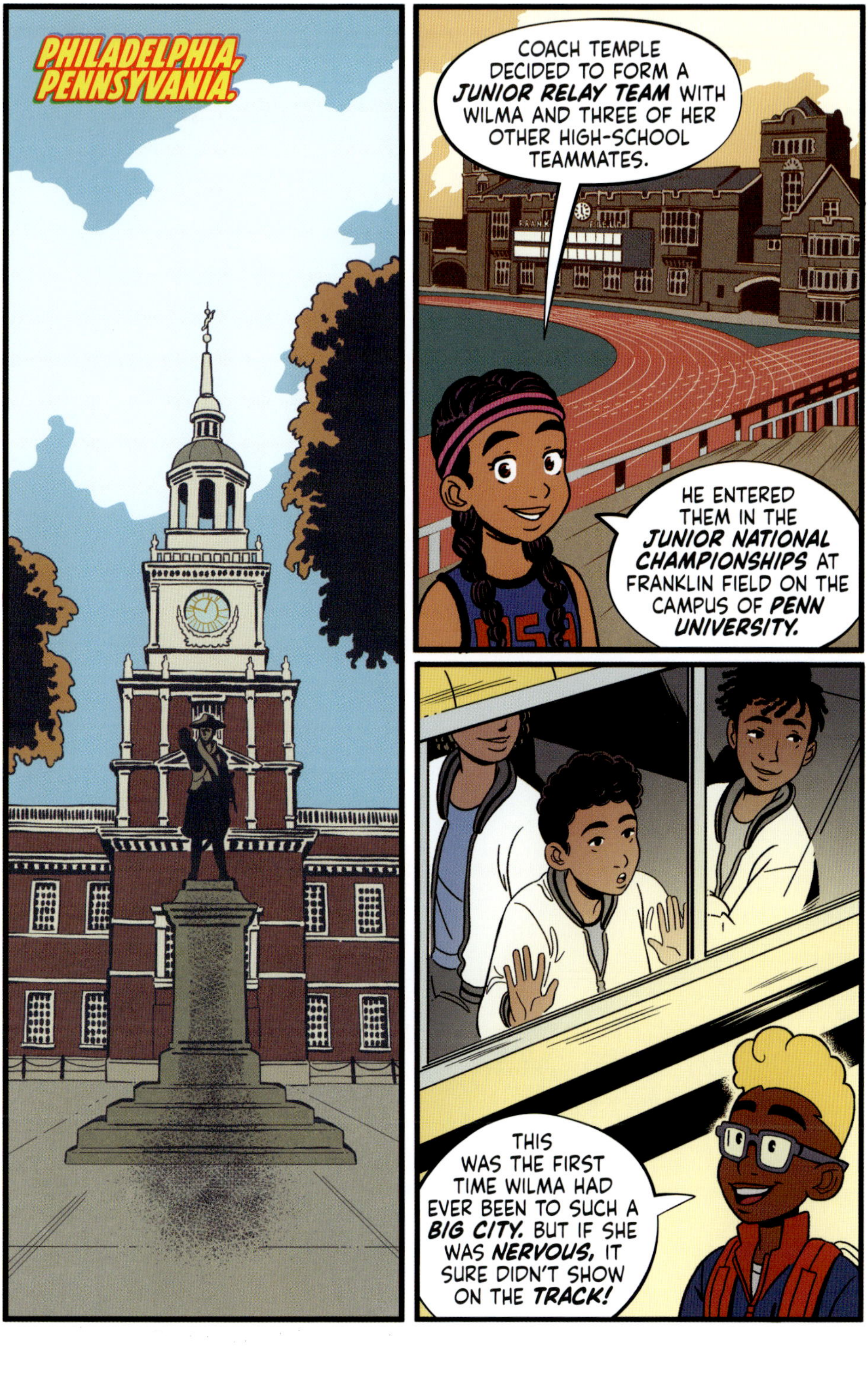
PHILADELPHIA, PENNSYVANIA.
COACH TEMPLE DECIDED TO FORM A JUNIOR RELAY TEAM WITH WILMA AND THREE OF HER OTHER HIGH-SCHOOL TEAMMATES.
HE ENTERED THEM IN THE JUNIOR NATIONAL CHAMPIONSHIPS AT FRANKLIN FIELD ON THE CAMPUS OF PENN UNIVERSITY.
THIS WAS THE FIRST TIME WILMA HAD EVER BEEN TO SUCH A BIG CITY. BUT IF SHE WAS NERVOUS, IT SURE DIDN'T SHOW ON THE TRACK!

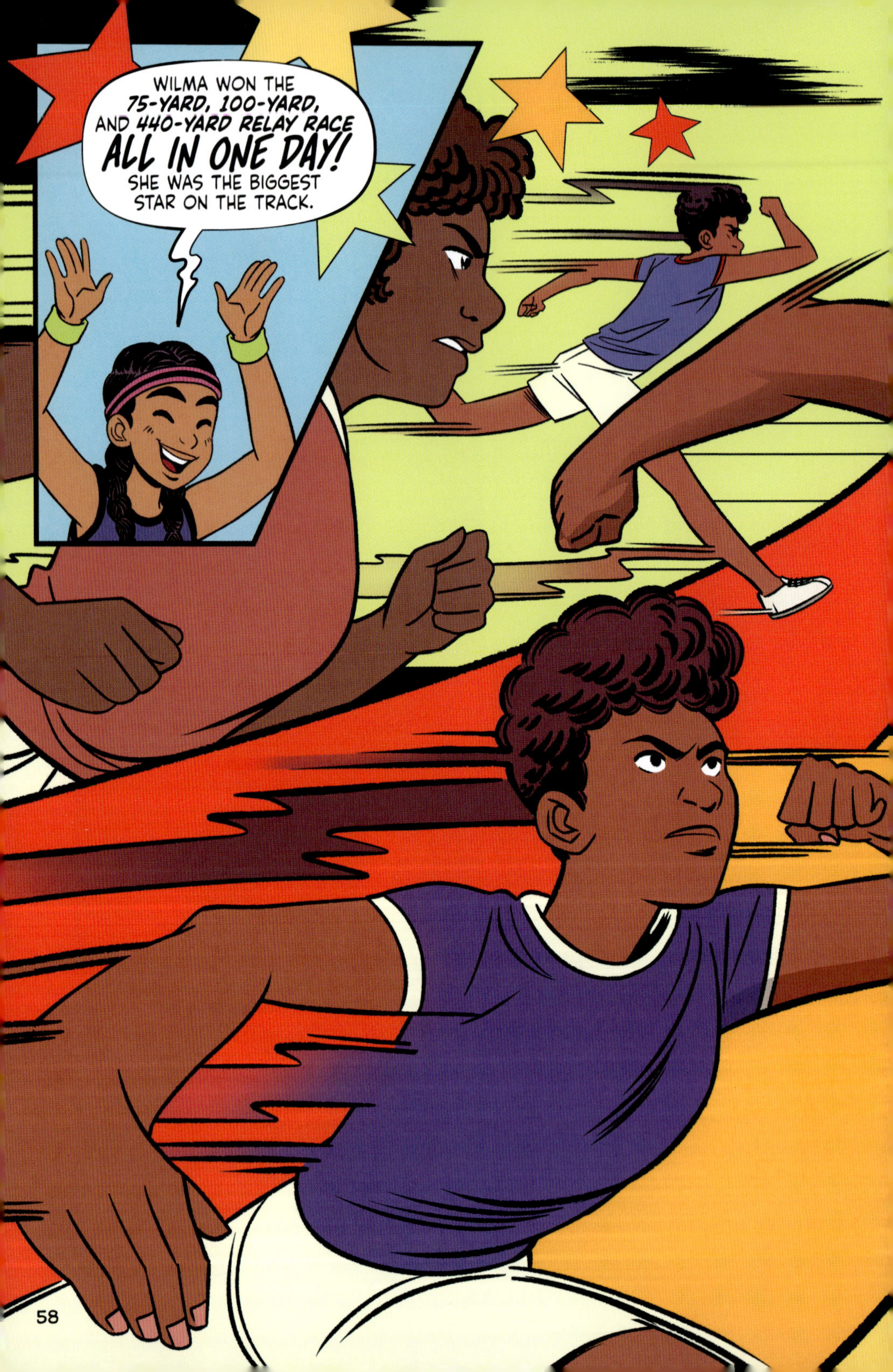
WILMA WON THE 75-YARD, 100-YARD, AND 440-YARD RELAY RACE ALL IN ONE DAY! SHE WAS THE BIGGEST STAR ON THE TRACK.

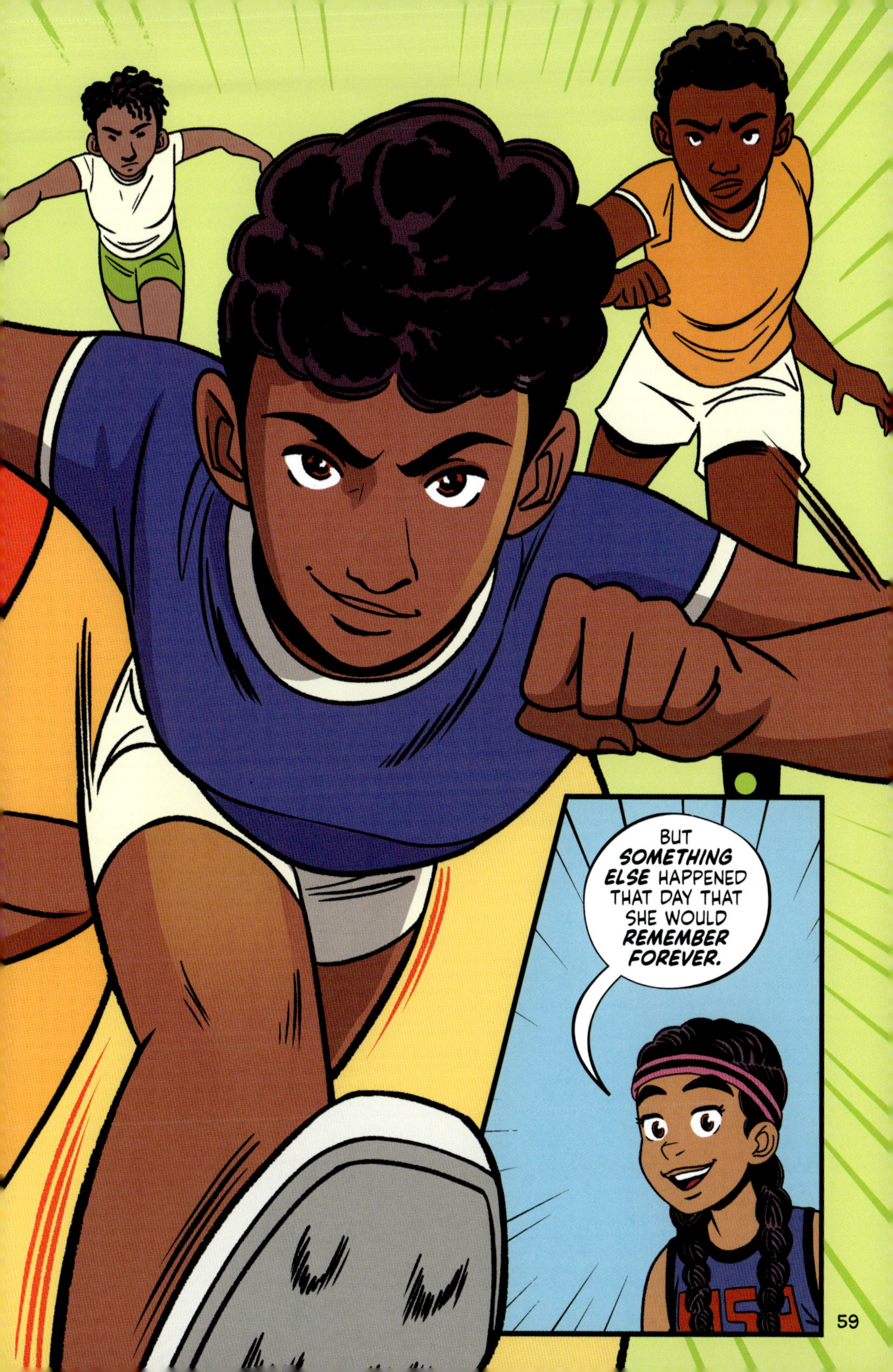
BUT SOMETHING ELSE HAPPENED THAT DAY THAT SHE WOULD REMEMBER FOREVER.

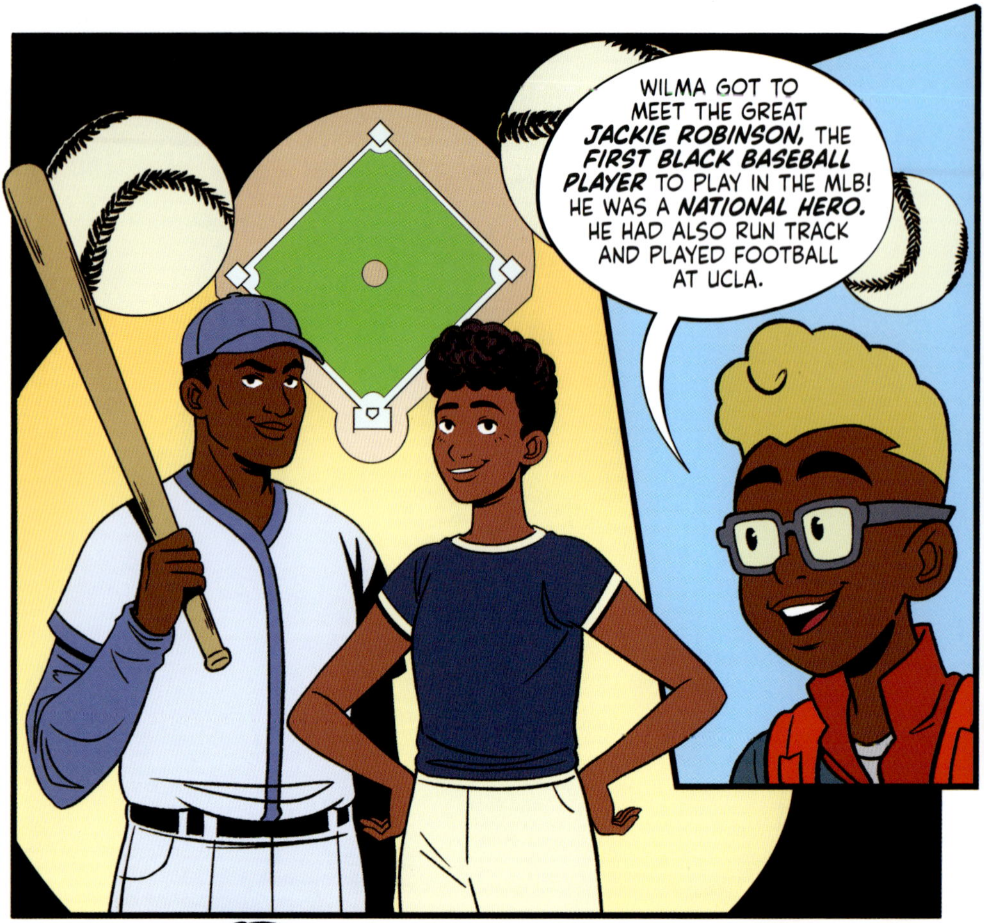
WILMA GOT TO MEET THE GREAT ***JACKIE ROBINSON,*** THE ***FIRST BLACK BASEBALL PLAYER*** TO PLAY IN THE MLB! HE WAS A ***NATIONAL HERO.*** HE HAD ALSO RUN TRACK AND PLAYED FOOTBALL AT UCLA.

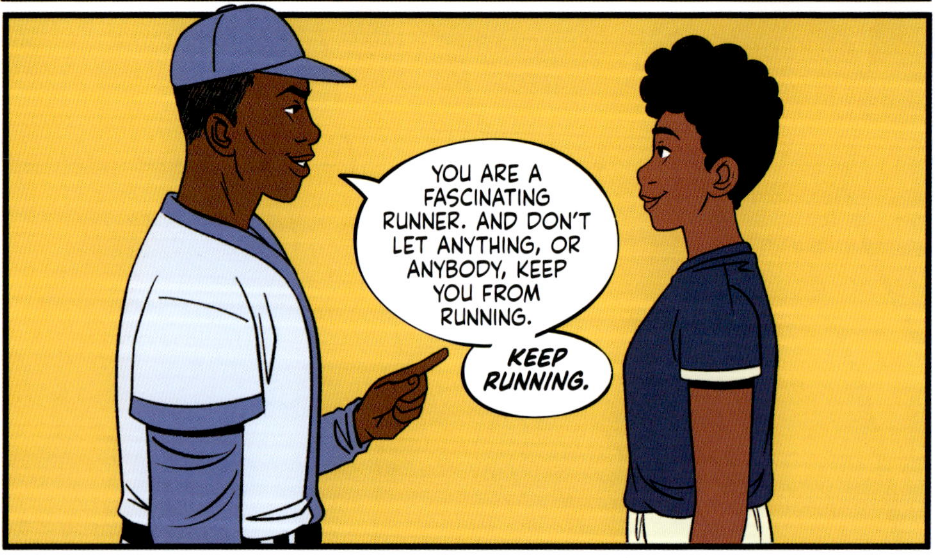
YOU ARE A FASCINATING RUNNER. AND DON'T LET ANYTHING, OR ANYBODY, KEEP YOU FROM RUNNING.
KEEP RUNNING.

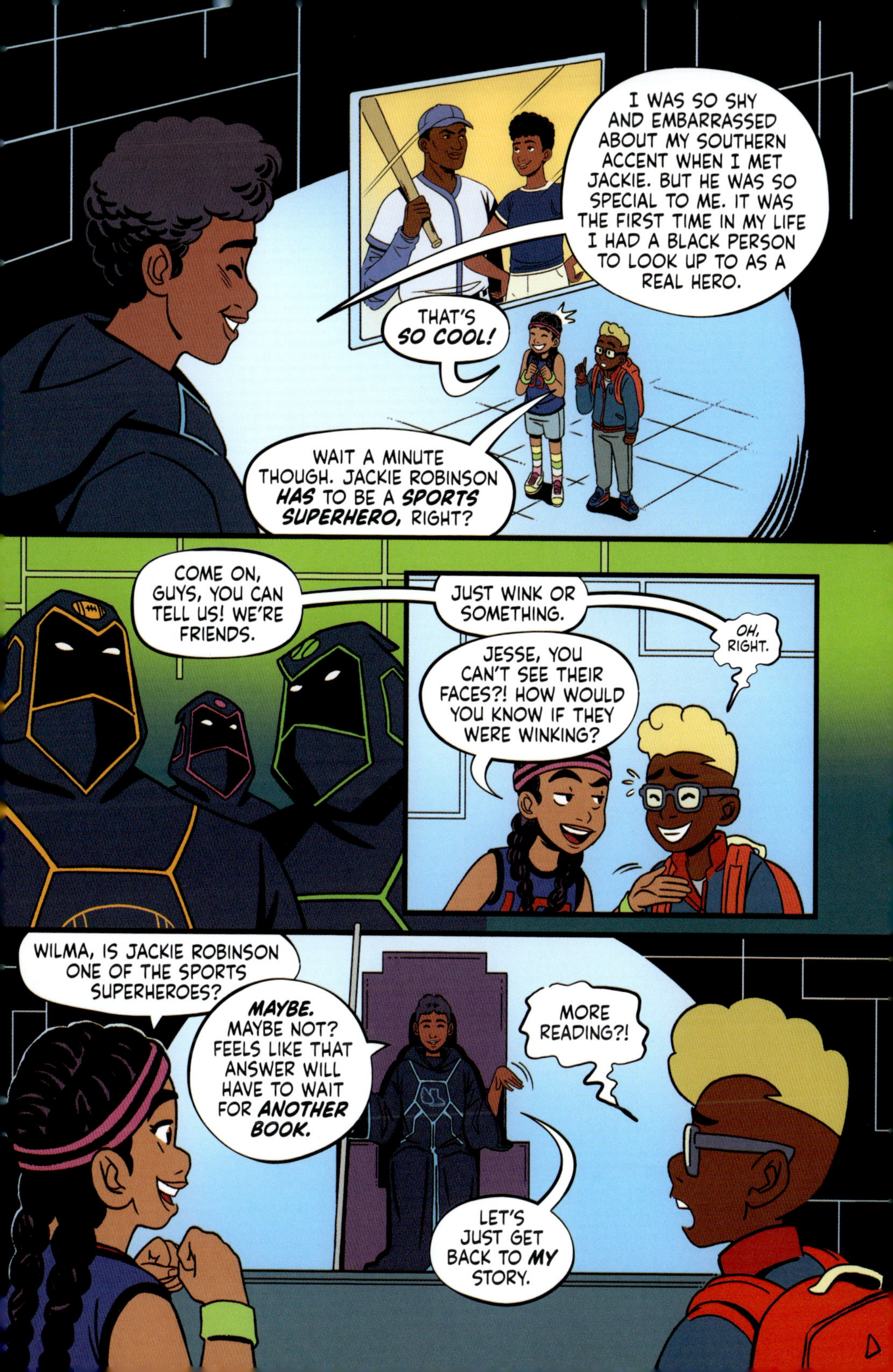
I WAS SO SHY AND EMBARRASSED ABOUT MY SOUTHERN ACCENT WHEN I MET JACKIE. BUT HE WAS SO SPECIAL TO ME. IT WAS THE FIRST TIME IN MY LIFE I HAD A BLACK PERSON TO LOOK UP TO AS A REAL HERO.
THAT'S *SO COOL!*
WAIT A MINUTE THOUGH. JACKIE ROBINSON ***HAS*** TO BE A ***SPORTS SUPERHERO,*** RIGHT?
COME ON, GUYS, YOU CAN TELL US! WE'RE FRIENDS.
JUST WINK OR SOMETHING.
OH, RIGHT.
JESSE, YOU CAN'T SEE THEIR FACES?! HOW WOULD YOU KNOW IF THEY WERE WINKING?
WILMA, IS JACKIE ROBINSON ONE OF THE SPORTS SUPERHEROES?
MAYBE. MAYBE NOT? FEELS LIKE THAT ANSWER WILL HAVE TO WAIT FOR ***ANOTHER BOOK.***
MORE READING?!
LET'S JUST GET BACK TO ***MY*** STORY.

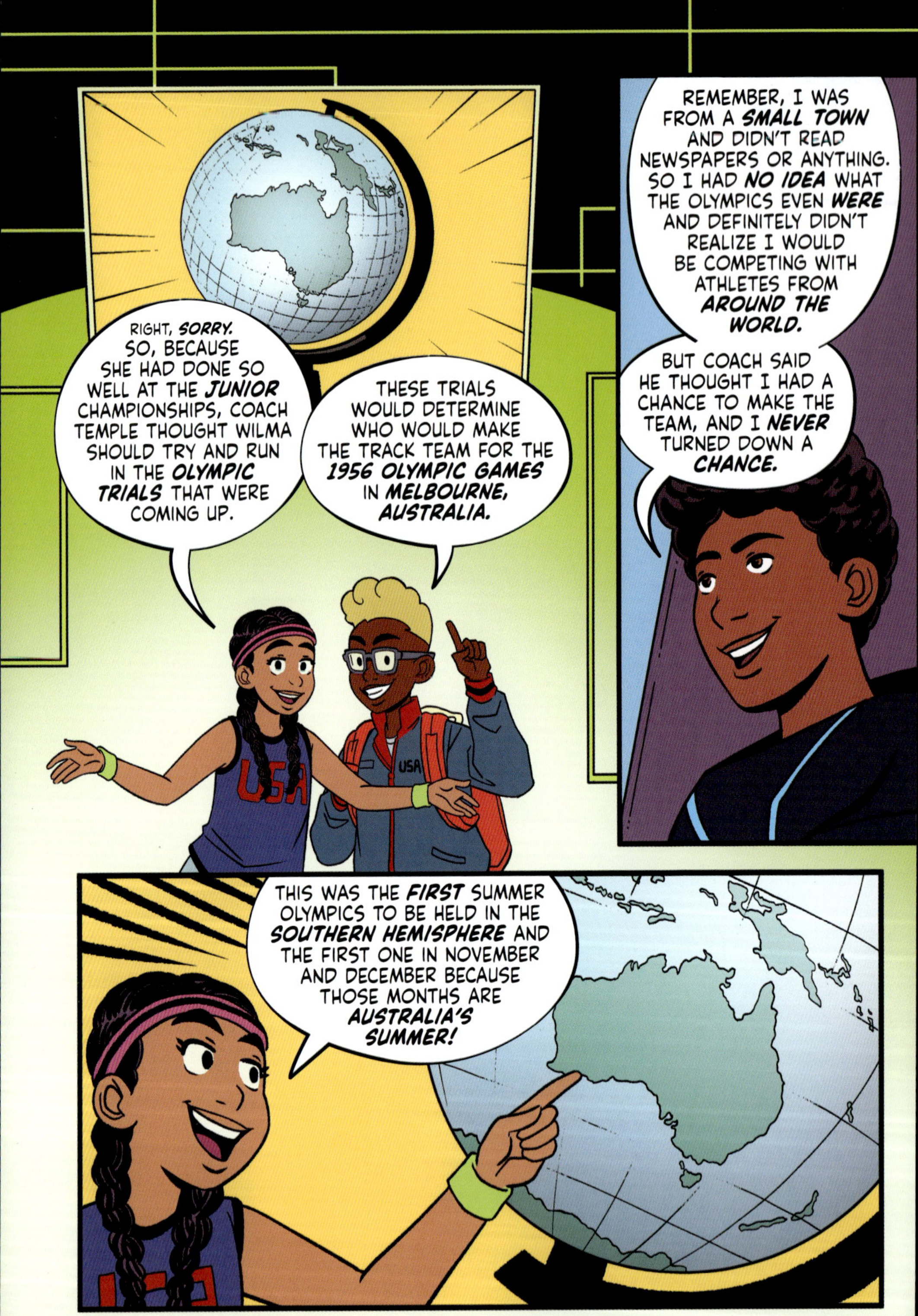
RIGHT, SORRY. SO, BECAUSE SHE HAD DONE SO WELL AT THE JUNIOR CHAMPIONSHIPS, COACH TEMPLE THOUGHT WILMA SHOULD TRY AND RUN IN THE OLYMPIC TRIALS THAT WERE COMING UP.
THESE TRIALS WOULD DETERMINE WHO WOULD MAKE THE TRACK TEAM FOR THE 1956 OLYMPIC GAMES IN MELBOURNE, AUSTRALIA.
REMEMBER, I WAS FROM A SMALL TOWN AND DIDN'T READ NEWSPAPERS OR ANYTHING. SO I HAD NO IDEA WHAT THE OLYMPICS EVEN WERE AND DEFINITELY DIDN'T REALIZE I WOULD BE COMPETING WITH ATHLETES FROM AROUND THE WORLD.
BUT COACH SAID HE THOUGHT I HAD A CHANCE TO MAKE THE TEAM, AND I NEVER TURNED DOWN A CHANCE.
USA
USA
THIS WAS THE FIRST SUMMER OLYMPICS TO BE HELD IN THE SOUTHERN HEMISPHERE AND THE FIRST ONE IN NOVEMBER AND DECEMBER BECAUSE THOSE MONTHS ARE AUSTRALIA'S SUMMER!

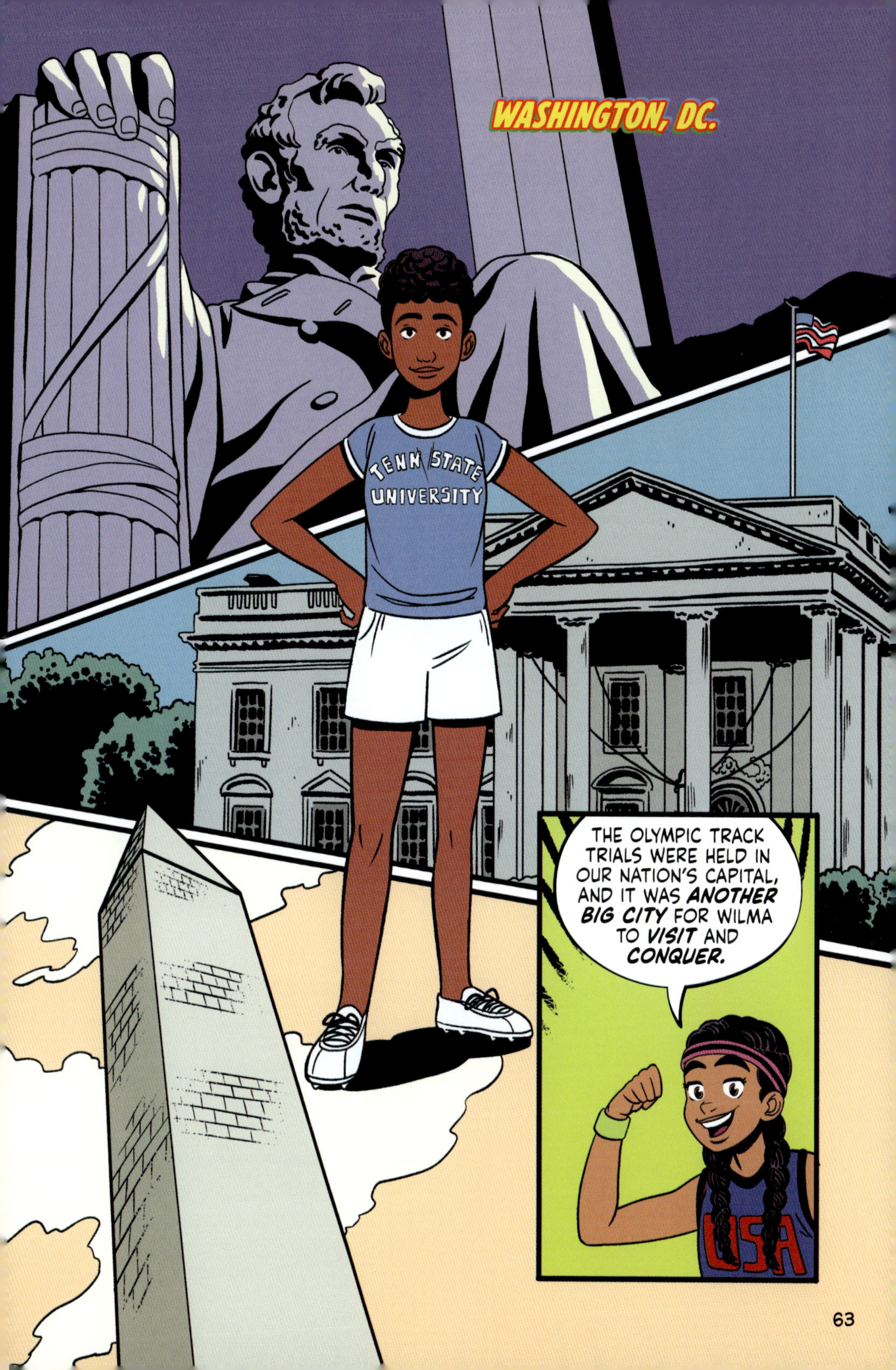
WASHINGTON, DC.
TENN STATE UNIVERSITY
THE OLYMPIC TRACK TRIALS WERE HELD IN OUR NATION'S CAPITAL, AND IT WAS ***ANOTHER BIG CITY*** FOR WILMA TO ***VISIT*** AND ***CONQUER.***
USA

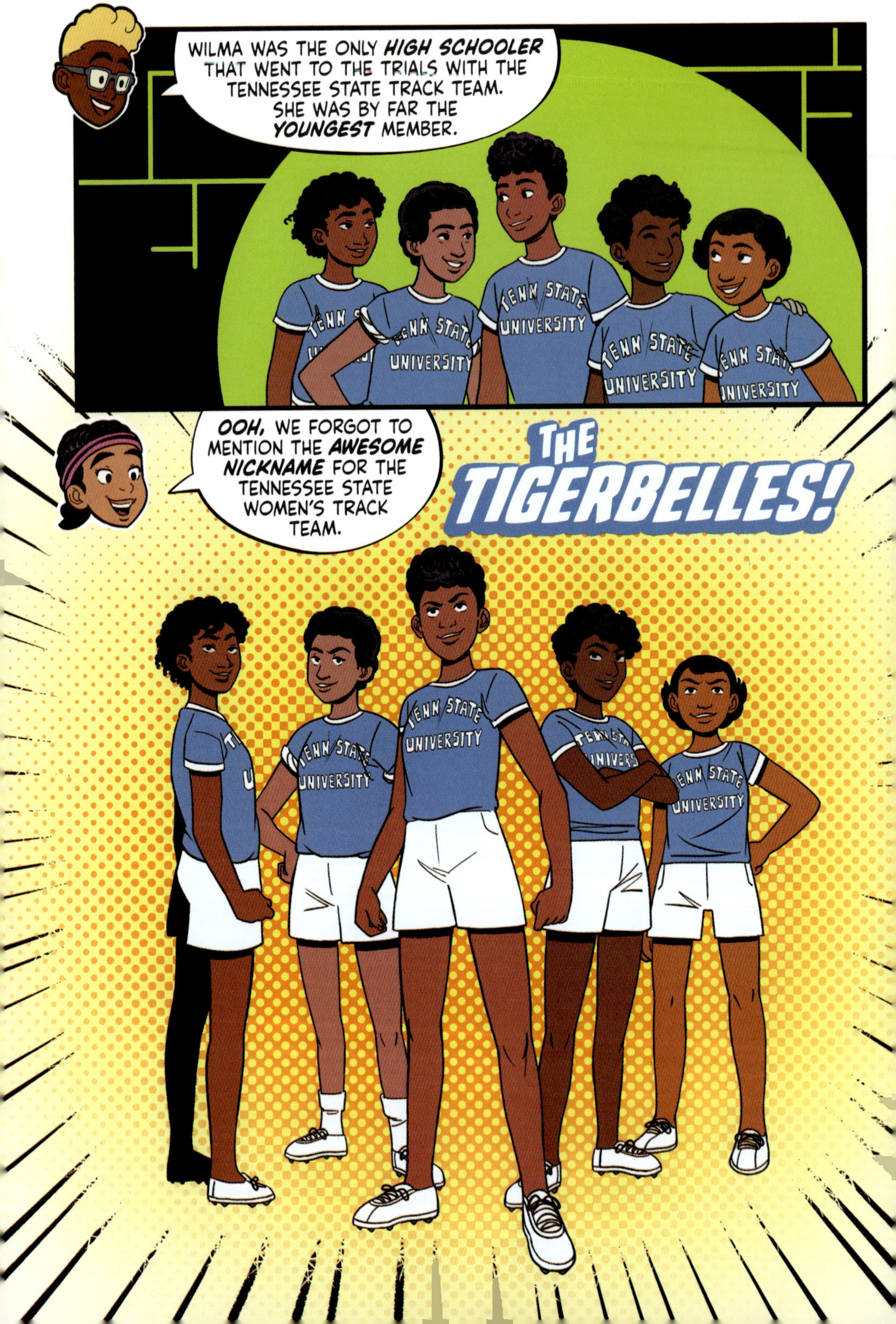
WILMA WAS THE ONLY HIGH SCHOOLER THAT WENT TO THE TRIALS WITH THE TENNESSEE STATE TRACK TEAM. SHE WAS BY FAR THE YOUNGEST MEMBER.
TENN STATE UNIVERSITY
OOH, WE FORGOT TO MENTION THE AWESOME NICKNAME FOR THE TENNESSEE STATE WOMEN'S TRACK TEAM.
THE TIGERBELLES!
TENN STATE UNIVERSITY

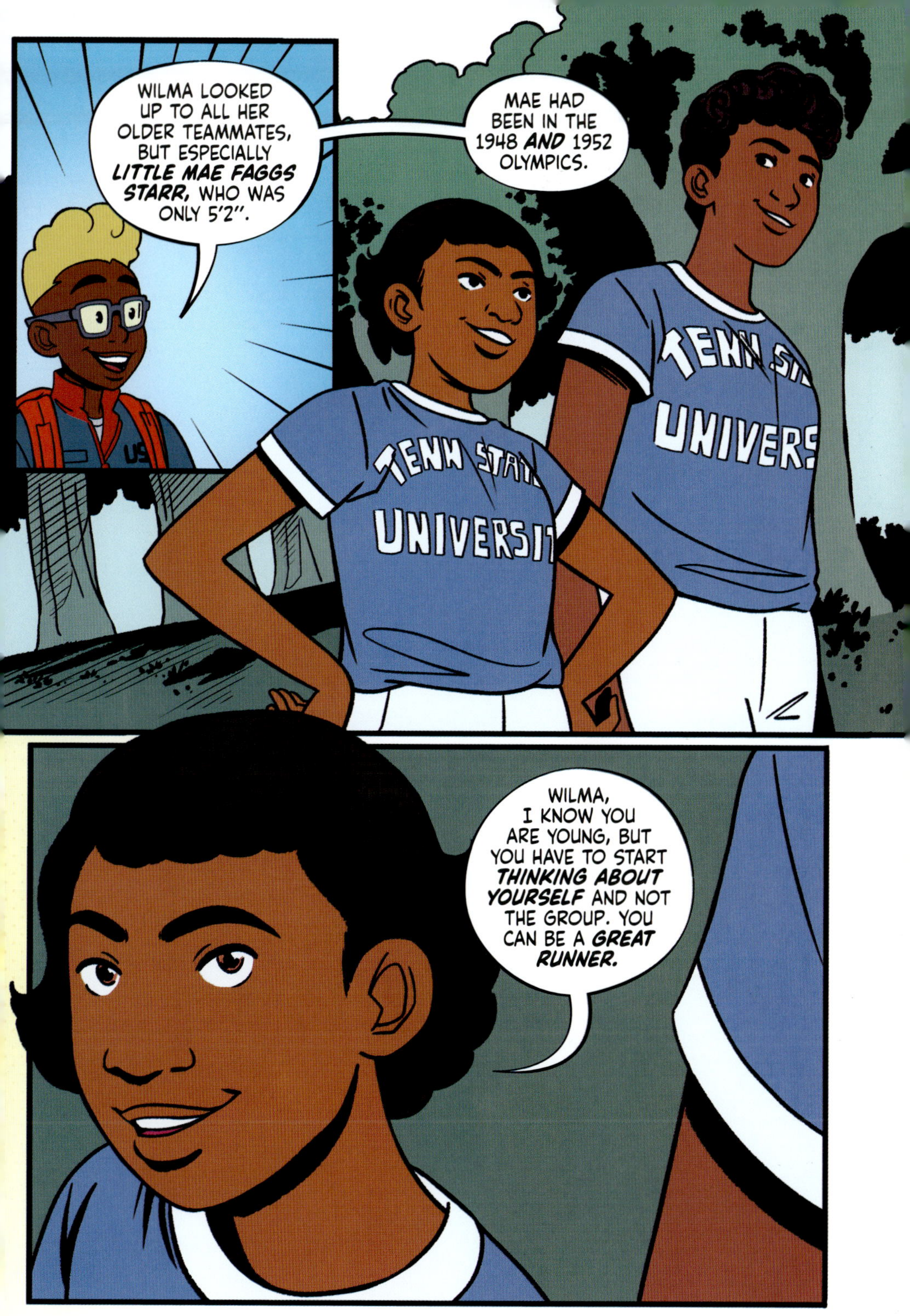
WILMA LOOKED UP TO ALL HER OLDER TEAMMATES, BUT ESPECIALLY ***LITTLE MAE FAGGS STARR,*** WHO WAS ONLY 5'2".
MAE HAD BEEN IN THE 1948 ***AND*** 1952 OLYMPICS.
TENN STATE UNIVERSITY
WILMA, I KNOW YOU ARE YOUNG, BUT YOU HAVE TO START ***THINKING ABOUT YOURSELF*** AND NOT THE GROUP. YOU CAN BE A ***GREAT RUNNER.***

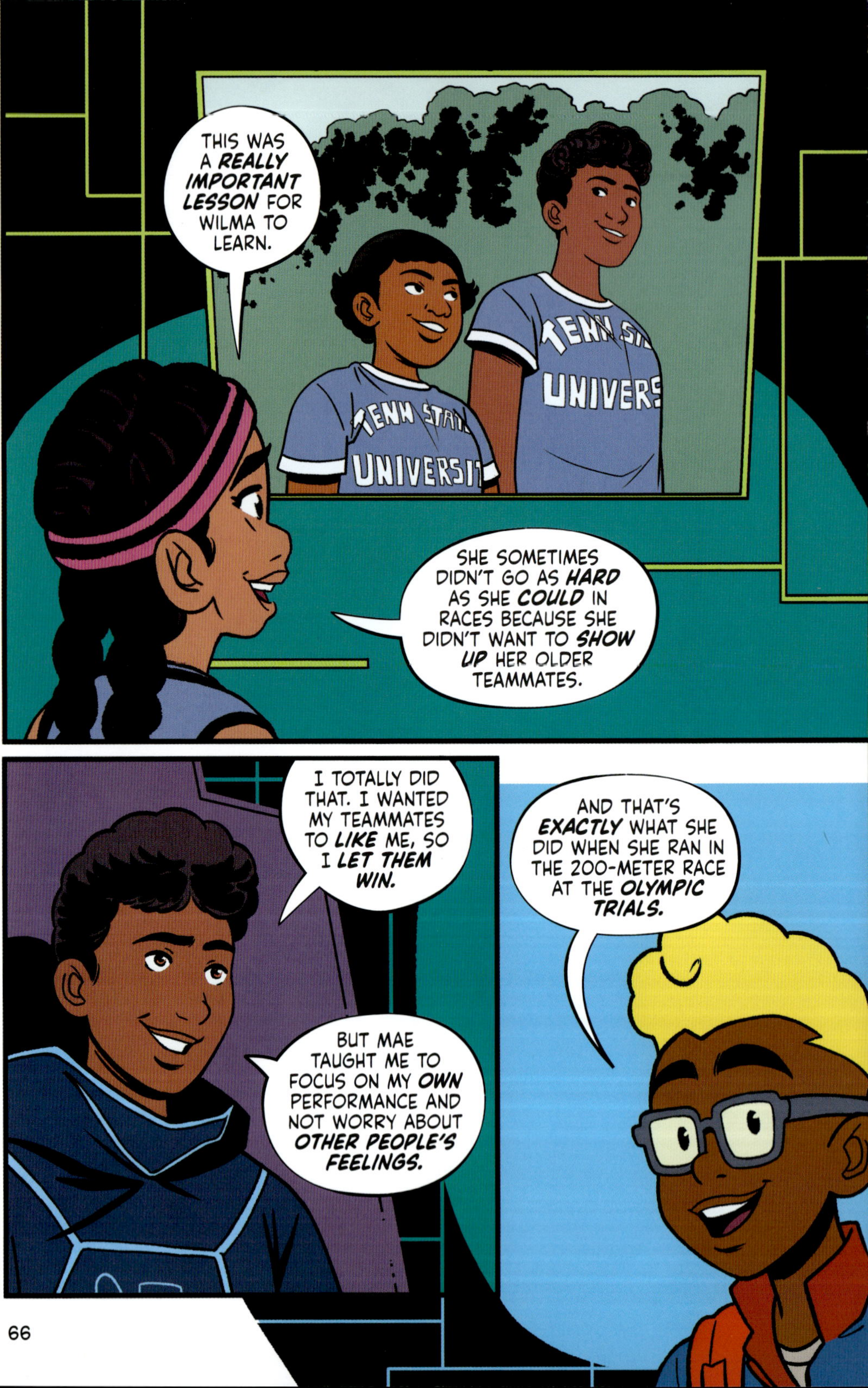
THIS WAS A REALLY IMPORTANT LESSON FOR WILMA TO LEARN.
TENN STATE UNIVERSIT
SHE SOMETIMES DIDN'T GO AS HARD AS SHE COULD IN RACES BECAUSE SHE DIDN'T WANT TO SHOW UP HER OLDER TEAMMATES.
I TOTALLY DID THAT. I WANTED MY TEAMMATES TO LIKE ME, SO I LET THEM WIN.
BUT MAE TAUGHT ME TO FOCUS ON MY OWN PERFORMANCE AND NOT WORRY ABOUT OTHER PEOPLE'S FEELINGS.
AND THAT'S EXACTLY WHAT SHE DID WHEN SHE RAN IN THE 200-METER RACE AT THE OLYMPIC TRIALS.

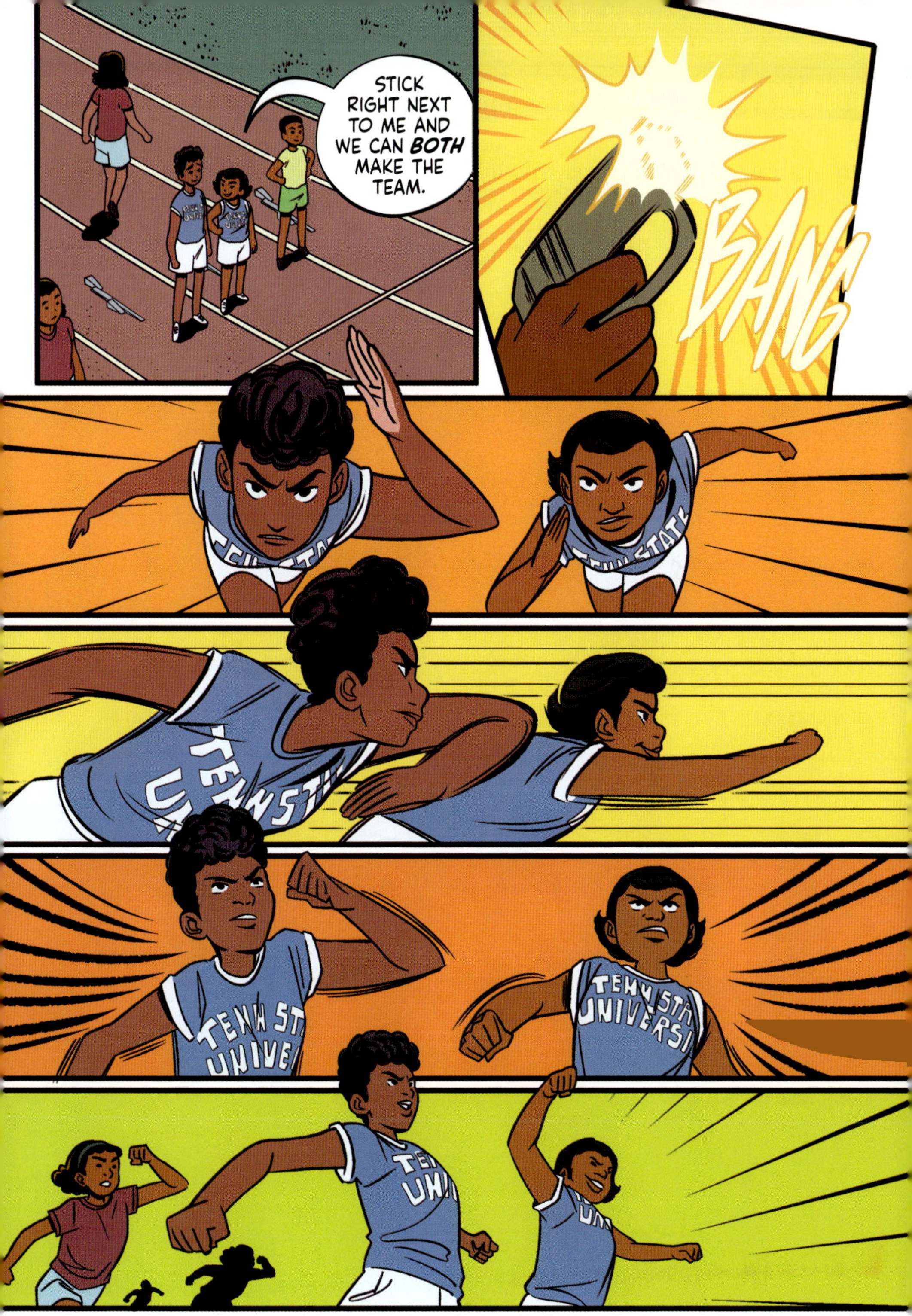
STICK RIGHT NEXT TO ME AND WE CAN *BOTH* MAKE THE TEAM.
BANG

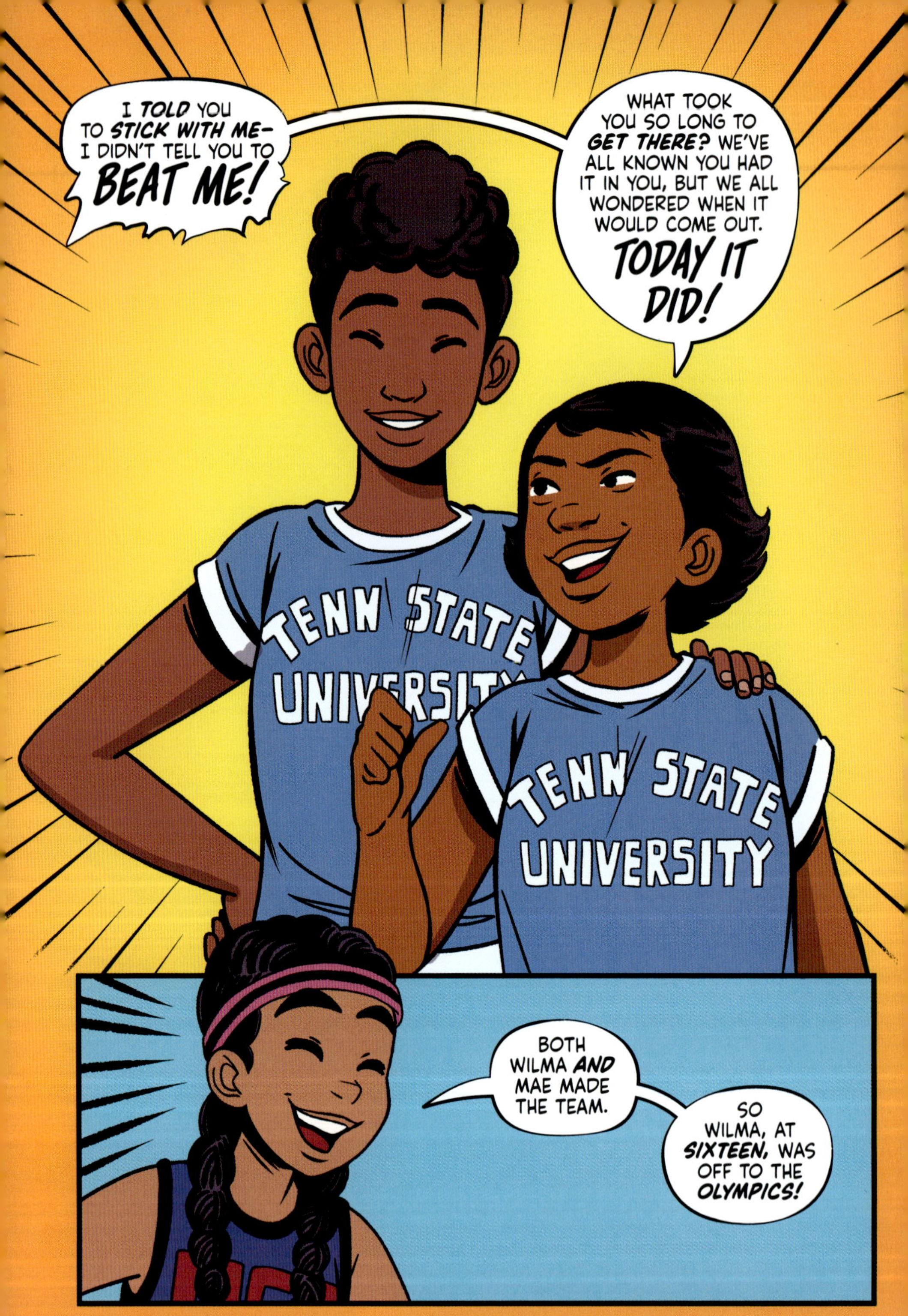
I TOLD YOU TO STICK WITH ME– I DIDN'T TELL YOU TO BEAT ME!
WHAT TOOK YOU SO LONG TO GET THERE? WE'VE ALL KNOWN YOU HAD IT IN YOU, BUT WE ALL WONDERED WHEN IT WOULD COME OUT. TODAY IT DID!
TENN STATE UNIVERSITY
TENN STATE UNIVERSITY
BOTH WILMA AND MAE MADE THE TEAM.
SO WILMA, AT SIXTEEN, WAS OFF TO THE OLYMPICS!

CHAPTER EIGHT

AUSTRALIA

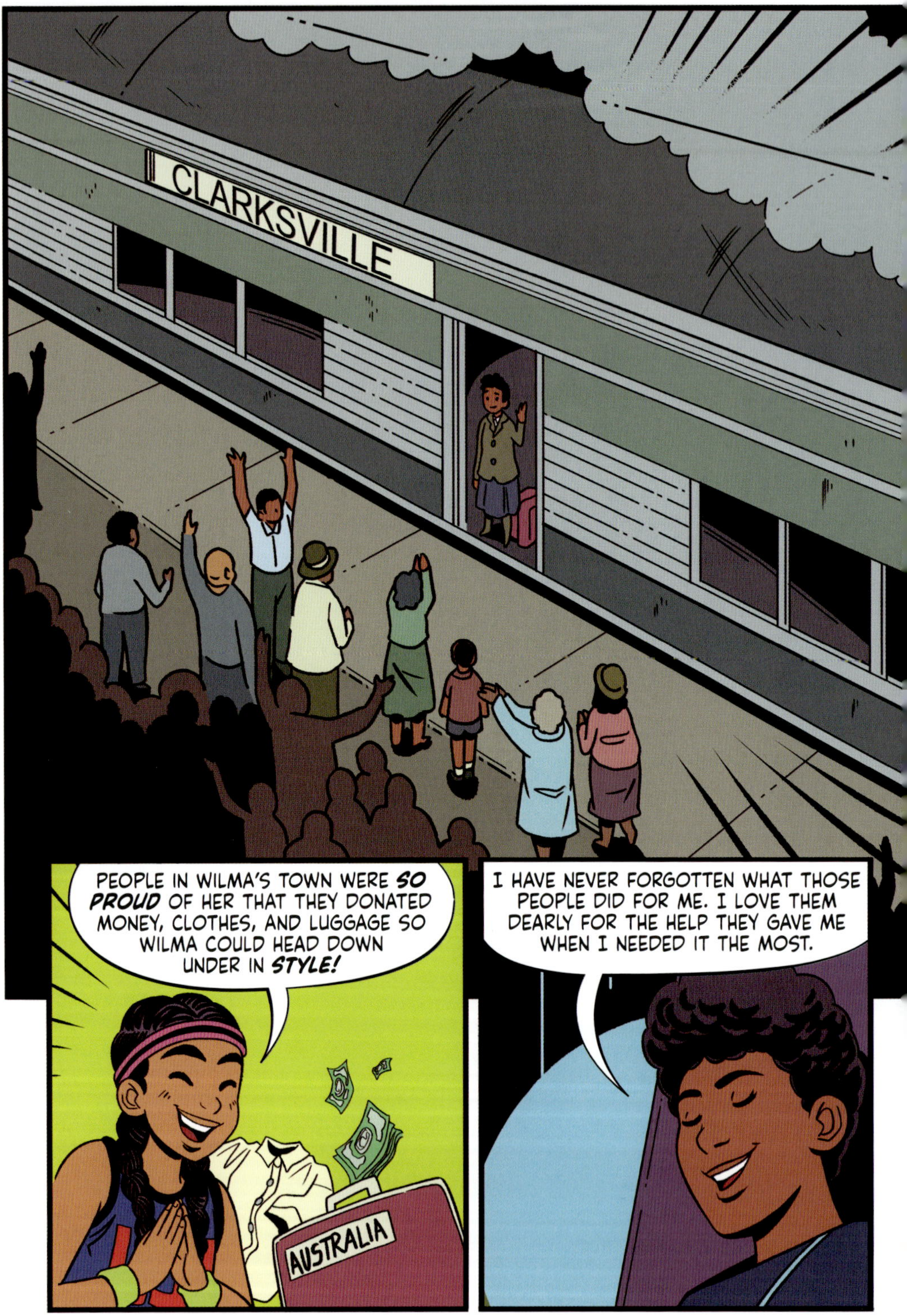
CLARKSVILLE
PEOPLE IN WILMA'S TOWN WERE SO PROUD OF HER THAT THEY DONATED MONEY, CLOTHES, AND LUGGAGE SO WILMA COULD HEAD DOWN UNDER IN STYLE!
AUSTRALIA
I HAVE NEVER FORGOTTEN WHAT THOSE PEOPLE DID FOR ME. I LOVE THEM DEARLY FOR THE HELP THEY GAVE ME WHEN I NEEDED IT THE MOST.

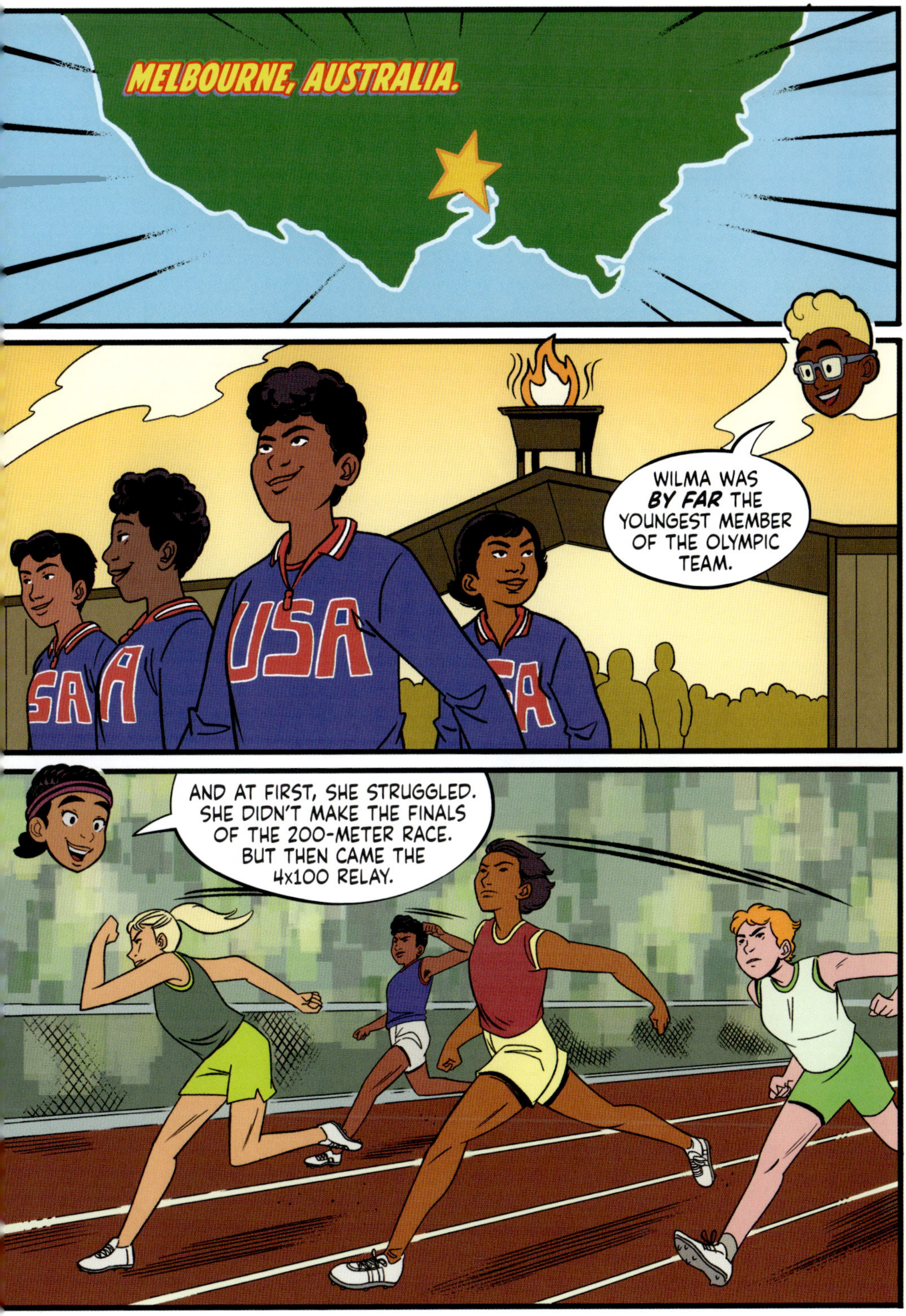
MELBOURNE, AUSTRALIA.
WILMA WAS BY FAR THE YOUNGEST MEMBER OF THE OLYMPIC TEAM.
USA
AND AT FIRST, SHE STRUGGLED. SHE DIDN'T MAKE THE FINALS OF THE 200-METER RACE. BUT THEN CAME THE 4x100 RELAY.

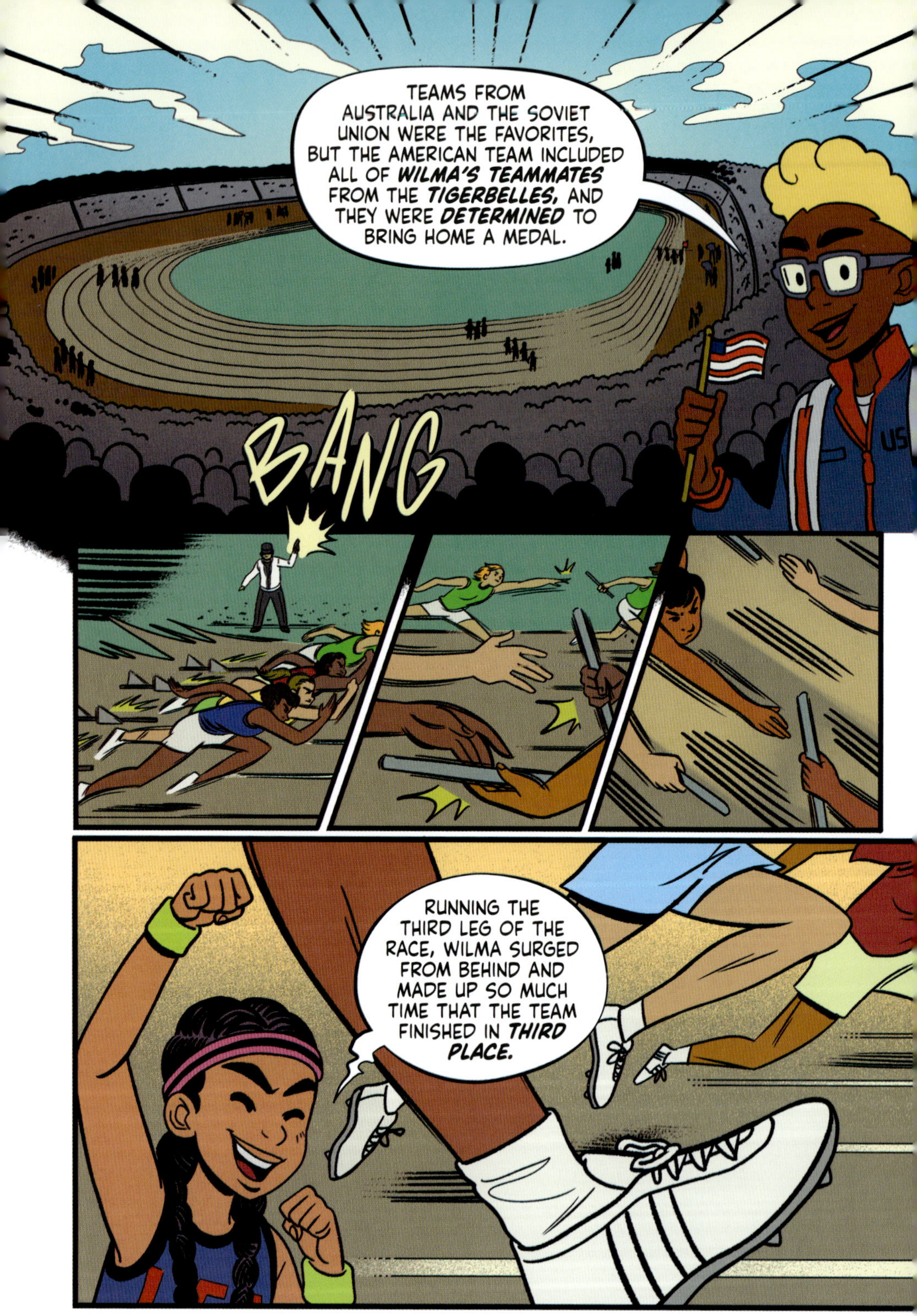
TEAMS FROM AUSTRALIA AND THE SOVIET UNION WERE THE FAVORITES, BUT THE AMERICAN TEAM INCLUDED ALL OF WILMA'S TEAMMATES FROM THE TIGERBELLES, AND THEY WERE DETERMINED TO BRING HOME A MEDAL.
BANG
RUNNING THE THIRD LEG OF THE RACE, WILMA SURGED FROM BEHIND AND MADE UP SO MUCH TIME THAT THE TEAM FINISHED IN THIRD PLACE.

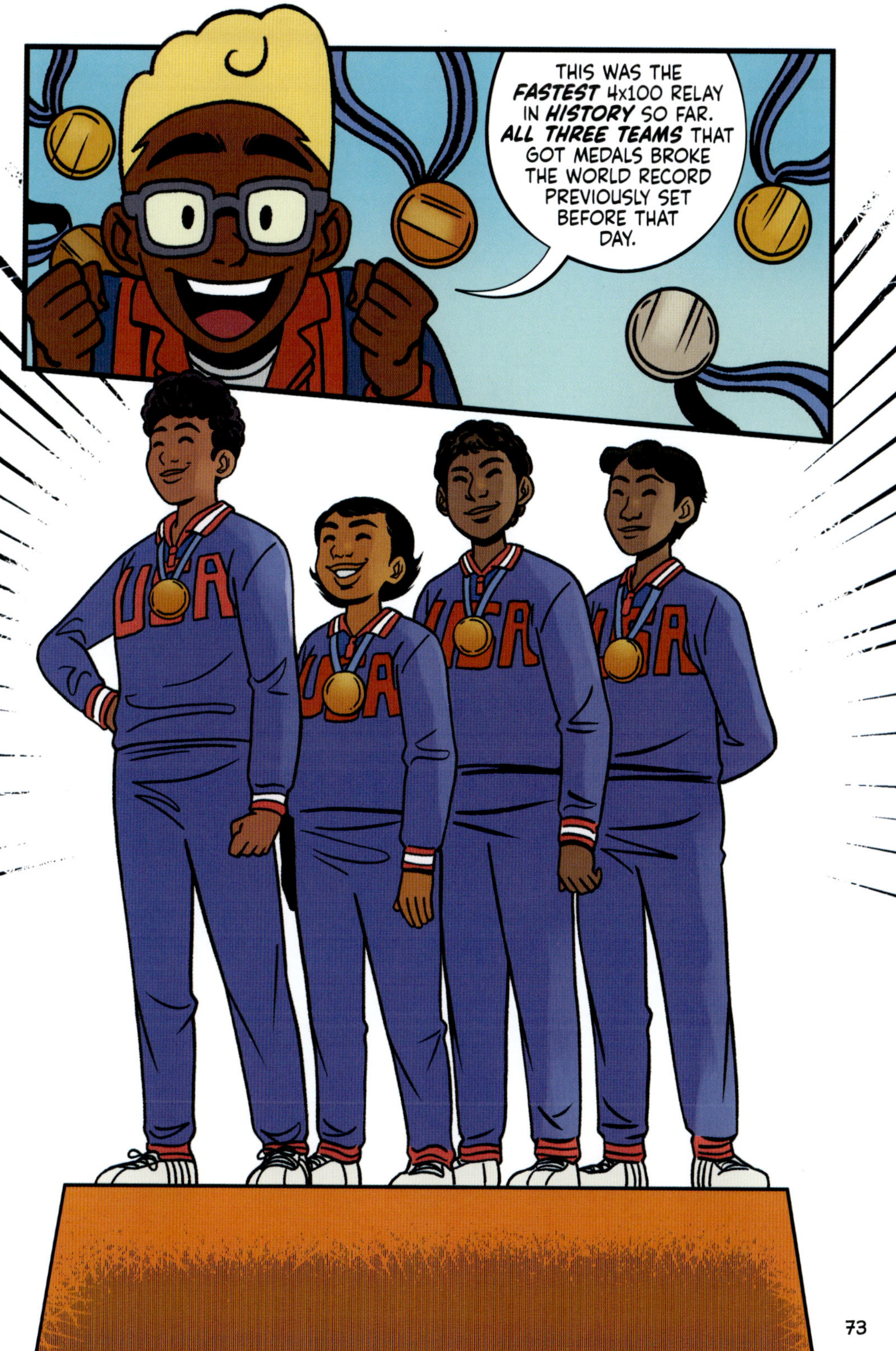
THIS WAS THE FASTEST 4x100 RELAY IN HISTORY SO FAR. ALL THREE TEAMS THAT GOT MEDALS BROKE THE WORLD RECORD PREVIOUSLY SET BEFORE THAT DAY.

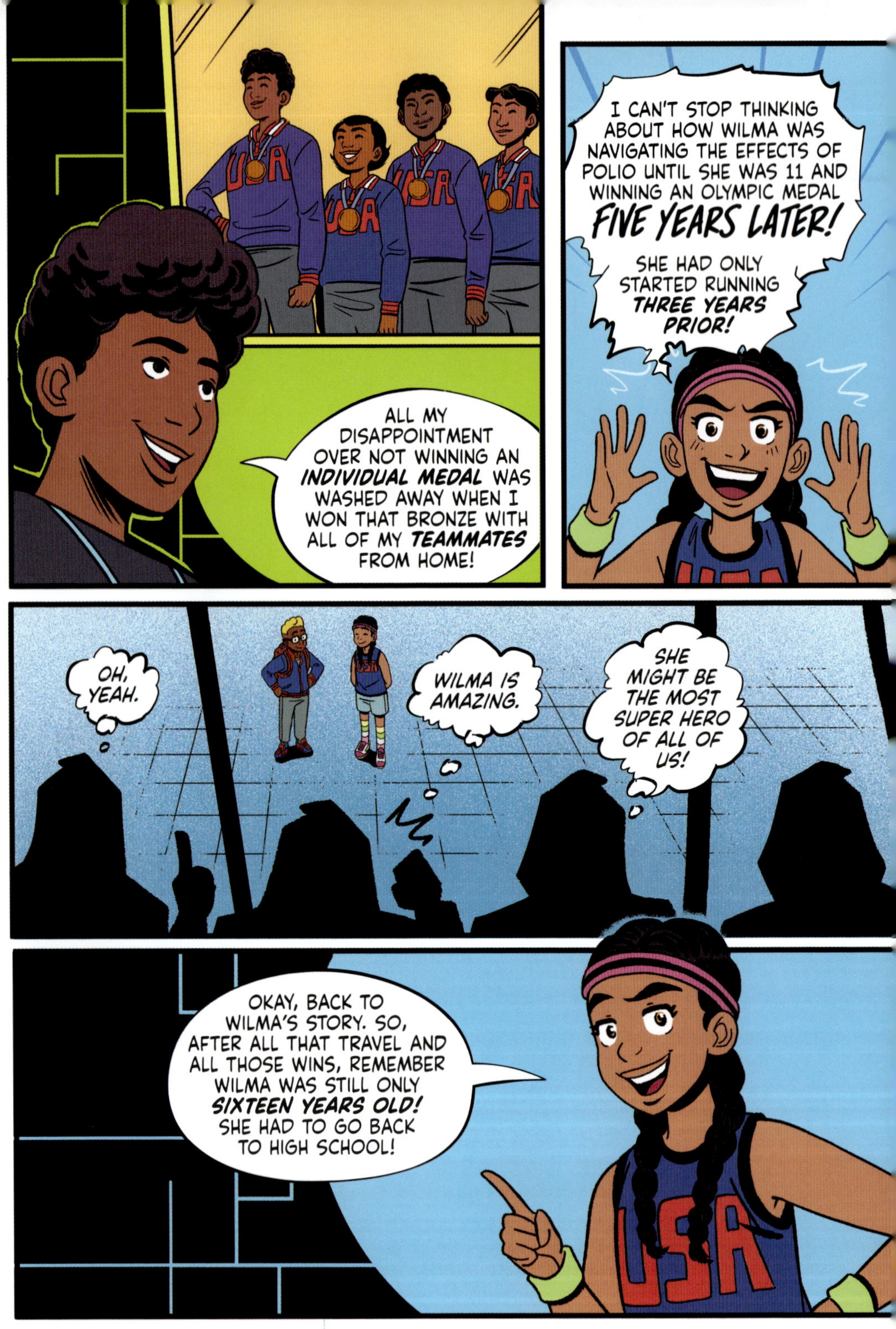
ALL MY DISAPPOINTMENT OVER NOT WINNING AN INDIVIDUAL MEDAL WAS WASHED AWAY WHEN I WON THAT BRONZE WITH ALL OF MY TEAMMATES FROM HOME!
I CAN'T STOP THINKING ABOUT HOW WILMA WAS NAVIGATING THE EFFECTS OF POLIO UNTIL SHE WAS 11 AND WINNING AN OLYMPIC MEDAL FIVE YEARS LATER!
SHE HAD ONLY STARTED RUNNING THREE YEARS PRIOR!
OH, YEAH.
WILMA IS AMAZING.
SHE MIGHT BE THE MOST SUPER HERO OF ALL OF US!
OKAY, BACK TO WILMA'S STORY. SO, AFTER ALL THAT TRAVEL AND ALL THOSE WINS, REMEMBER WILMA WAS STILL ONLY SIXTEEN YEARS OLD! SHE HAD TO GO BACK TO HIGH SCHOOL!

CHAPTER NINE

BACK TO HIGH SCHOOL!

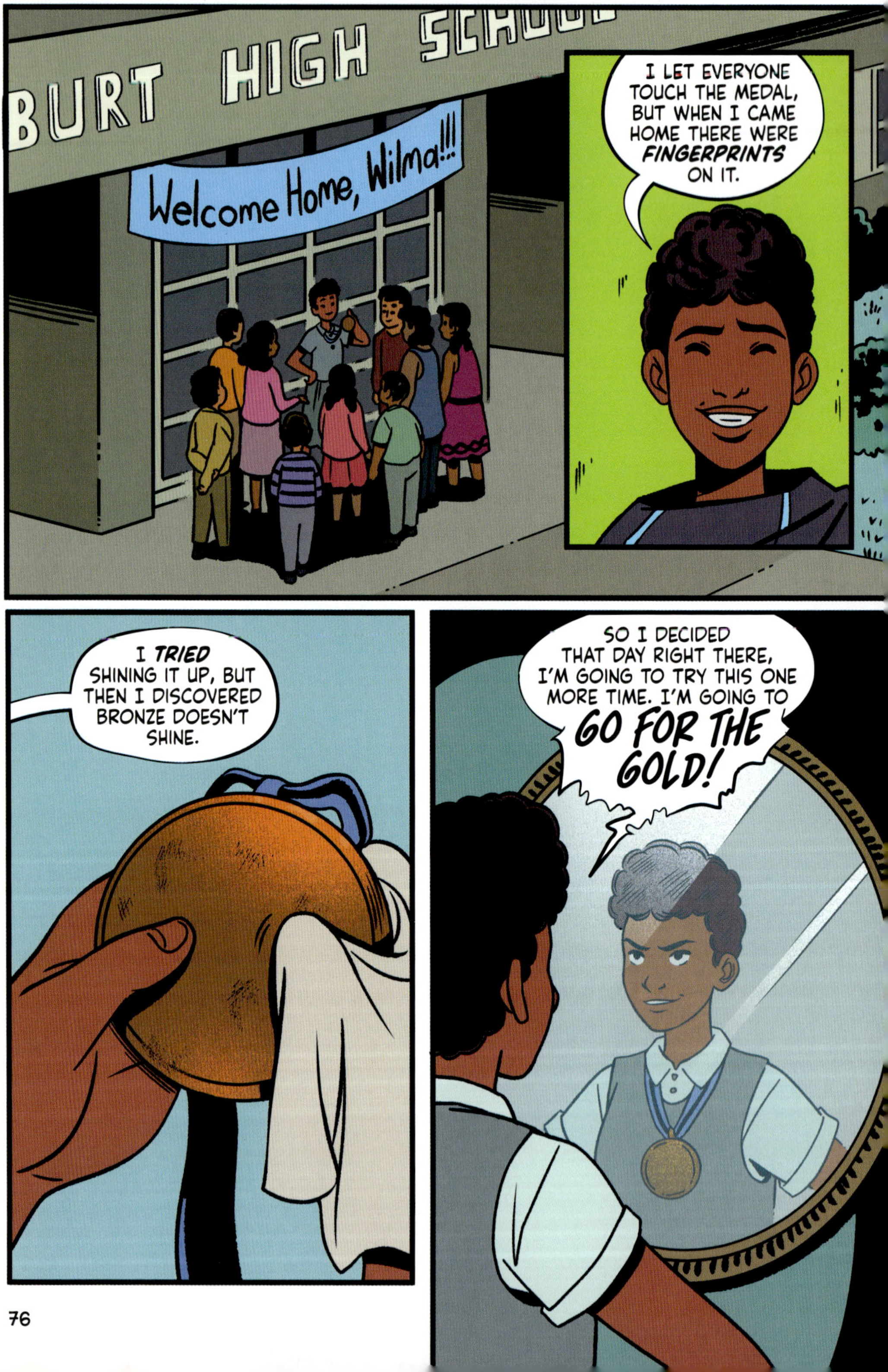
BURT HIGH SCHOOL
Welcome Home, Wilma!!!
I LET EVERYONE TOUCH THE MEDAL, BUT WHEN I CAME HOME THERE WERE *FINGERPRINTS* ON IT.
I *TRIED* SHINING IT UP, BUT THEN I DISCOVERED BRONZE DOESN'T SHINE.
SO I DECIDED THAT DAY RIGHT THERE, I'M GOING TO TRY THIS ONE MORE TIME. I'M GOING TO **GO FOR THE GOLD!**

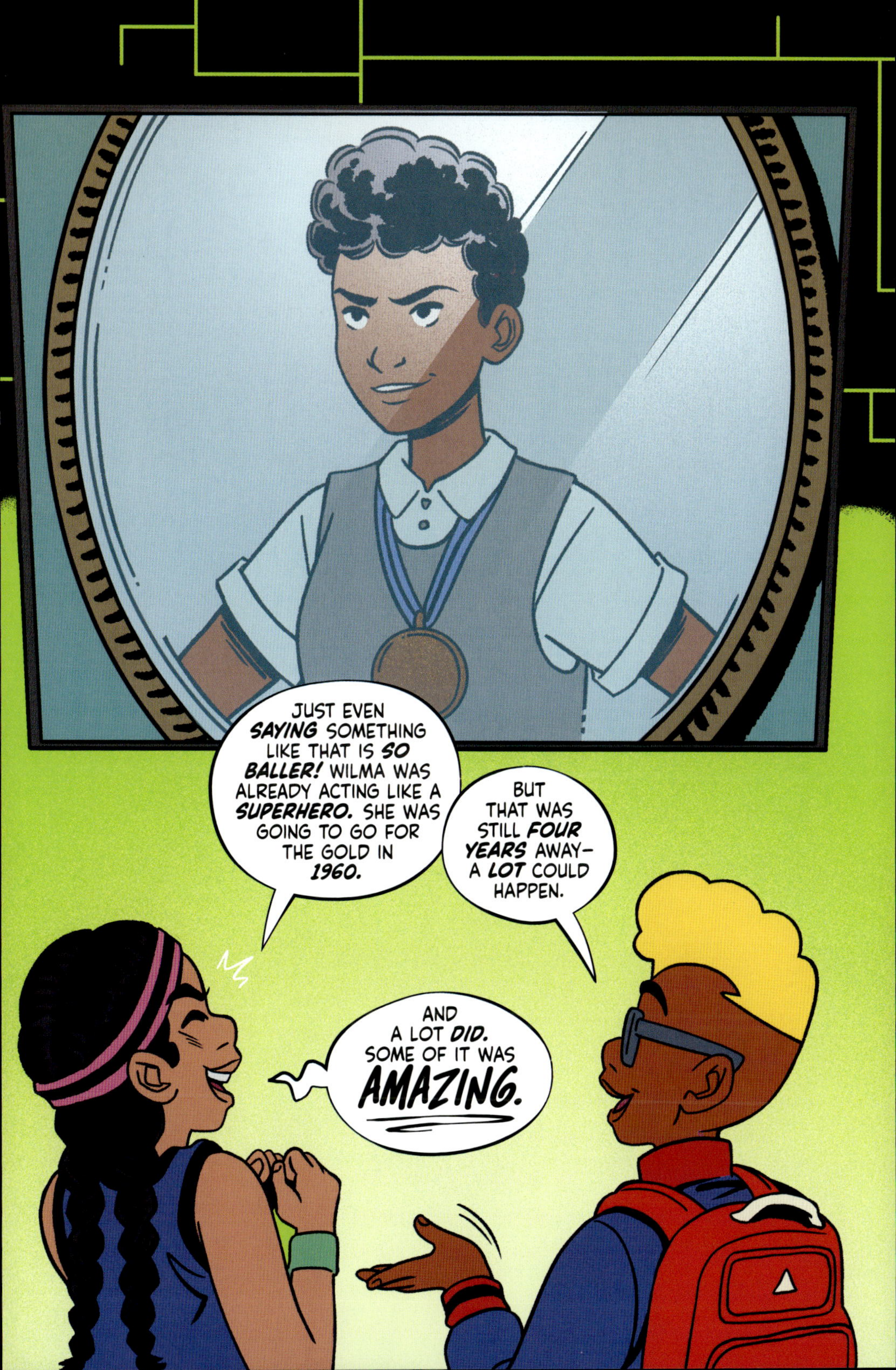
JUST EVEN SAYING SOMETHING LIKE THAT IS SO BALLER! WILMA WAS ALREADY ACTING LIKE A SUPERHERO. SHE WAS GOING TO GO FOR THE GOLD IN 1960.
BUT THAT WAS STILL FOUR YEARS AWAY– A LOT COULD HAPPEN.
AND A LOT DID. SOME OF IT WAS AMAZING.

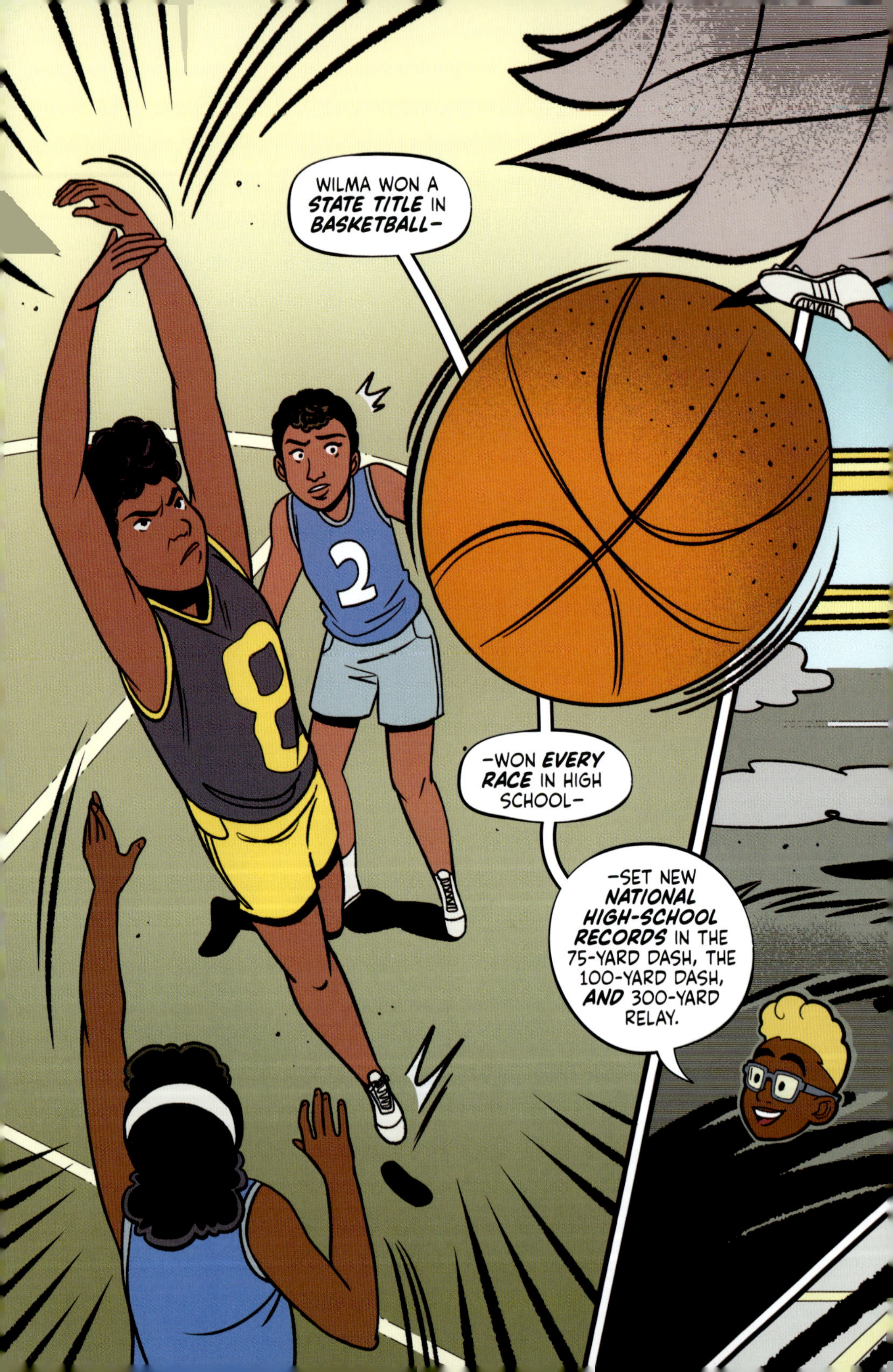
WILMA WON A STATE TITLE IN BASKETBALL—
—WON EVERY RACE IN HIGH SCHOOL—
—SET NEW NATIONAL HIGH-SCHOOL RECORDS IN THE 75-YARD DASH, THE 100-YARD DASH, AND 300-YARD RELAY.

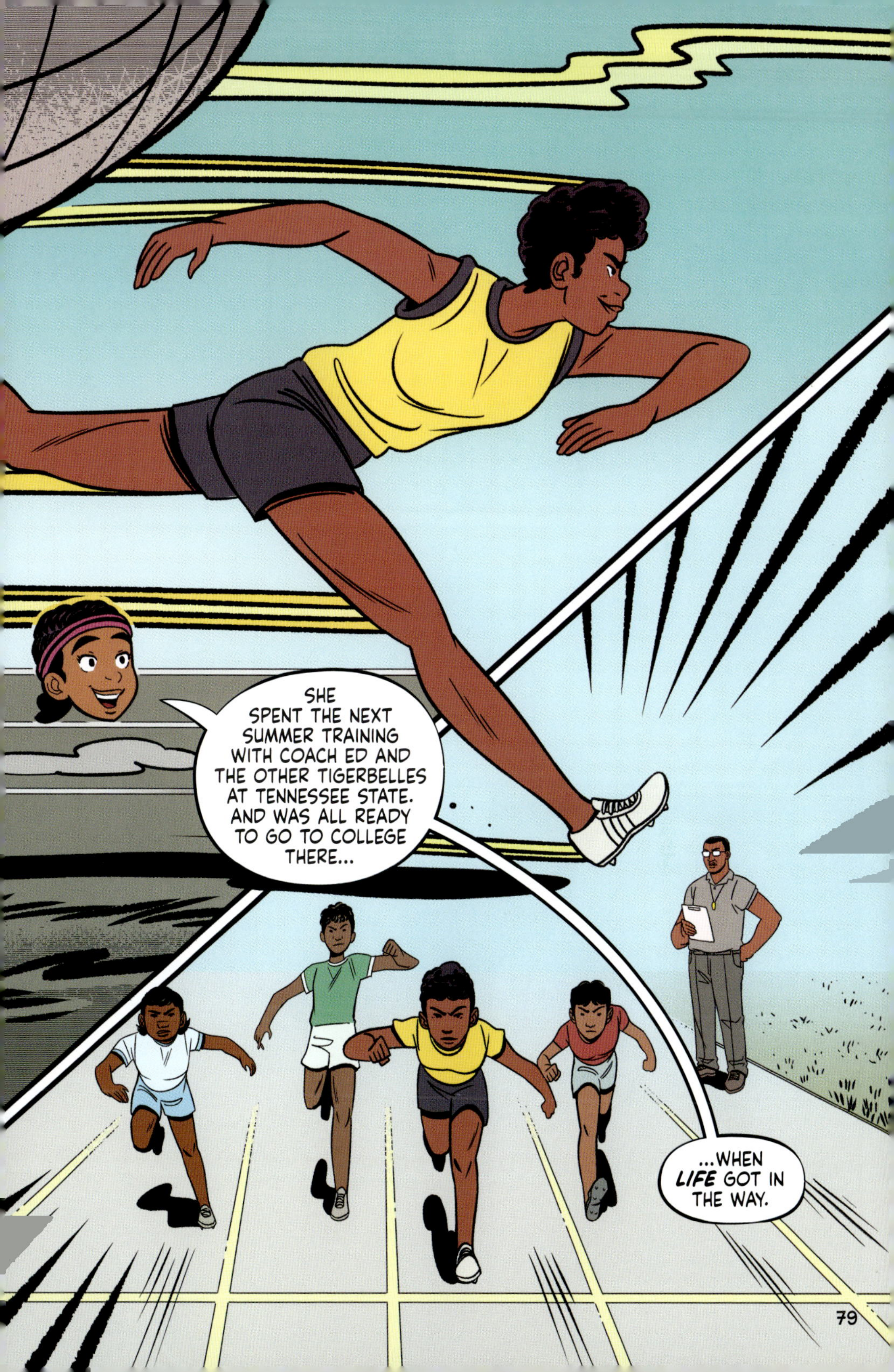
SHE SPENT THE NEXT SUMMER TRAINING WITH COACH ED AND THE OTHER TIGERBELLES AT TENNESSEE STATE. AND WAS ALL READY TO GO TO COLLEGE THERE...
...WHEN *LIFE* GOT IN THE WAY.

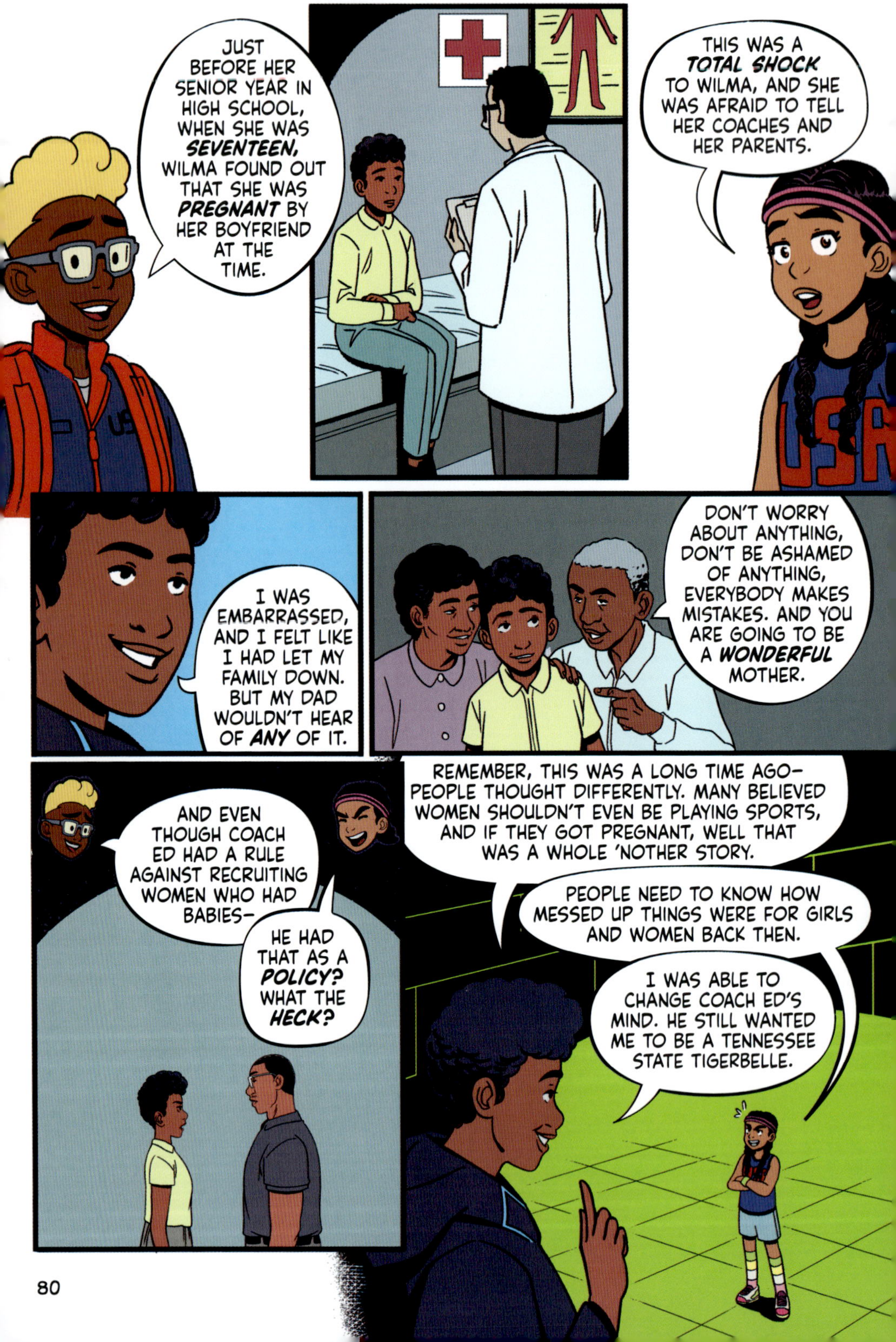
JUST BEFORE HER SENIOR YEAR IN HIGH SCHOOL, WHEN SHE WAS ***SEVENTEEN,*** WILMA FOUND OUT THAT SHE WAS ***PREGNANT*** BY HER BOYFRIEND AT THE TIME.
THIS WAS A ***TOTAL SHOCK*** TO WILMA, AND SHE WAS AFRAID TO TELL HER COACHES AND HER PARENTS.
I WAS EMBARRASSED, AND I FELT LIKE I HAD LET MY FAMILY DOWN. BUT MY DAD WOULDN'T HEAR OF ***ANY*** OF IT.
DON'T WORRY ABOUT ANYTHING, DON'T BE ASHAMED OF ANYTHING, EVERYBODY MAKES MISTAKES. AND YOU ARE GOING TO BE A ***WONDERFUL*** MOTHER.
AND EVEN THOUGH COACH ED HAD A RULE AGAINST RECRUITING WOMEN WHO HAD BABIES—
HE HAD THAT AS A ***POLICY?*** WHAT THE ***HECK?***
REMEMBER, THIS WAS A LONG TIME AGO—PEOPLE THOUGHT DIFFERENTLY. MANY BELIEVED WOMEN SHOULDN'T EVEN BE PLAYING SPORTS, AND IF THEY GOT PREGNANT, WELL THAT WAS A WHOLE 'NOTHER STORY.
PEOPLE NEED TO KNOW HOW MESSED UP THINGS WERE FOR GIRLS AND WOMEN BACK THEN.
I WAS ABLE TO CHANGE COACH ED'S MIND. HE STILL WANTED ME TO BE A TENNESSEE STATE TIGERBELLE.

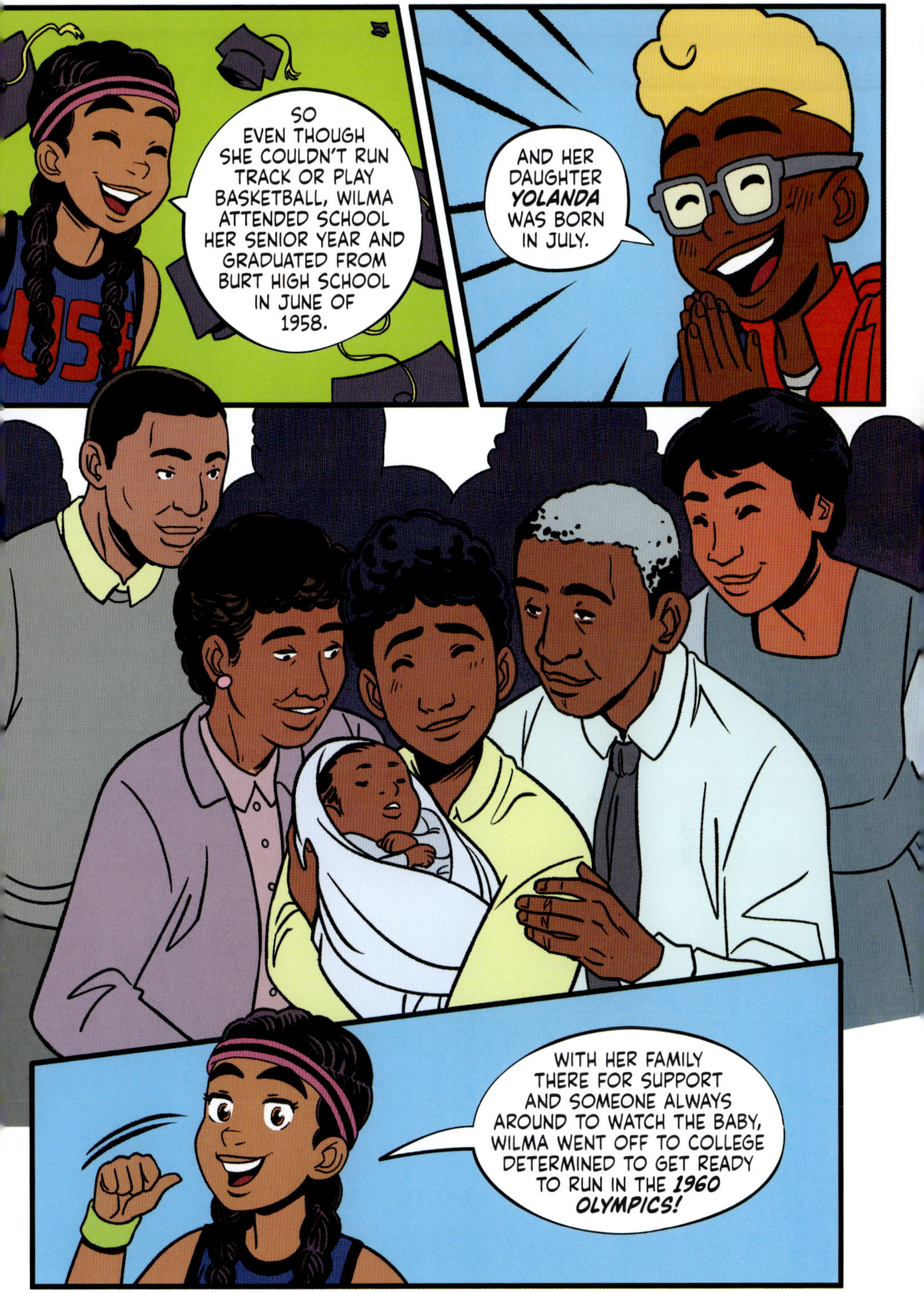
SO EVEN THOUGH SHE COULDN'T RUN TRACK OR PLAY BASKETBALL, WILMA ATTENDED SCHOOL HER SENIOR YEAR AND GRADUATED FROM BURT HIGH SCHOOL IN JUNE OF 1958.
AND HER DAUGHTER ***YOLANDA*** WAS BORN IN JULY.
WITH HER FAMILY THERE FOR SUPPORT AND SOMEONE ALWAYS AROUND TO WATCH THE BABY, WILMA WENT OFF TO COLLEGE DETERMINED TO GET READY TO RUN IN THE ***1960 OLYMPICS!***

CHAPTER TEN

RUN TO GLORY!

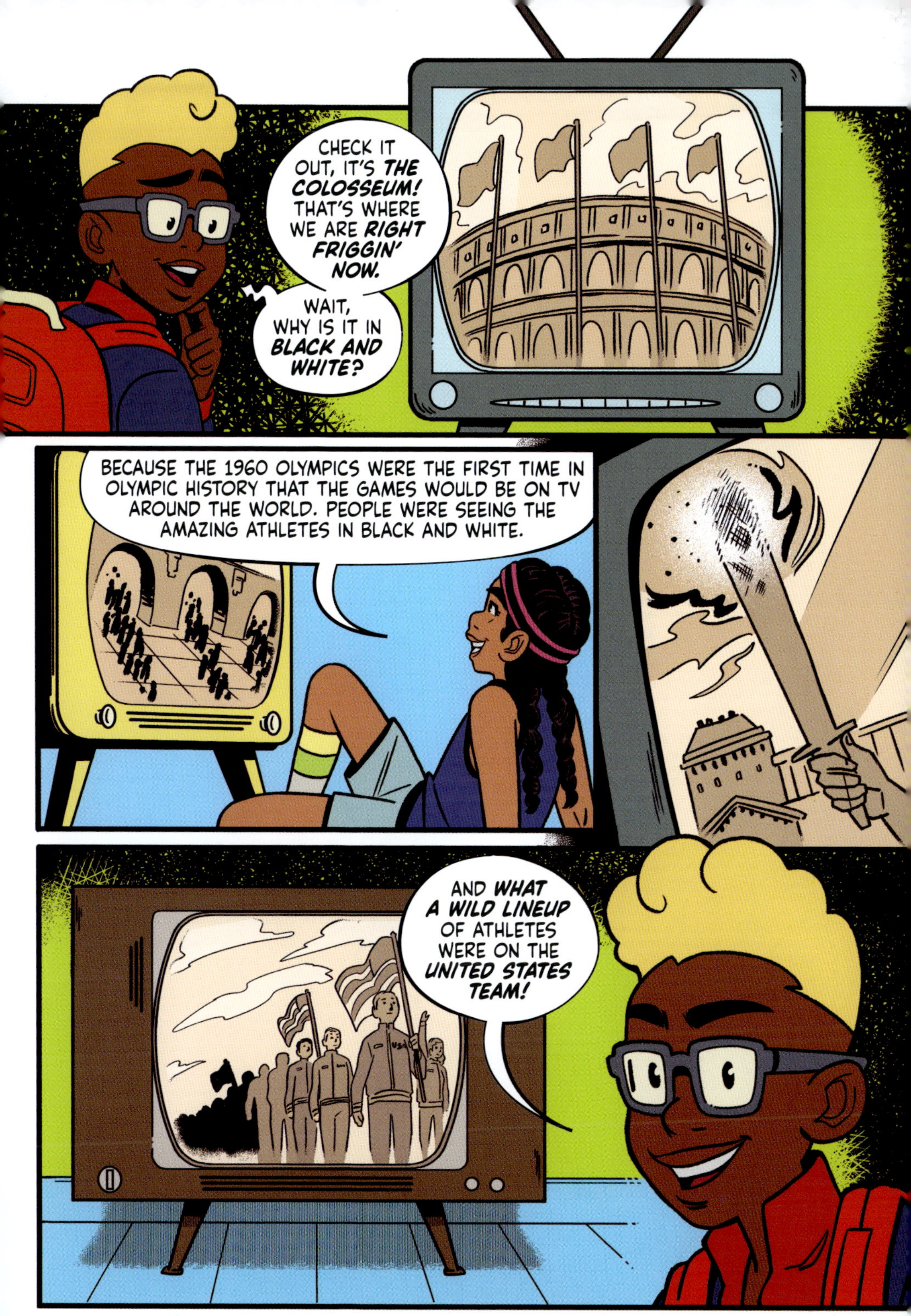
CHECK IT OUT, IT'S THE COLOSSEUM! THAT'S WHERE WE ARE RIGHT FRIGGIN' NOW.
WAIT, WHY IS IT IN BLACK AND WHITE?
BECAUSE THE 1960 OLYMPICS WERE THE FIRST TIME IN OLYMPIC HISTORY THAT THE GAMES WOULD BE ON TV AROUND THE WORLD. PEOPLE WERE SEEING THE AMAZING ATHLETES IN BLACK AND WHITE.
AND WHAT A WILD LINEUP OF ATHLETES WERE ON THE UNITED STATES TEAM!
USA

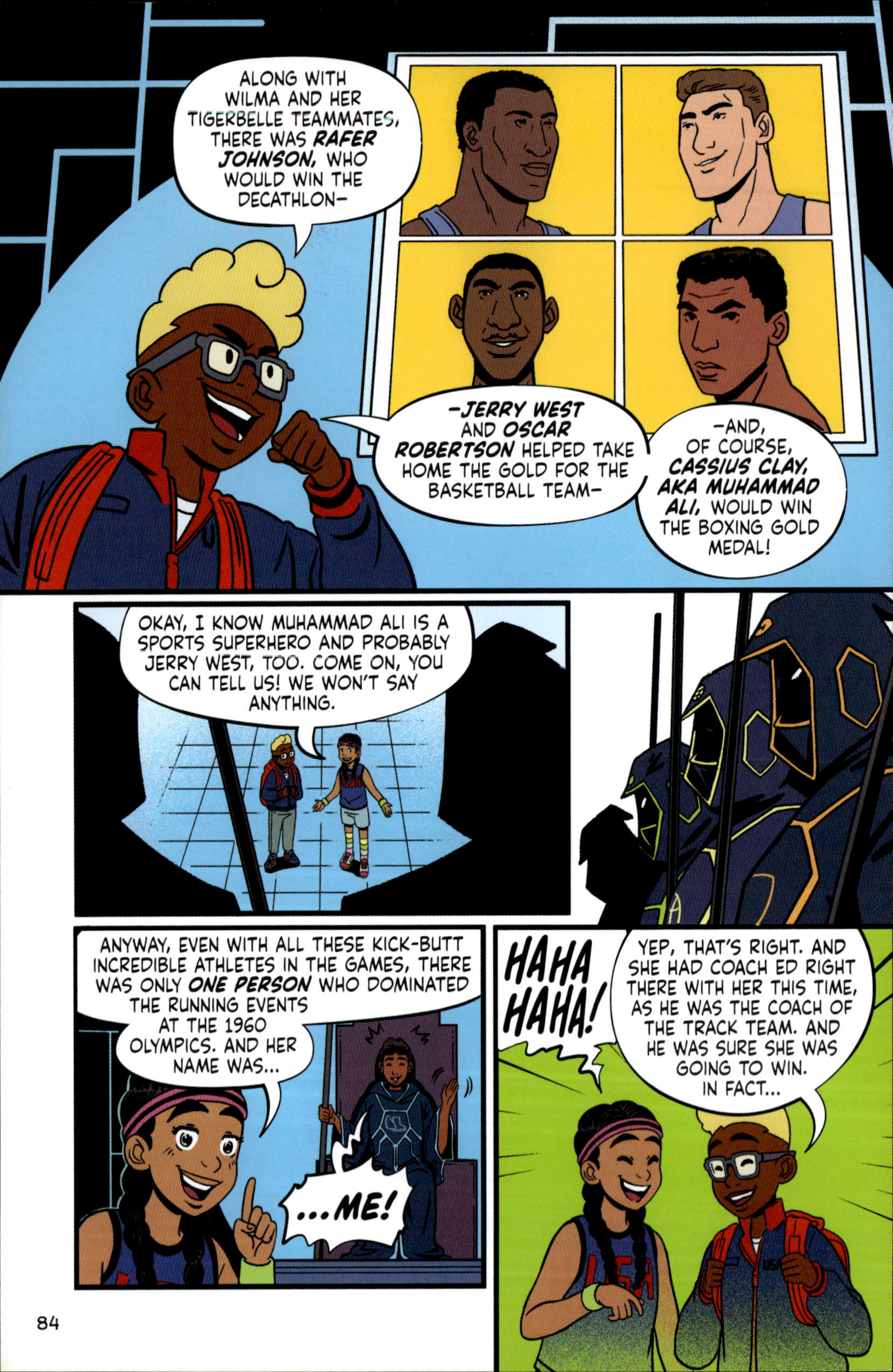
ALONG WITH WILMA AND HER TIGERBELLE TEAMMATES, THERE WAS RAFER JOHNSON, WHO WOULD WIN THE DECATHLON—
—JERRY WEST AND OSCAR ROBERTSON HELPED TAKE HOME THE GOLD FOR THE BASKETBALL TEAM—
—AND, OF COURSE, CASSIUS CLAY, AKA MUHAMMAD ALI, WOULD WIN THE BOXING GOLD MEDAL!
OKAY, I KNOW MUHAMMAD ALI IS A SPORTS SUPERHERO AND PROBABLY JERRY WEST, TOO. COME ON, YOU CAN TELL US! WE WON'T SAY ANYTHING.
ANYWAY, EVEN WITH ALL THESE KICK-BUTT INCREDIBLE ATHLETES IN THE GAMES, THERE WAS ONLY ONE PERSON WHO DOMINATED THE RUNNING EVENTS AT THE 1960 OLYMPICS. AND HER NAME WAS...
...ME!
HAHA HAHA!
YEP, THAT'S RIGHT. AND SHE HAD COACH ED RIGHT THERE WITH HER THIS TIME, AS HE WAS THE COACH OF THE TRACK TEAM. AND HE WAS SURE SHE WAS GOING TO WIN. IN FACT...

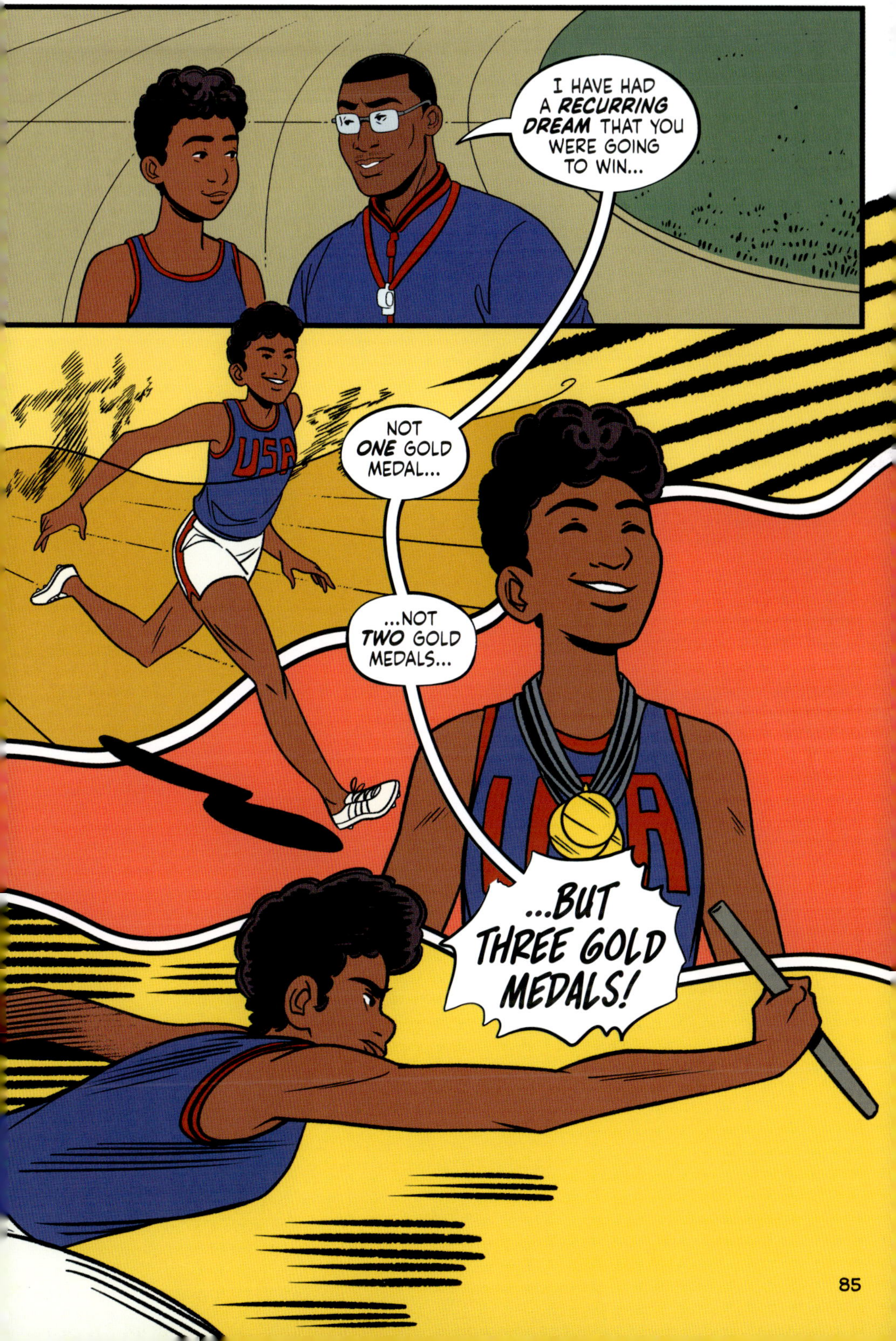
I HAVE HAD A RECURRING DREAM THAT YOU WERE GOING TO WIN...
NOT ONE GOLD MEDAL...
...NOT TWO GOLD MEDALS...
...BUT THREE GOLD MEDALS!
USA

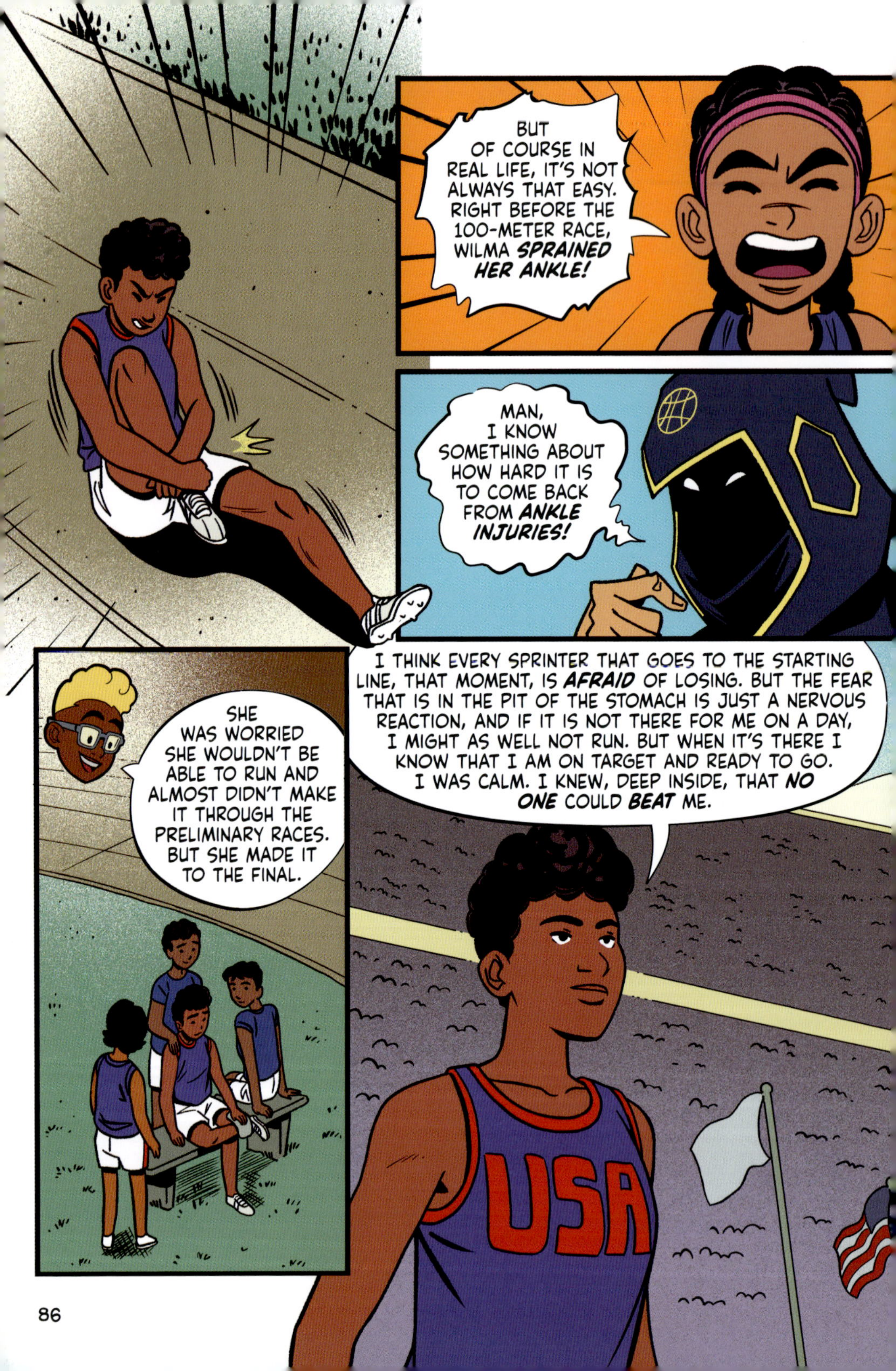
BUT OF COURSE IN REAL LIFE, IT'S NOT ALWAYS THAT EASY. RIGHT BEFORE THE 100-METER RACE, WILMA SPRAINED HER ANKLE!
MAN, I KNOW SOMETHING ABOUT HOW HARD IT IS TO COME BACK FROM ANKLE INJURIES!
SHE WAS WORRIED SHE WOULDN'T BE ABLE TO RUN AND ALMOST DIDN'T MAKE IT THROUGH THE PRELIMINARY RACES. BUT SHE MADE IT TO THE FINAL.
I THINK EVERY SPRINTER THAT GOES TO THE STARTING LINE, THAT MOMENT, IS AFRAID OF LOSING. BUT THE FEAR THAT IS IN THE PIT OF THE STOMACH IS JUST A NERVOUS REACTION, AND IF IT IS NOT THERE FOR ME ON A DAY, I MIGHT AS WELL NOT RUN. BUT WHEN IT'S THERE I KNOW THAT I AM ON TARGET AND READY TO GO. I WAS CALM. I KNEW, DEEP INSIDE, THAT NO ONE COULD BEAT ME.
USA

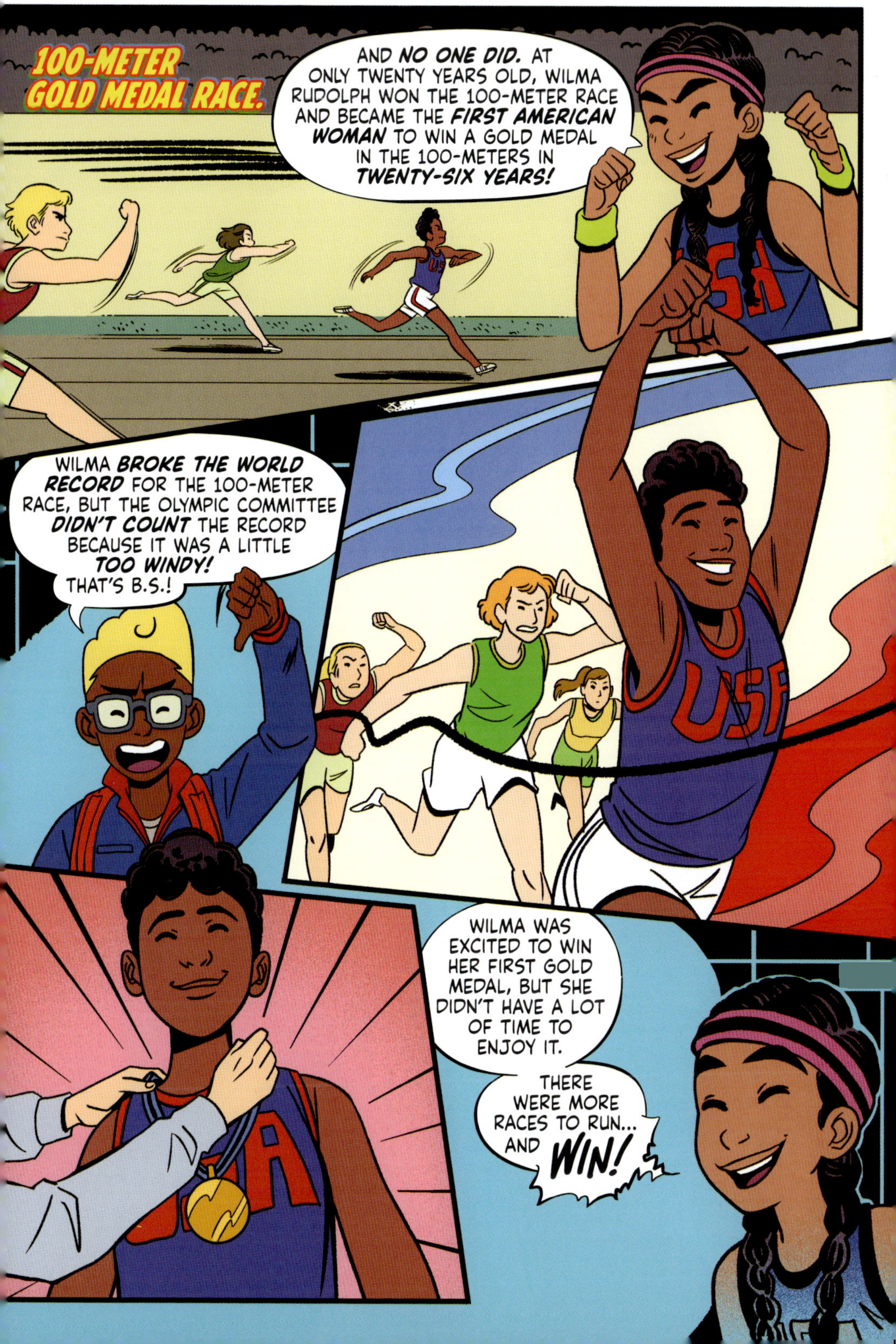
100-METER GOLD MEDAL RACE.
AND NO ONE DID. AT ONLY TWENTY YEARS OLD, WILMA RUDOLPH WON THE 100-METER RACE AND BECAME THE FIRST AMERICAN WOMAN TO WIN A GOLD MEDAL IN THE 100-METERS IN TWENTY-SIX YEARS!
WILMA BROKE THE WORLD RECORD FOR THE 100-METER RACE, BUT THE OLYMPIC COMMITTEE DIDN'T COUNT THE RECORD BECAUSE IT WAS A LITTLE TOO WINDY! THAT'S B.S.!
WILMA WAS EXCITED TO WIN HER FIRST GOLD MEDAL, BUT SHE DIDN'T HAVE A LOT OF TIME TO ENJOY IT.
THERE WERE MORE RACES TO RUN... AND WIN!

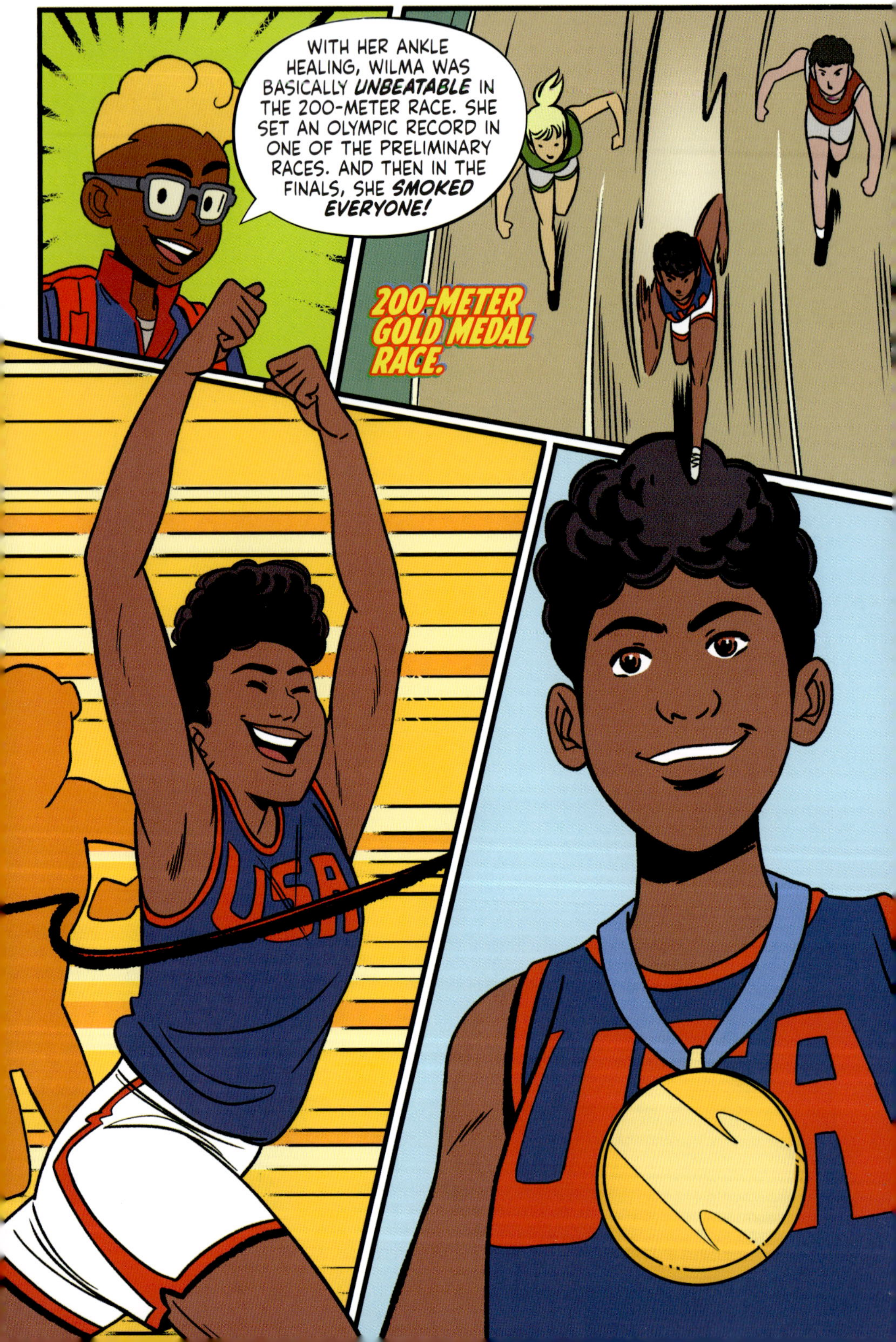
WITH HER ANKLE HEALING, WILMA WAS BASICALLY UNBEATABLE IN THE 200-METER RACE. SHE SET AN OLYMPIC RECORD IN ONE OF THE PRELIMINARY RACES. AND THEN IN THE FINALS, SHE SMOKED EVERYONE!
200-METER GOLD MEDAL RACE.
USA
USA

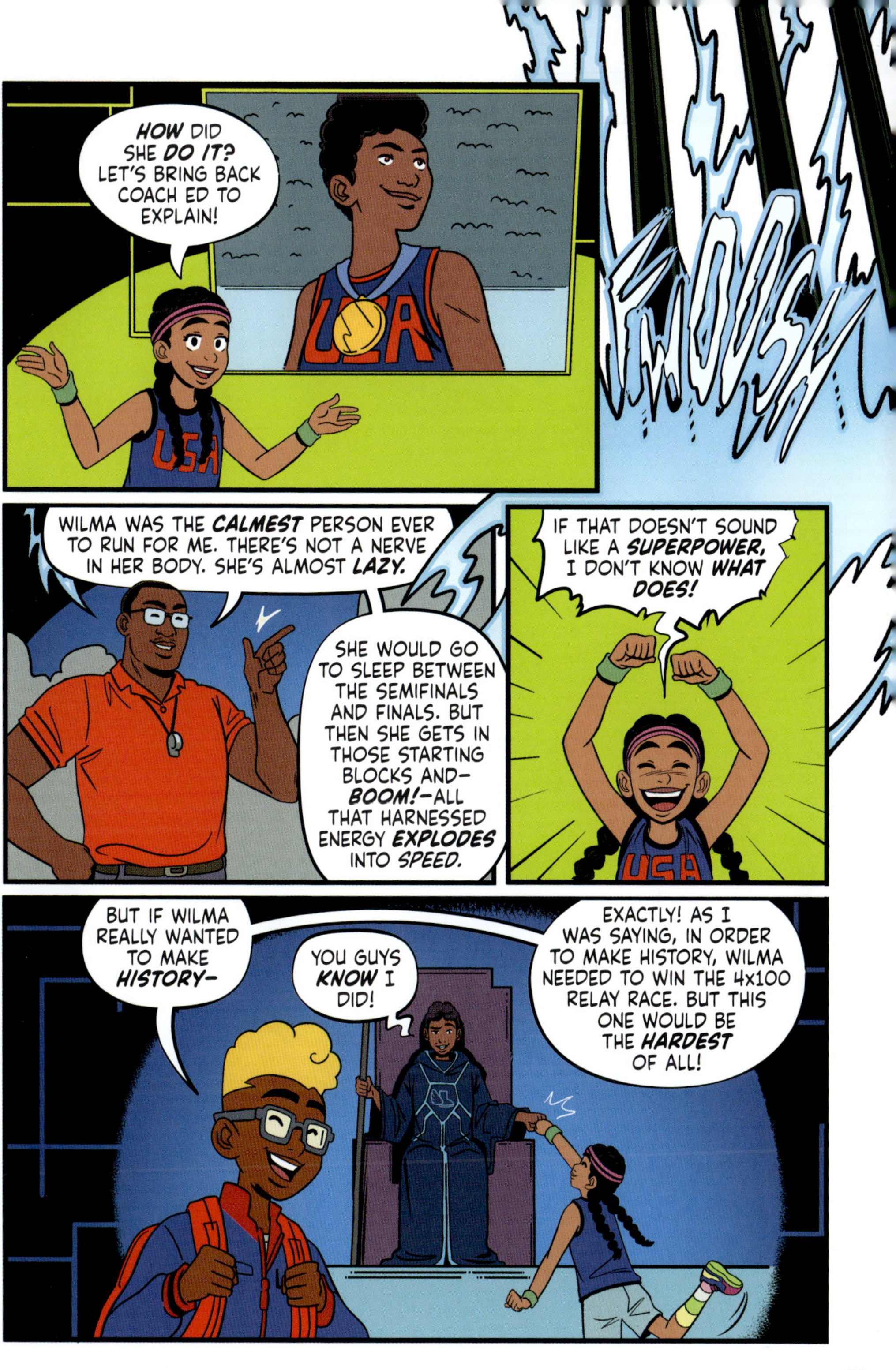

HOW DID SHE DO IT? LET'S BRING BACK COACH ED TO EXPLAIN!
FWOOSH
WILMA WAS THE CALMEST PERSON EVER TO RUN FOR ME. THERE'S NOT A NERVE IN HER BODY. SHE'S ALMOST LAZY.
SHE WOULD GO TO SLEEP BETWEEN THE SEMIFINALS AND FINALS. BUT THEN SHE GETS IN THOSE STARTING BLOCKS AND—BOOM!—ALL THAT HARNESSED ENERGY EXPLODES INTO SPEED.
IF THAT DOESN'T SOUND LIKE A SUPERPOWER, I DON'T KNOW WHAT DOES!
BUT IF WILMA REALLY WANTED TO MAKE HISTORY—
YOU GUYS KNOW I DID!
EXACTLY! AS I WAS SAYING, IN ORDER TO MAKE HISTORY, WILMA NEEDED TO WIN THE 4x100 RELAY RACE. BUT THIS ONE WOULD BE THE HARDEST OF ALL!

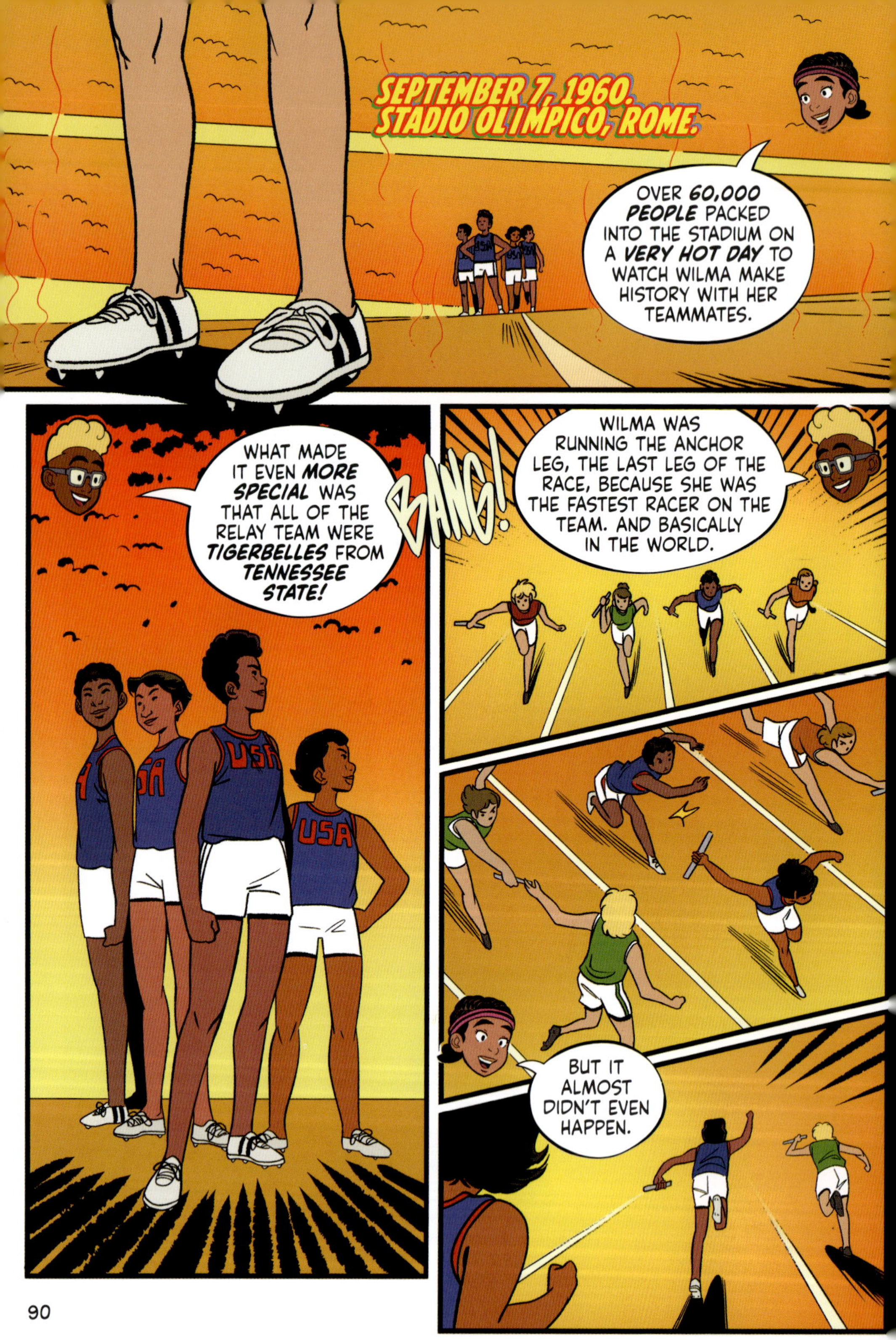

SEPTEMBER 7, 1960. STADIO OLIMPICO, ROME.
OVER 60,000 PEOPLE PACKED INTO THE STADIUM ON A VERY HOT DAY TO WATCH WILMA MAKE HISTORY WITH HER TEAMMATES.
WHAT MADE IT EVEN MORE SPECIAL WAS THAT ALL OF THE RELAY TEAM WERE TIGERBELLES FROM TENNESSEE STATE!
BANG!
WILMA WAS RUNNING THE ANCHOR LEG, THE LAST LEG OF THE RACE, BECAUSE SHE WAS THE FASTEST RACER ON THE TEAM. AND BASICALLY IN THE WORLD.
BUT IT ALMOST DIDN'T EVEN HAPPEN.

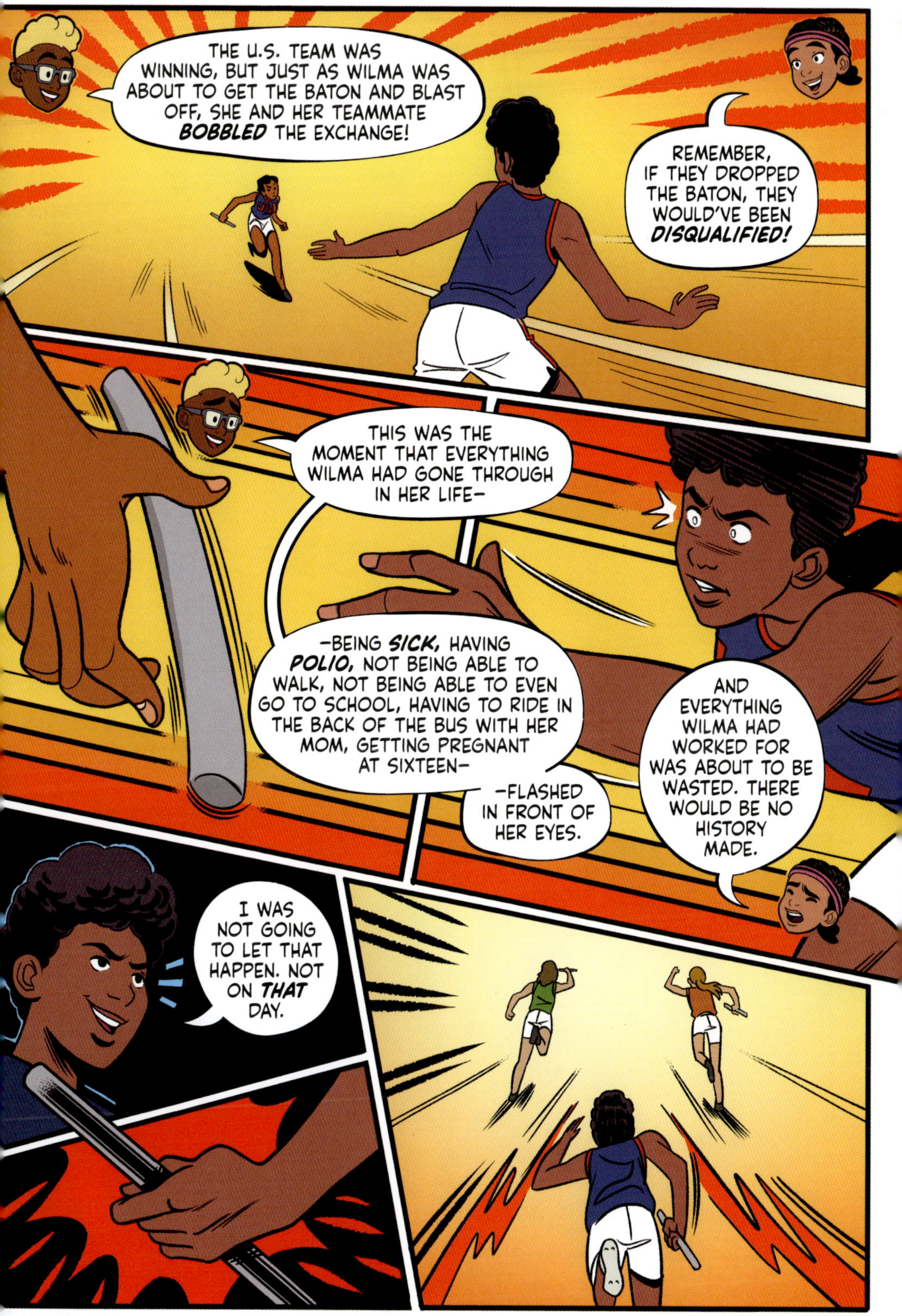
THE U.S. TEAM WAS WINNING, BUT JUST AS WILMA WAS ABOUT TO GET THE BATON AND BLAST OFF, SHE AND HER TEAMMATE **BOBBLED** THE EXCHANGE!
REMEMBER, IF THEY DROPPED THE BATON, THEY WOULD'VE BEEN **DISQUALIFIED!**
THIS WAS THE MOMENT THAT EVERYTHING WILMA HAD GONE THROUGH IN HER LIFE—
—BEING **SICK,** HAVING **POLIO,** NOT BEING ABLE TO WALK, NOT BEING ABLE TO EVEN GO TO SCHOOL, HAVING TO RIDE IN THE BACK OF THE BUS WITH HER MOM, GETTING PREGNANT AT SIXTEEN—
—FLASHED IN FRONT OF HER EYES.
AND EVERYTHING WILMA HAD WORKED FOR WAS ABOUT TO BE WASTED. THERE WOULD BE NO HISTORY MADE.
I WAS NOT GOING TO LET THAT HAPPEN. NOT ON **THAT** DAY.

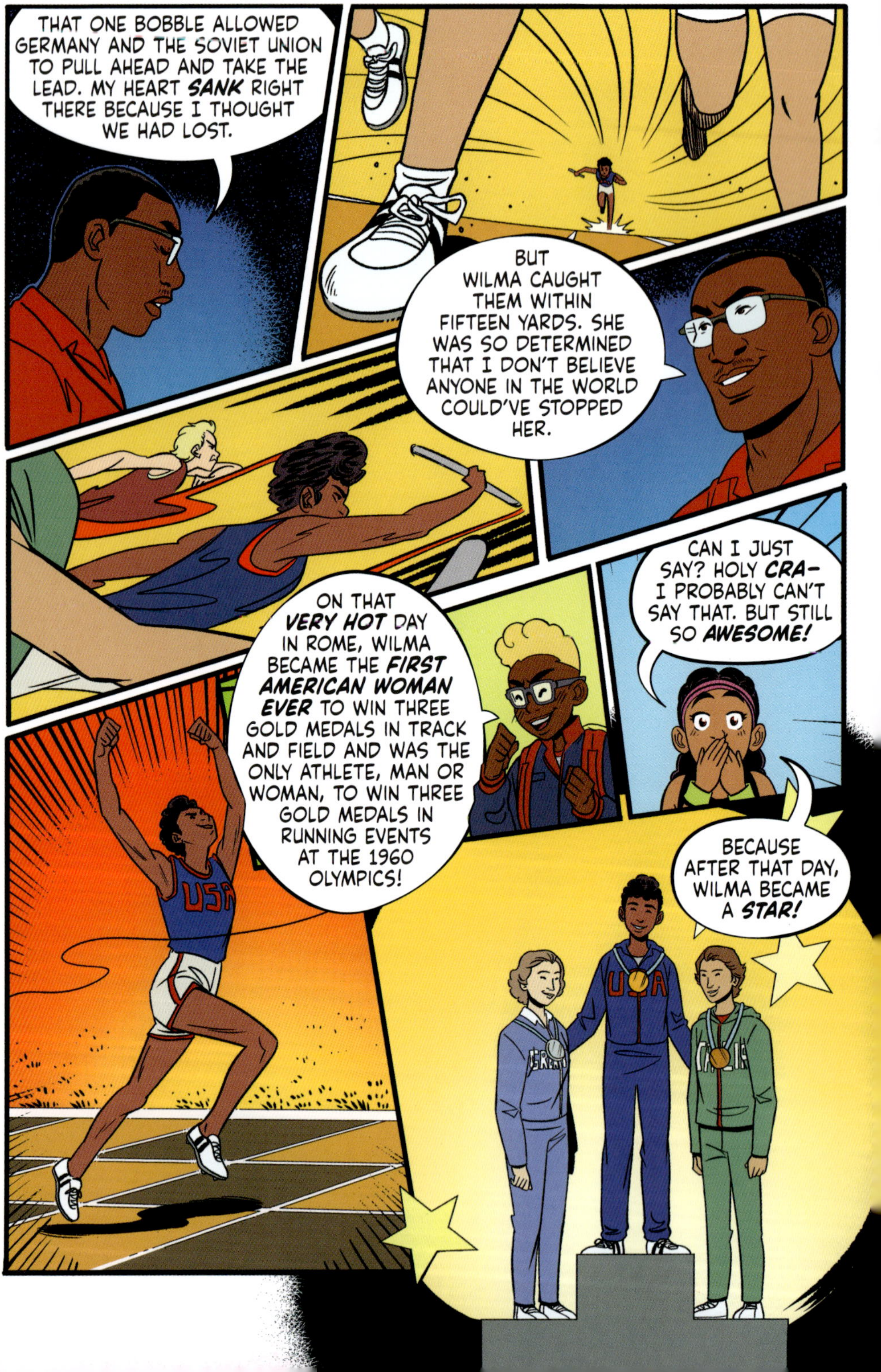
THAT ONE BOBBLE ALLOWED GERMANY AND THE SOVIET UNION TO PULL AHEAD AND TAKE THE LEAD. MY HEART **SANK** RIGHT THERE BECAUSE I THOUGHT WE HAD LOST.
BUT WILMA CAUGHT THEM WITHIN FIFTEEN YARDS. SHE WAS SO DETERMINED THAT I DON'T BELIEVE ANYONE IN THE WORLD COULD'VE STOPPED HER.
CAN I JUST SAY? HOLY **CRA–** I PROBABLY CAN'T SAY THAT. BUT STILL SO **AWESOME!**
ON THAT **VERY HOT** DAY IN ROME, WILMA BECAME THE **FIRST AMERICAN WOMAN EVER** TO WIN THREE GOLD MEDALS IN TRACK AND FIELD AND WAS THE ONLY ATHLETE, MAN OR WOMAN, TO WIN THREE GOLD MEDALS IN RUNNING EVENTS AT THE 1960 OLYMPICS!
BECAUSE AFTER THAT DAY, WILMA BECAME A **STAR!**
USA
USA

CHAPTER ELEVEN

A STAR IS BORN

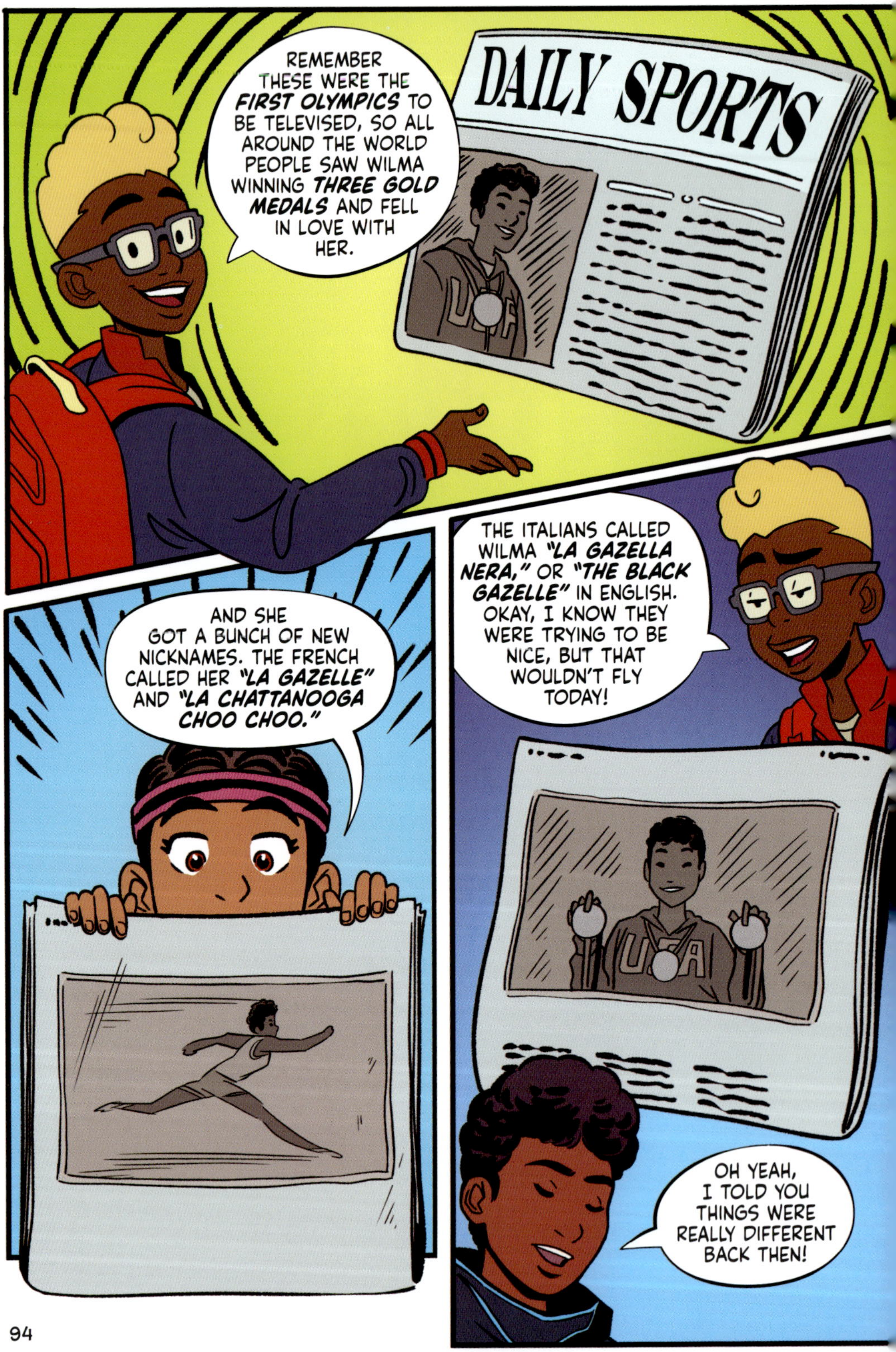
REMEMBER THESE WERE THE FIRST OLYMPICS TO BE TELEVISED, SO ALL AROUND THE WORLD PEOPLE SAW WILMA WINNING THREE GOLD MEDALS AND FELL IN LOVE WITH HER.
DAILY SPORTS
AND SHE GOT A BUNCH OF NEW NICKNAMES. THE FRENCH CALLED HER "LA GAZELLE" AND "LA CHATTANOOGA CHOO CHOO."
THE ITALIANS CALLED WILMA "LA GAZELLA NERA," OR "THE BLACK GAZELLE" IN ENGLISH. OKAY, I KNOW THEY WERE TRYING TO BE NICE, BUT THAT WOULDN'T FLY TODAY!
OH YEAH, I TOLD YOU THINGS WERE REALLY DIFFERENT BACK THEN!

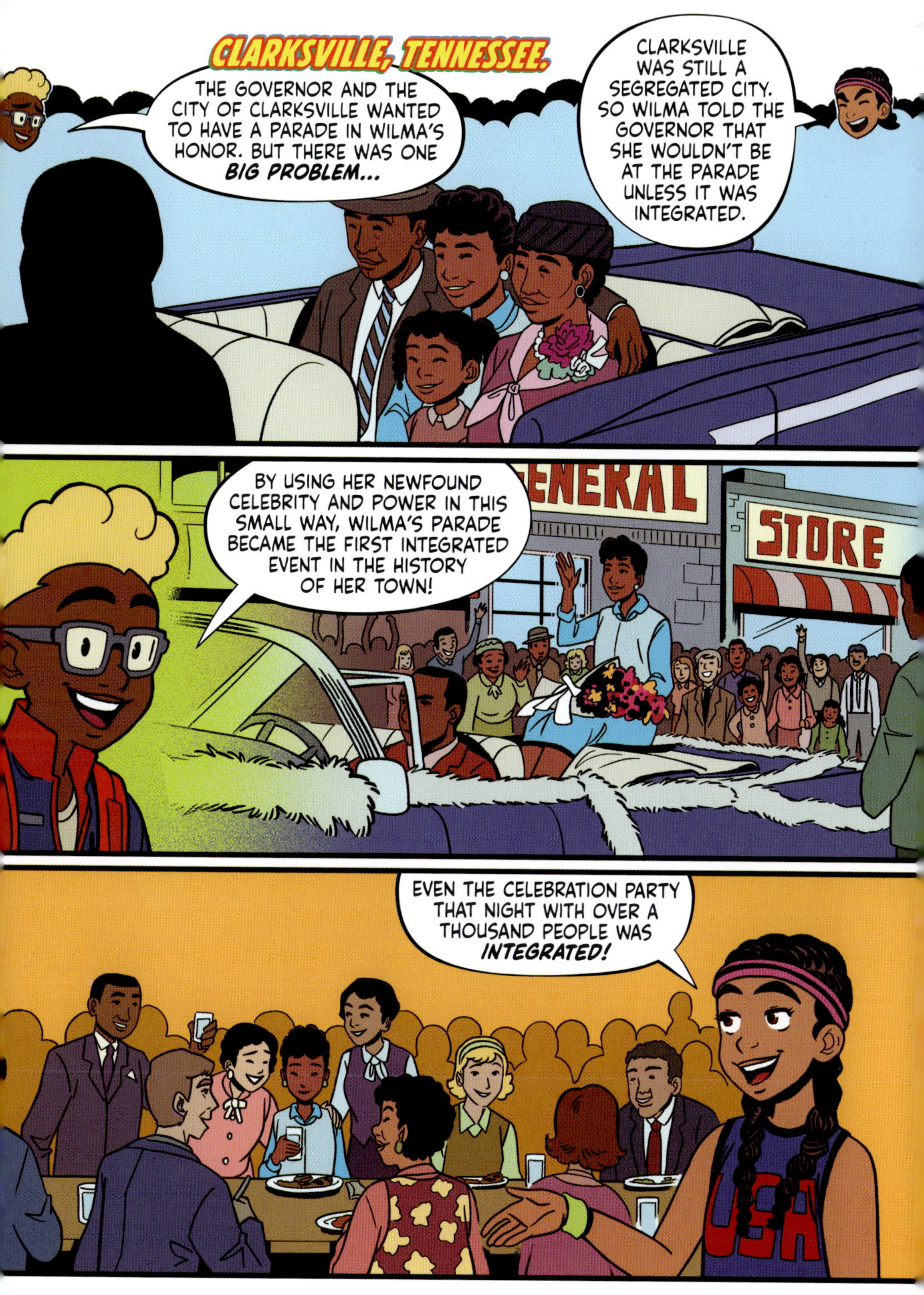

CLARKSVILLE, TENNESSEE.
THE GOVERNOR AND THE CITY OF CLARKSVILLE WANTED TO HAVE A PARADE IN WILMA'S HONOR. BUT THERE WAS ONE BIG PROBLEM...
CLARKSVILLE WAS STILL A SEGREGATED CITY. SO WILMA TOLD THE GOVERNOR THAT SHE WOULDN'T BE AT THE PARADE UNLESS IT WAS INTEGRATED.
BY USING HER NEWFOUND CELEBRITY AND POWER IN THIS SMALL WAY, WILMA'S PARADE BECAME THE FIRST INTEGRATED EVENT IN THE HISTORY OF HER TOWN!
ENERAL
STORE
EVEN THE CELEBRATION PARTY THAT NIGHT WITH OVER A THOUSAND PEOPLE WAS INTEGRATED!
USA

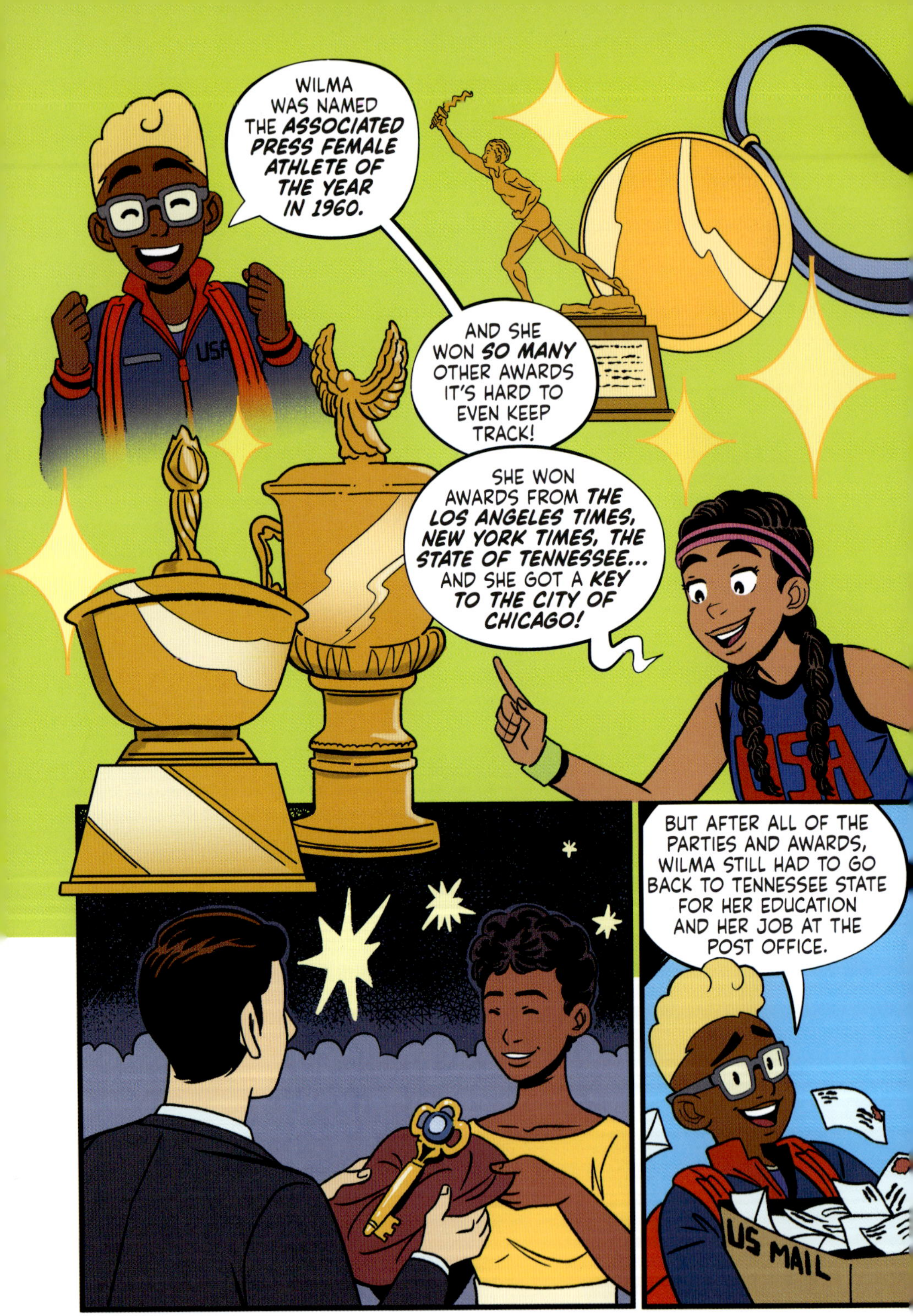
WILMA WAS NAMED THE ***ASSOCIATED PRESS FEMALE ATHLETE OF THE YEAR IN 1960.***
AND SHE WON ***SO MANY*** OTHER AWARDS IT'S HARD TO EVEN KEEP TRACK!
SHE WON AWARDS FROM ***THE LOS ANGELES TIMES, NEW YORK TIMES, THE STATE OF TENNESSEE...*** AND SHE GOT A ***KEY TO THE CITY OF CHICAGO!***
BUT AFTER ALL OF THE PARTIES AND AWARDS, WILMA STILL HAD TO GO BACK TO TENNESSEE STATE FOR HER EDUCATION AND HER JOB AT THE POST OFFICE.
US MAIL

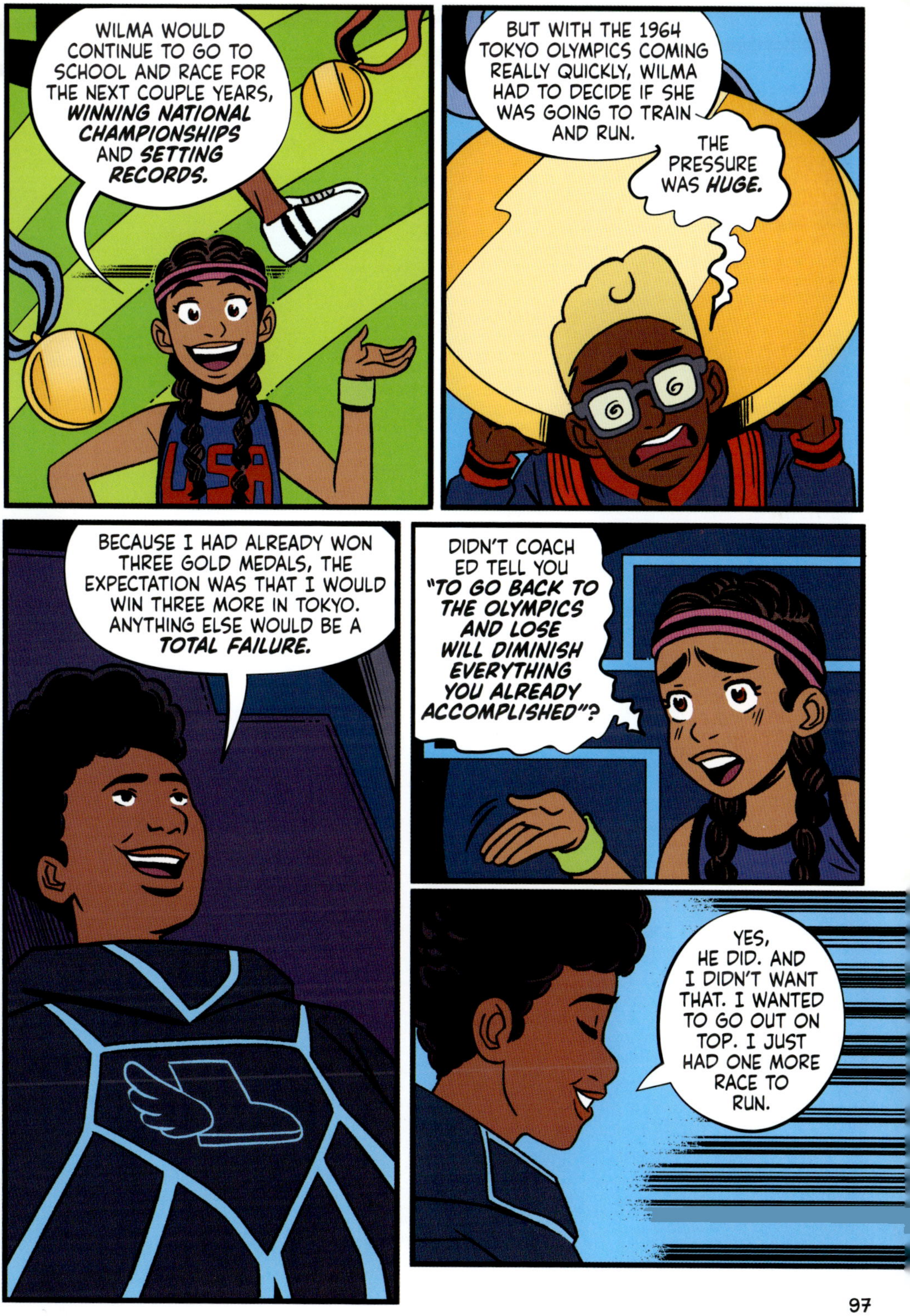
WILMA WOULD CONTINUE TO GO TO SCHOOL AND RACE FOR THE NEXT COUPLE YEARS, ***WINNING NATIONAL CHAMPIONSHIPS*** AND ***SETTING RECORDS.***
BUT WITH THE 1964 TOKYO OLYMPICS COMING REALLY QUICKLY, WILMA HAD TO DECIDE IF SHE WAS GOING TO TRAIN AND RUN.
THE PRESSURE WAS ***HUGE.***
BECAUSE I HAD ALREADY WON THREE GOLD MEDALS, THE EXPECTATION WAS THAT I WOULD WIN THREE MORE IN TOKYO. ANYTHING ELSE WOULD BE A ***TOTAL FAILURE.***
DIDN'T COACH ED TELL YOU ***"TO GO BACK TO THE OLYMPICS AND LOSE WILL DIMINISH EVERYTHING YOU ALREADY ACCOMPLISHED"?***
YES, HE DID. AND I DIDN'T WANT THAT. I WANTED TO GO OUT ON TOP. I JUST HAD ONE MORE RACE TO RUN.

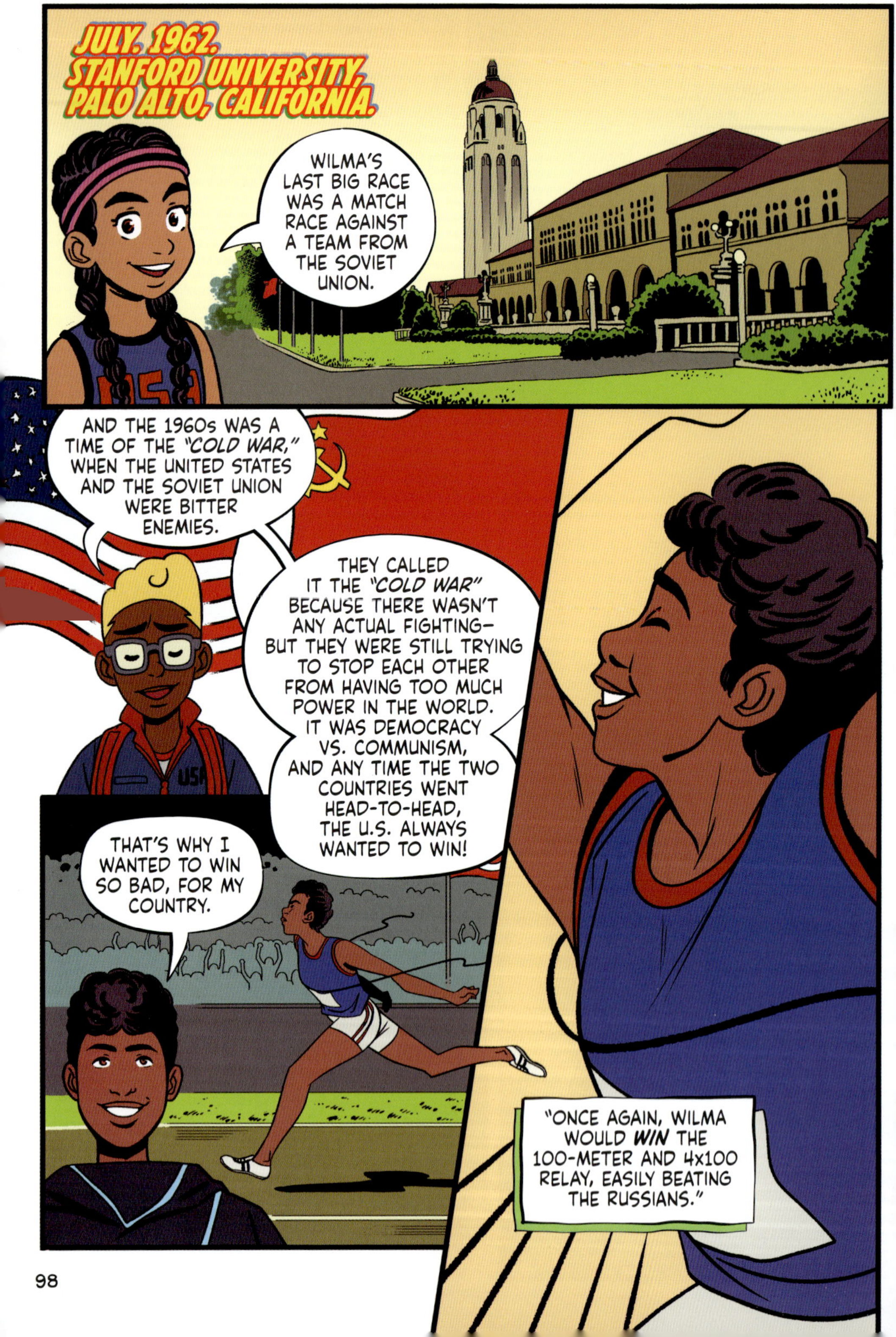
JULY, 1962.
STANFORD UNIVERSITY,
PALO ALTO, CALIFORNIA.
WILMA'S LAST BIG RACE WAS A MATCH RACE AGAINST A TEAM FROM THE SOVIET UNION.
AND THE 1960s WAS A TIME OF THE "COLD WAR," WHEN THE UNITED STATES AND THE SOVIET UNION WERE BITTER ENEMIES.
THEY CALLED IT THE "COLD WAR" BECAUSE THERE WASN'T ANY ACTUAL FIGHTING– BUT THEY WERE STILL TRYING TO STOP EACH OTHER FROM HAVING TOO MUCH POWER IN THE WORLD. IT WAS DEMOCRACY VS. COMMUNISM, AND ANY TIME THE TWO COUNTRIES WENT HEAD-TO-HEAD, THE U.S. ALWAYS WANTED TO WIN!
THAT'S WHY I WANTED TO WIN SO BAD, FOR MY COUNTRY.
"ONCE AGAIN, WILMA WOULD WIN THE 100-METER AND 4x100 RELAY, EASILY BEATING THE RUSSIANS."

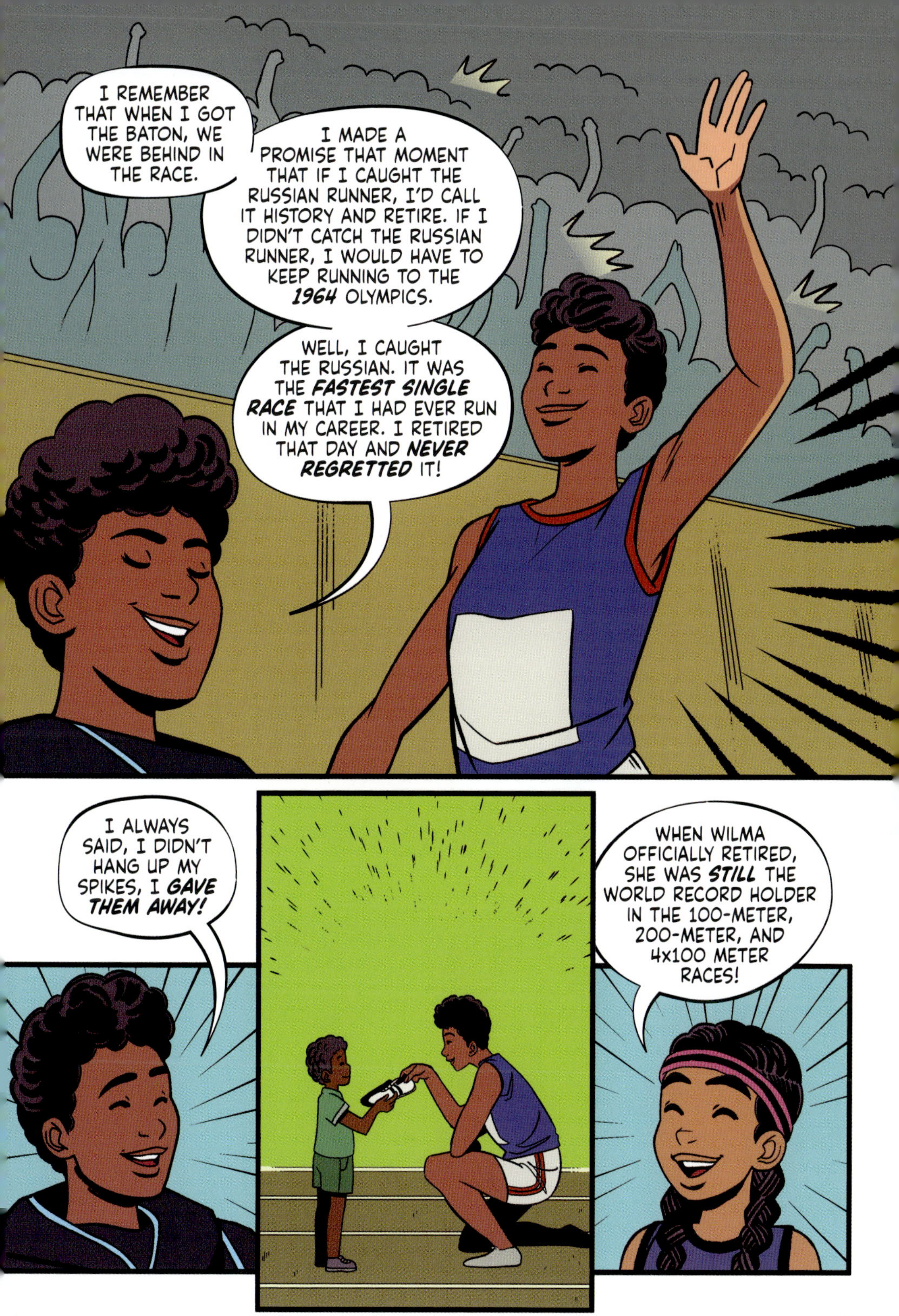
I REMEMBER THAT WHEN I GOT THE BATON, WE WERE BEHIND IN THE RACE.
I MADE A PROMISE THAT MOMENT THAT IF I CAUGHT THE RUSSIAN RUNNER, I'D CALL IT HISTORY AND RETIRE. IF I DIDN'T CATCH THE RUSSIAN RUNNER, I WOULD HAVE TO KEEP RUNNING TO THE *1964* OLYMPICS.
WELL, I CAUGHT THE RUSSIAN. IT WAS THE ***FASTEST SINGLE RACE*** THAT I HAD EVER RUN IN MY CAREER. I RETIRED THAT DAY AND ***NEVER REGRETTED*** IT!
I ALWAYS SAID, I DIDN'T HANG UP MY SPIKES, I ***GAVE THEM AWAY!***
WHEN WILMA OFFICIALLY RETIRED, SHE WAS ***STILL*** THE WORLD RECORD HOLDER IN THE 100-METER, 200-METER, AND 4x100 METER RACES!

CHAPTER TWELVE

ME, US, WE

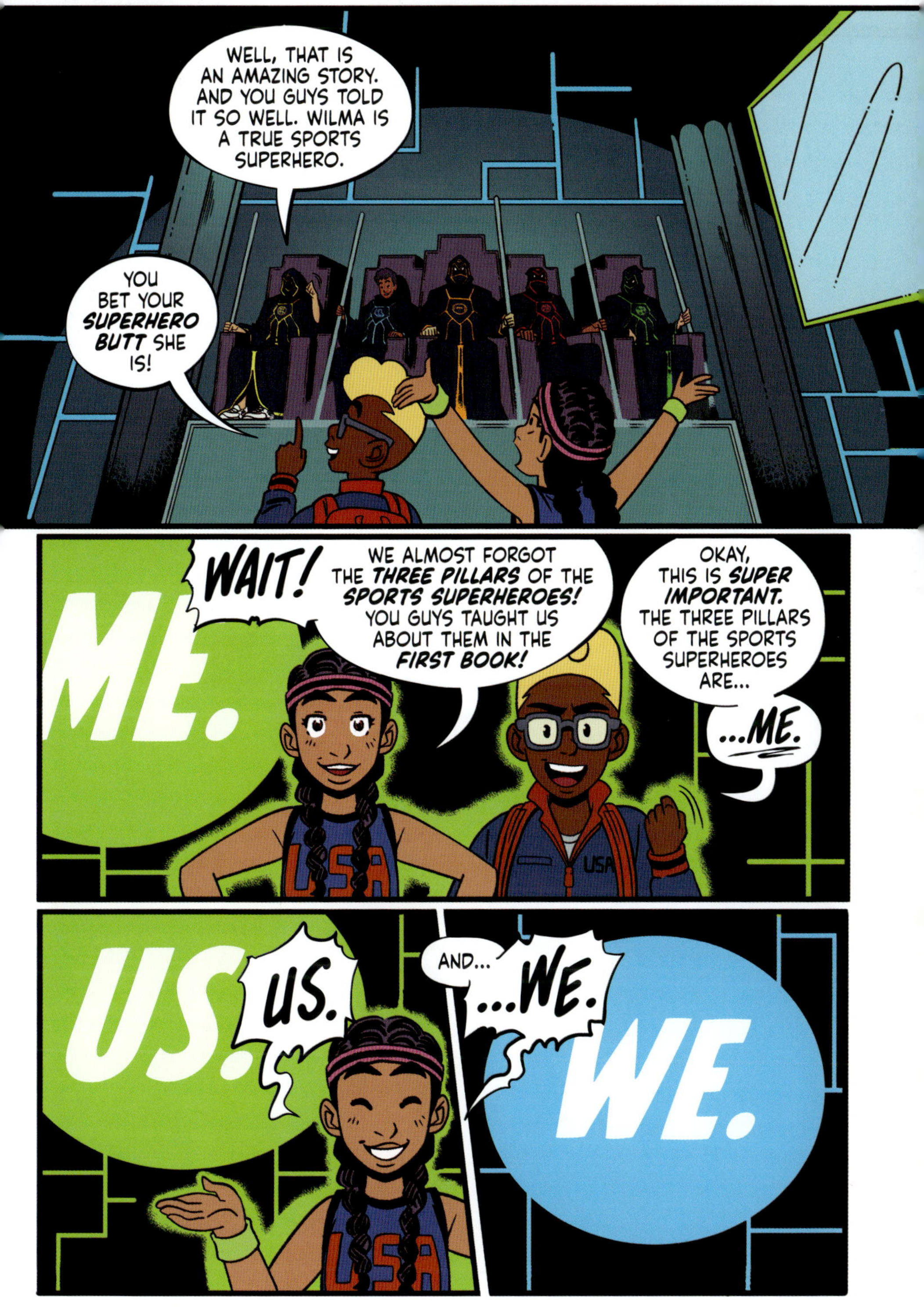
WELL, THAT IS AN AMAZING STORY. AND YOU GUYS TOLD IT SO WELL. WILMA IS A TRUE SPORTS SUPERHERO.
YOU BET YOUR *SUPERHERO BUTT* SHE IS!
WAIT!
WE ALMOST FORGOT THE *THREE PILLARS* OF THE *SPORTS SUPERHEROES!* YOU GUYS TAUGHT US ABOUT THEM IN THE *FIRST BOOK!*
OKAY, THIS IS *SUPER IMPORTANT.* THE THREE PILLARS OF THE SPORTS SUPERHEROES ARE...
...ME.
ME.
US.
US.
AND...
...WE.
WE.

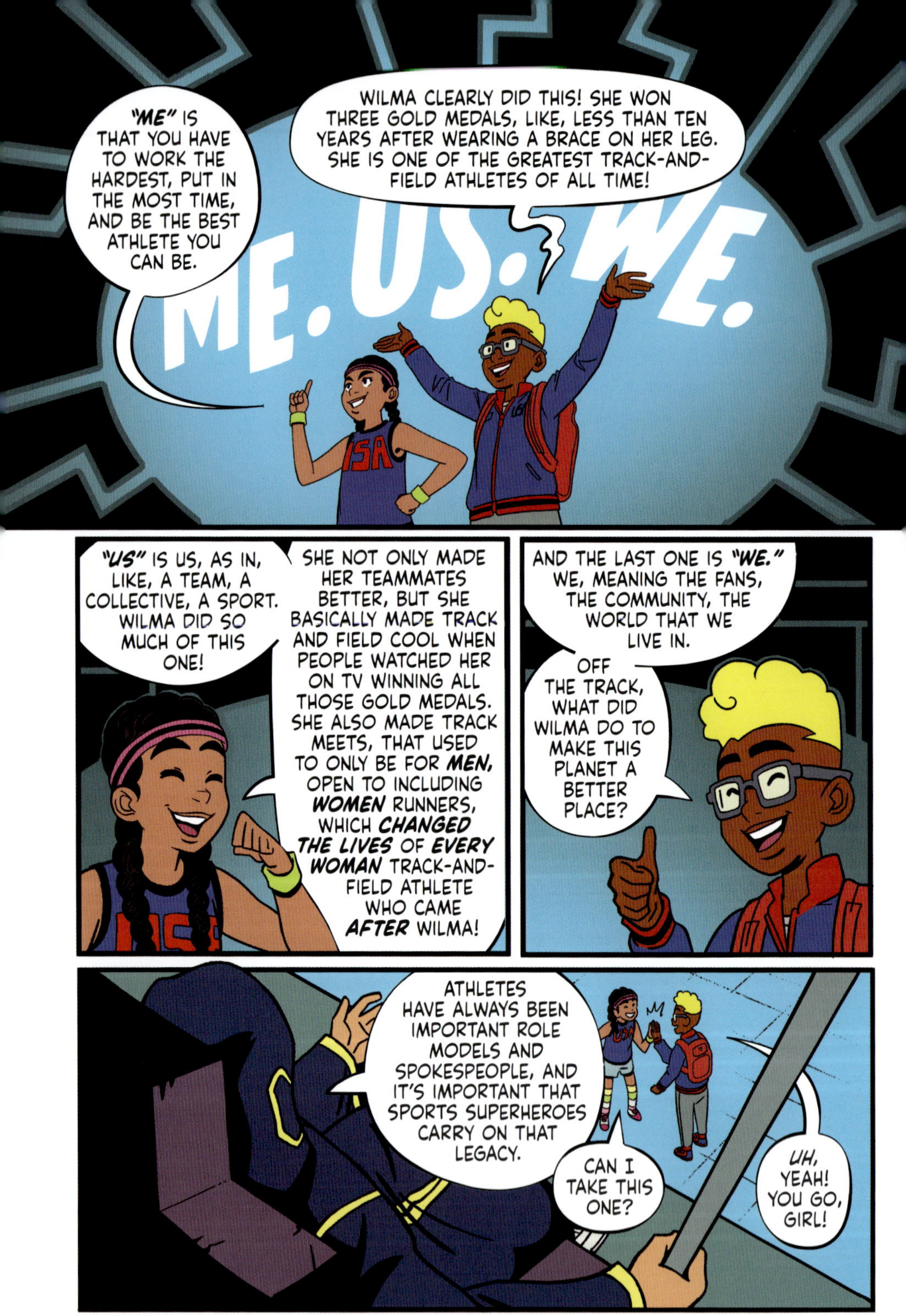
"ME" IS THAT YOU HAVE TO WORK THE HARDEST, PUT IN THE MOST TIME, AND BE THE BEST ATHLETE YOU CAN BE.
WILMA CLEARLY DID THIS! SHE WON THREE GOLD MEDALS, LIKE, LESS THAN TEN YEARS AFTER WEARING A BRACE ON HER LEG. SHE IS ONE OF THE GREATEST TRACK-AND-FIELD ATHLETES OF ALL TIME!
ME. US. WE.
"US" IS US, AS IN, LIKE, A TEAM, A COLLECTIVE, A SPORT. WILMA DID SO MUCH OF THIS ONE!
SHE NOT ONLY MADE HER TEAMMATES BETTER, BUT SHE BASICALLY MADE TRACK AND FIELD COOL WHEN PEOPLE WATCHED HER ON TV WINNING ALL THOSE GOLD MEDALS. SHE ALSO MADE TRACK MEETS, THAT USED TO ONLY BE FOR MEN, OPEN TO INCLUDING WOMEN RUNNERS, WHICH CHANGED THE LIVES OF EVERY WOMAN TRACK-AND-FIELD ATHLETE WHO CAME AFTER WILMA!
AND THE LAST ONE IS "WE." WE, MEANING THE FANS, THE COMMUNITY, THE WORLD THAT WE LIVE IN.
OFF THE TRACK, WHAT DID WILMA DO TO MAKE THIS PLANET A BETTER PLACE?
ATHLETES HAVE ALWAYS BEEN IMPORTANT ROLE MODELS AND SPOKESPEOPLE, AND IT'S IMPORTANT THAT SPORTS SUPERHEROES CARRY ON THAT LEGACY.
CAN I TAKE THIS ONE?
UH, YEAH! YOU GO, GIRL!

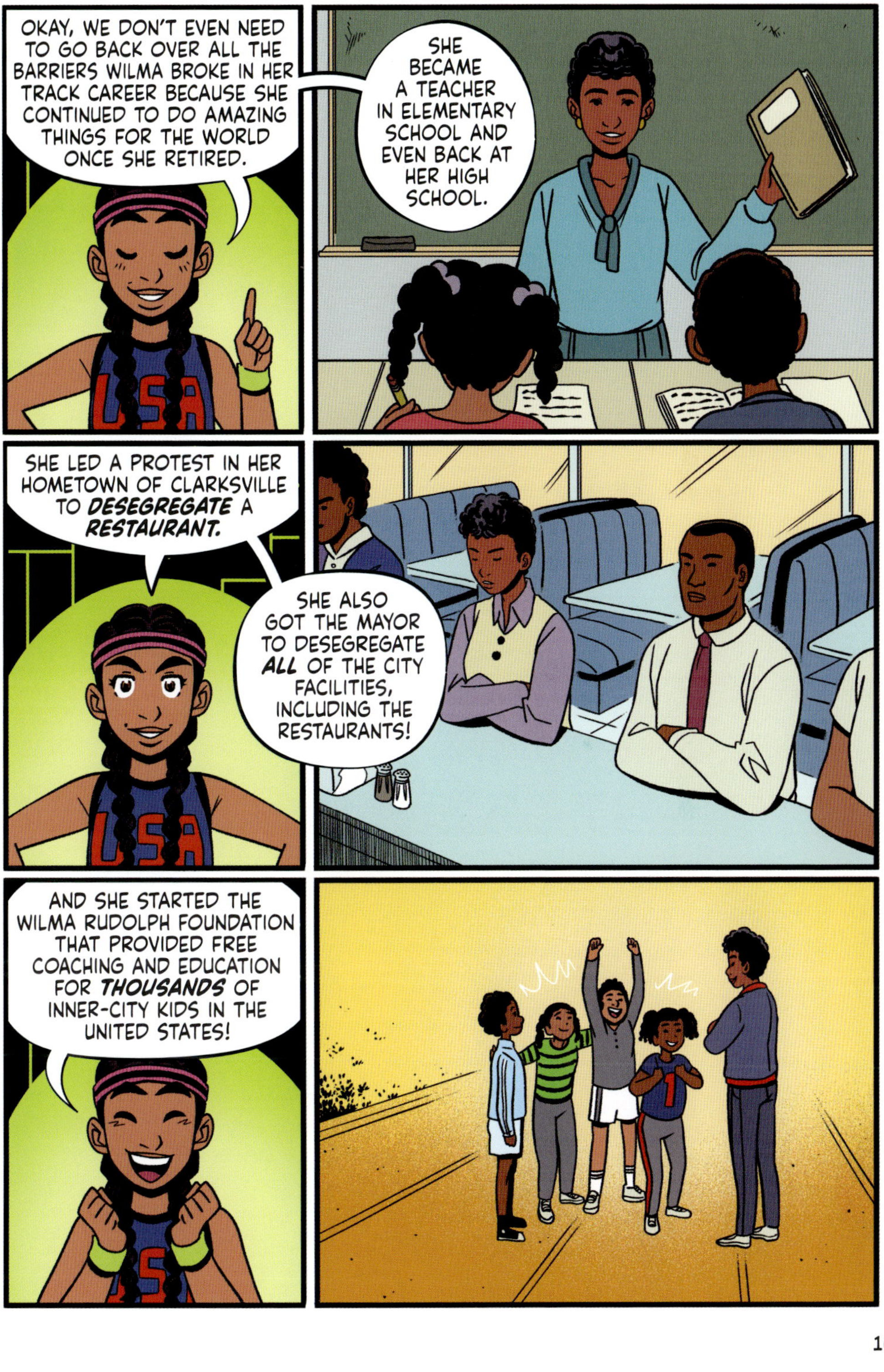
OKAY, WE DON'T EVEN NEED TO GO BACK OVER ALL THE BARRIERS WILMA BROKE IN HER TRACK CAREER BECAUSE SHE CONTINUED TO DO AMAZING THINGS FOR THE WORLD ONCE SHE RETIRED.
SHE BECAME A TEACHER IN ELEMENTARY SCHOOL AND EVEN BACK AT HER HIGH SCHOOL.
SHE LED A PROTEST IN HER HOMETOWN OF CLARKSVILLE TO DESEGREGATE A RESTAURANT.
SHE ALSO GOT THE MAYOR TO DESEGREGATE ALL OF THE CITY FACILITIES, INCLUDING THE RESTAURANTS!
AND SHE STARTED THE WILMA RUDOLPH FOUNDATION THAT PROVIDED FREE COACHING AND EDUCATION FOR THOUSANDS OF INNER-CITY KIDS IN THE UNITED STATES!

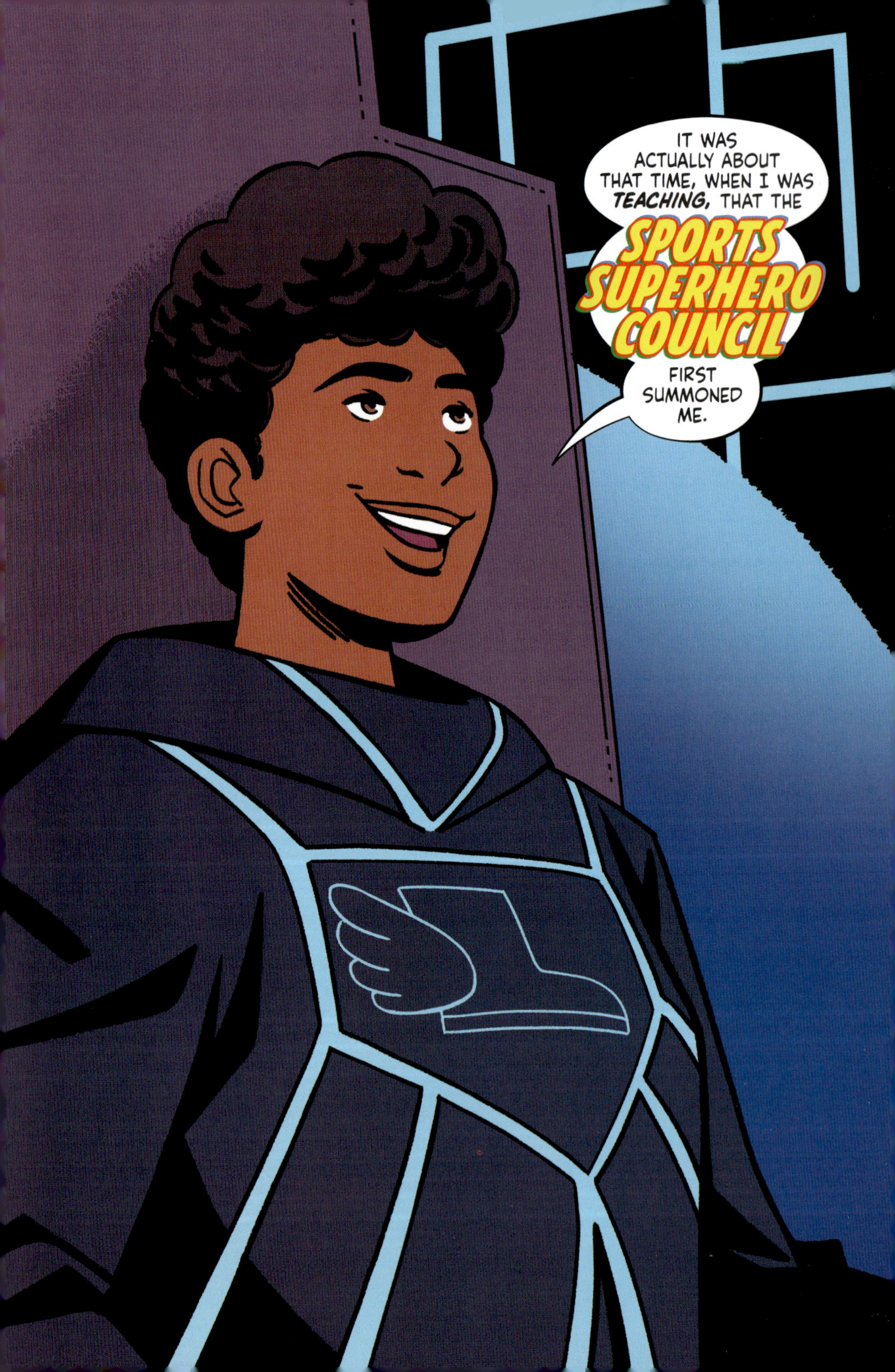
IT WAS ACTUALLY ABOUT THAT TIME, WHEN I WAS *TEACHING,* THAT THE SPORTS SUPERHERO COUNCIL FIRST SUMMONED ME.

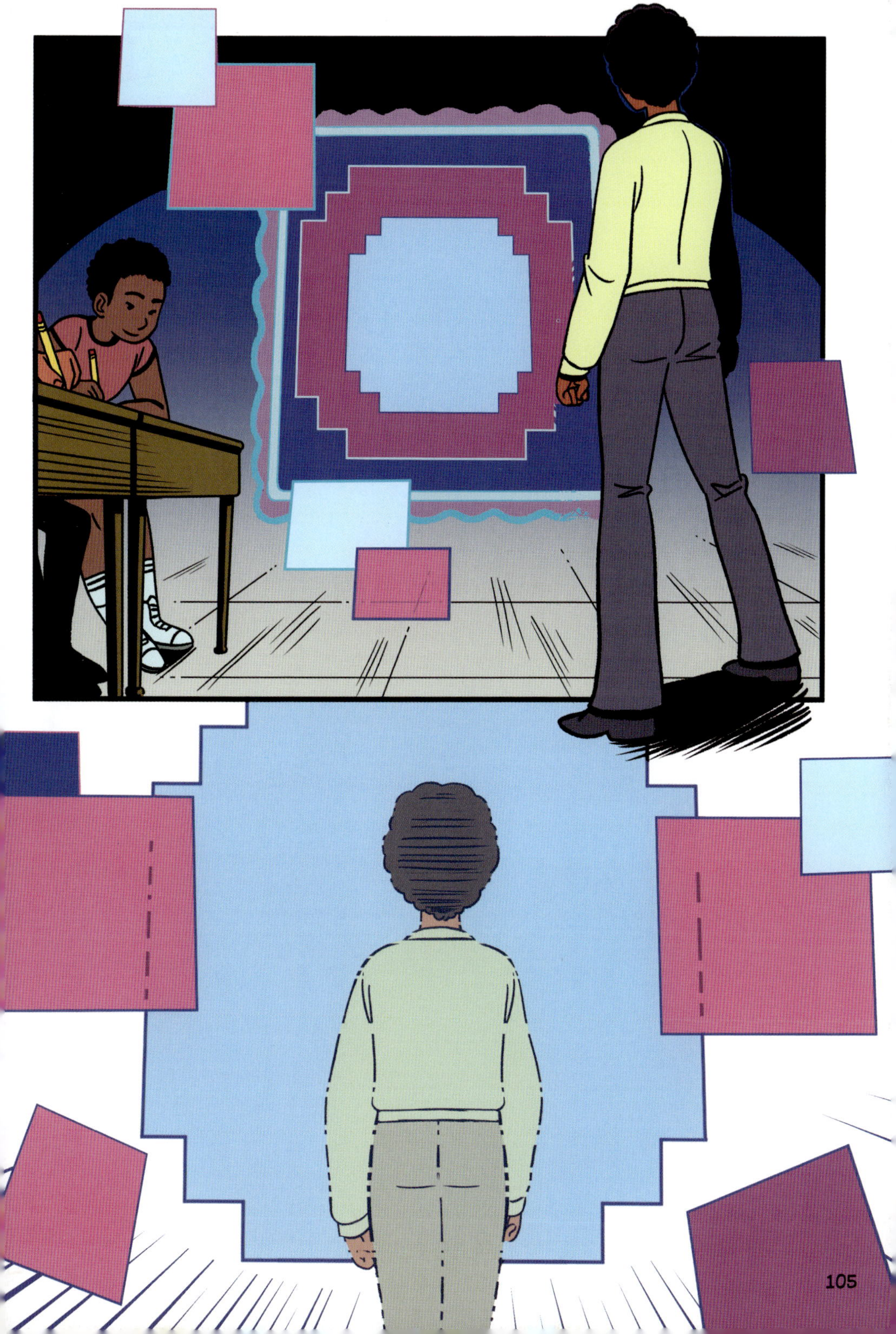

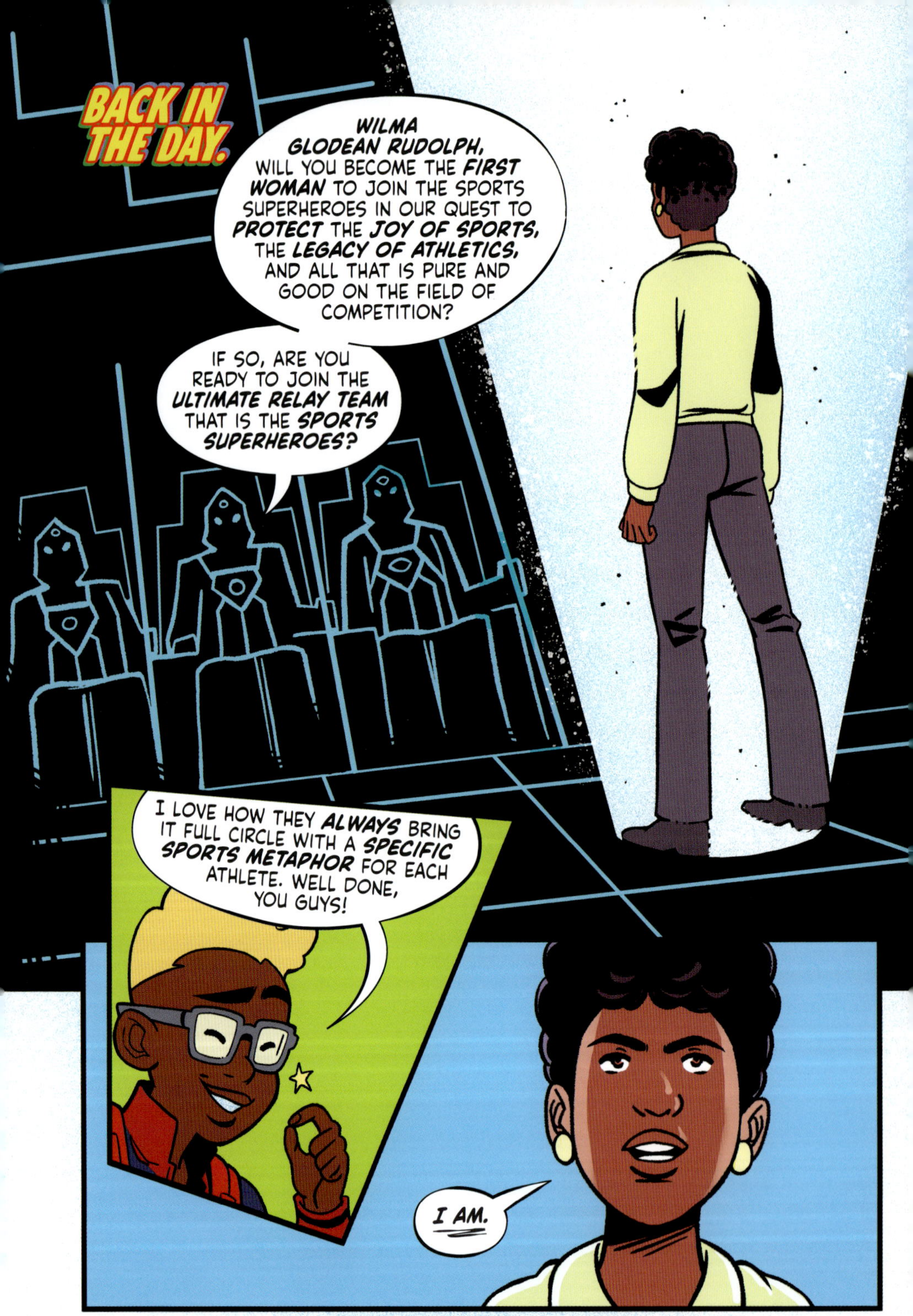
BACK IN THE DAY.
WILMA GLODEAN RUDOLPH, WILL YOU BECOME THE FIRST WOMAN TO JOIN THE SPORTS SUPERHEROES IN OUR QUEST TO PROTECT THE JOY OF SPORTS, THE LEGACY OF ATHLETICS, AND ALL THAT IS PURE AND GOOD ON THE FIELD OF COMPETITION?
IF SO, ARE YOU READY TO JOIN THE ULTIMATE RELAY TEAM THAT IS THE SPORTS SUPERHEROES?
I LOVE HOW THEY ALWAYS BRING IT FULL CIRCLE WITH A SPECIFIC SPORTS METAPHOR FOR EACH ATHLETE. WELL DONE, YOU GUYS!
I AM.

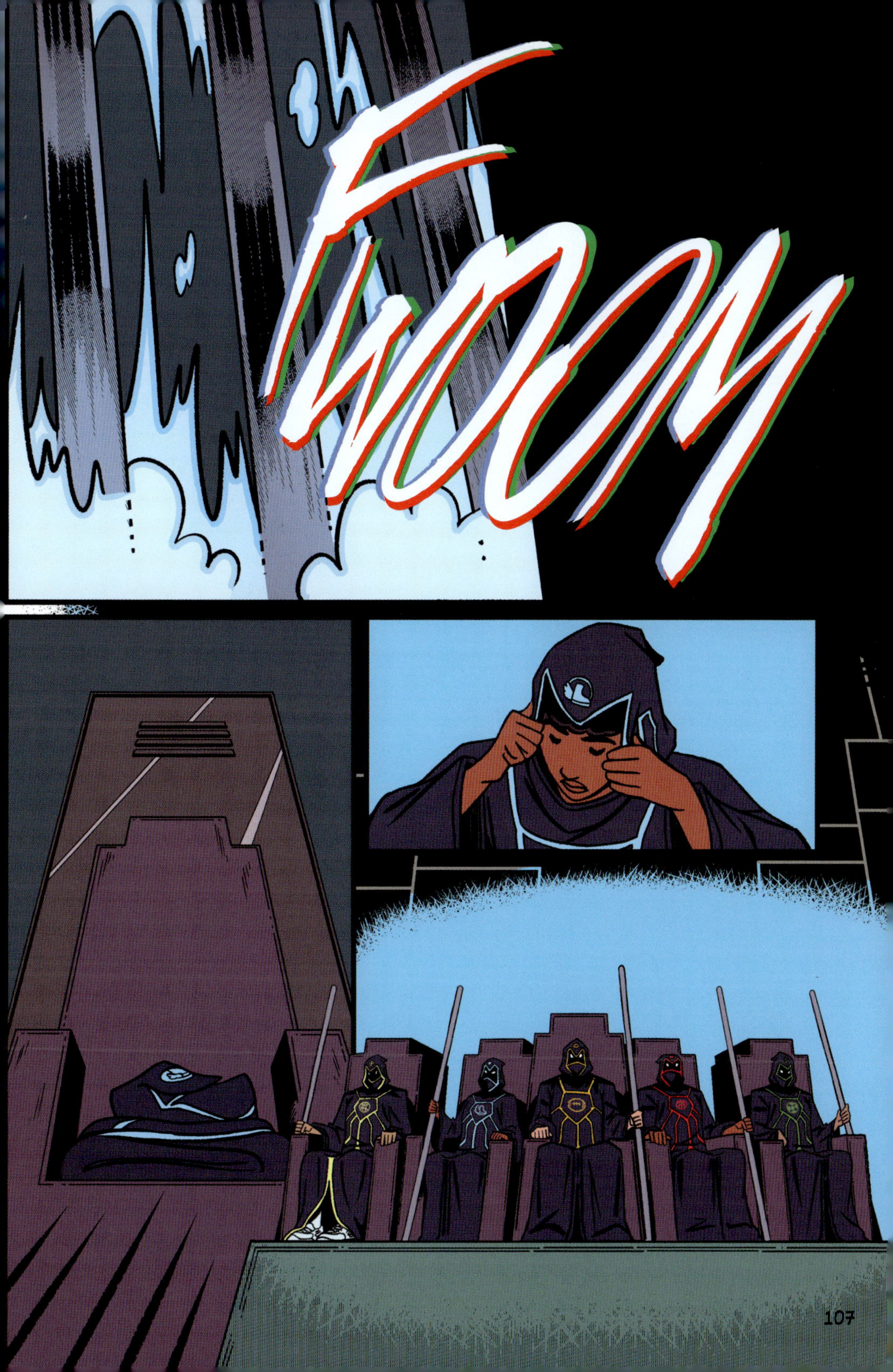
FWOOM

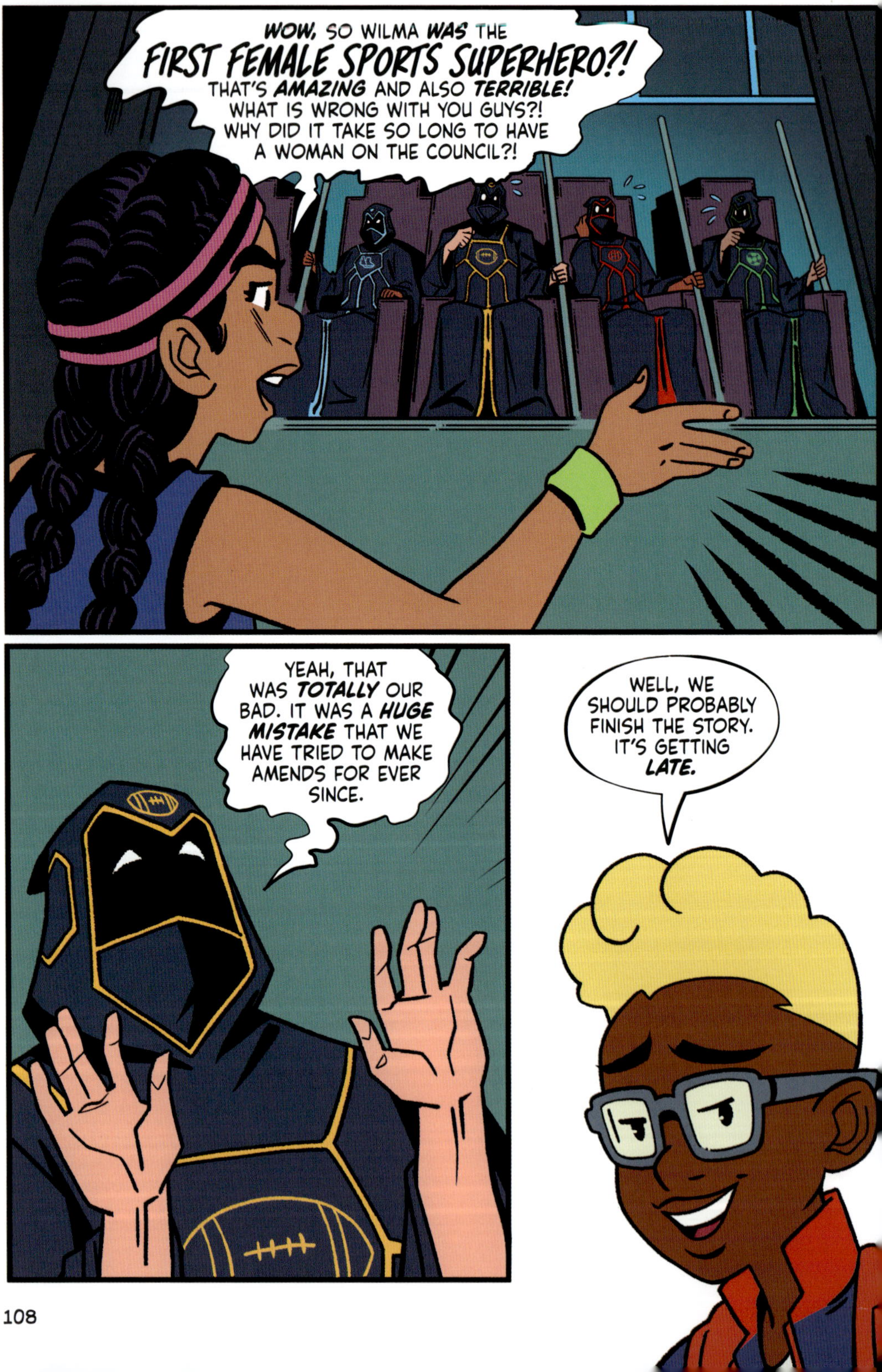
WOW, SO WILMA WAS THE FIRST FEMALE SPORTS SUPERHERO?! THAT'S AMAZING AND ALSO TERRIBLE! WHAT IS WRONG WITH YOU GUYS?! WHY DID IT TAKE SO LONG TO HAVE A WOMAN ON THE COUNCIL?!
YEAH, THAT WAS TOTALLY OUR BAD. IT WAS A HUGE MISTAKE THAT WE HAVE TRIED TO MAKE AMENDS FOR EVER SINCE.
WELL, WE SHOULD PROBABLY FINISH THE STORY. IT'S GETTING LATE.

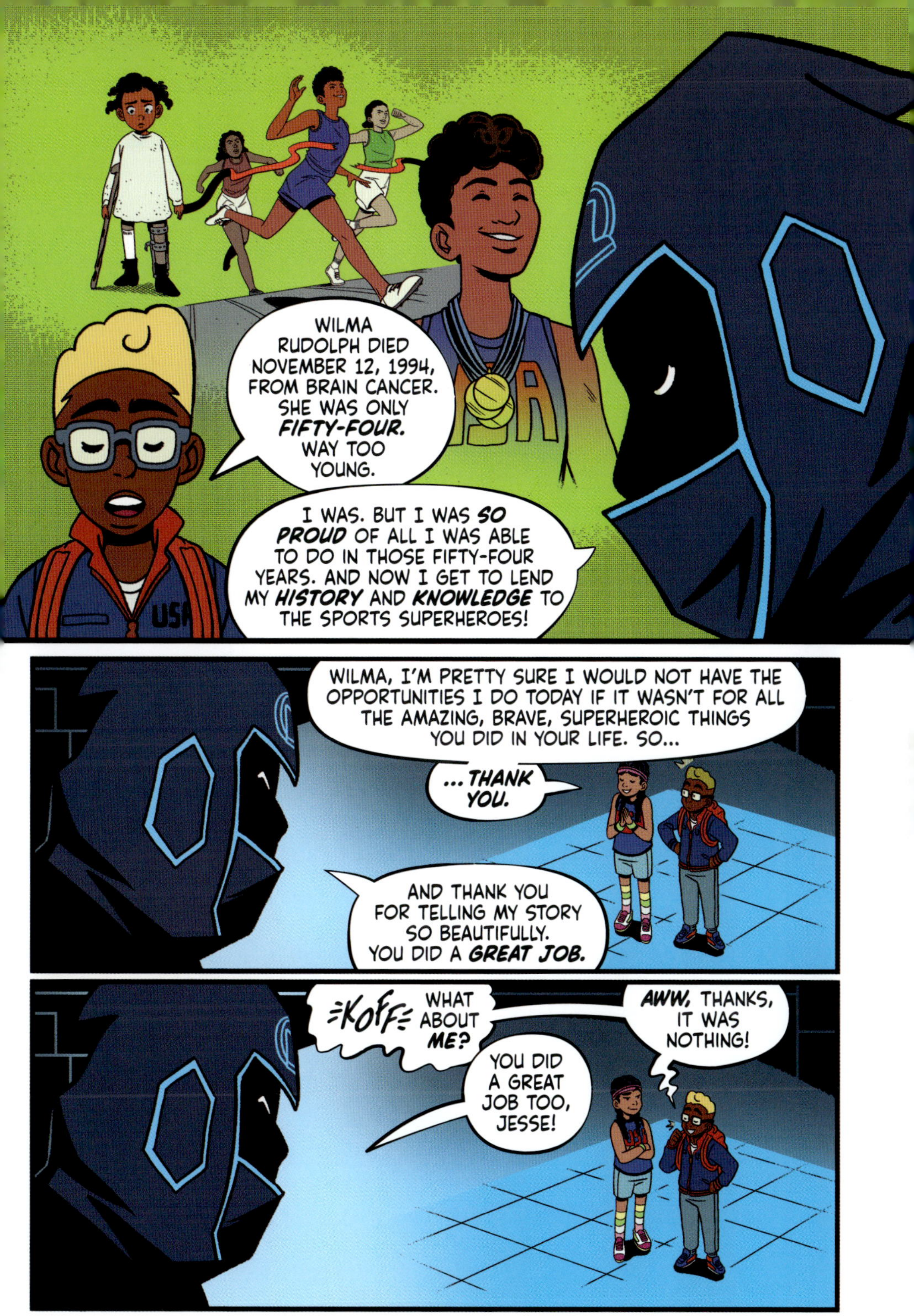
WILMA RUDOLPH DIED NOVEMBER 12, 1994, FROM BRAIN CANCER. SHE WAS ONLY ***FIFTY-FOUR.*** WAY TOO YOUNG.
I WAS. BUT I WAS ***SO PROUD*** OF ALL I WAS ABLE TO DO IN THOSE FIFTY-FOUR YEARS. AND NOW I GET TO LEND MY ***HISTORY*** AND ***KNOWLEDGE*** TO THE SPORTS SUPERHEROES!
WILMA, I'M PRETTY SURE I WOULD NOT HAVE THE OPPORTUNITIES I DO TODAY IF IT WASN'T FOR ALL THE AMAZING, BRAVE, SUPERHEROIC THINGS YOU DID IN YOUR LIFE. SO...
...THANK YOU.
AND THANK YOU FOR TELLING MY STORY SO BEAUTIFULLY. YOU DID A ***GREAT JOB.***
KOFF
WHAT ABOUT ***ME?***
AWW, THANKS, IT WAS NOTHING!
YOU DID A GREAT JOB TOO, JESSE!

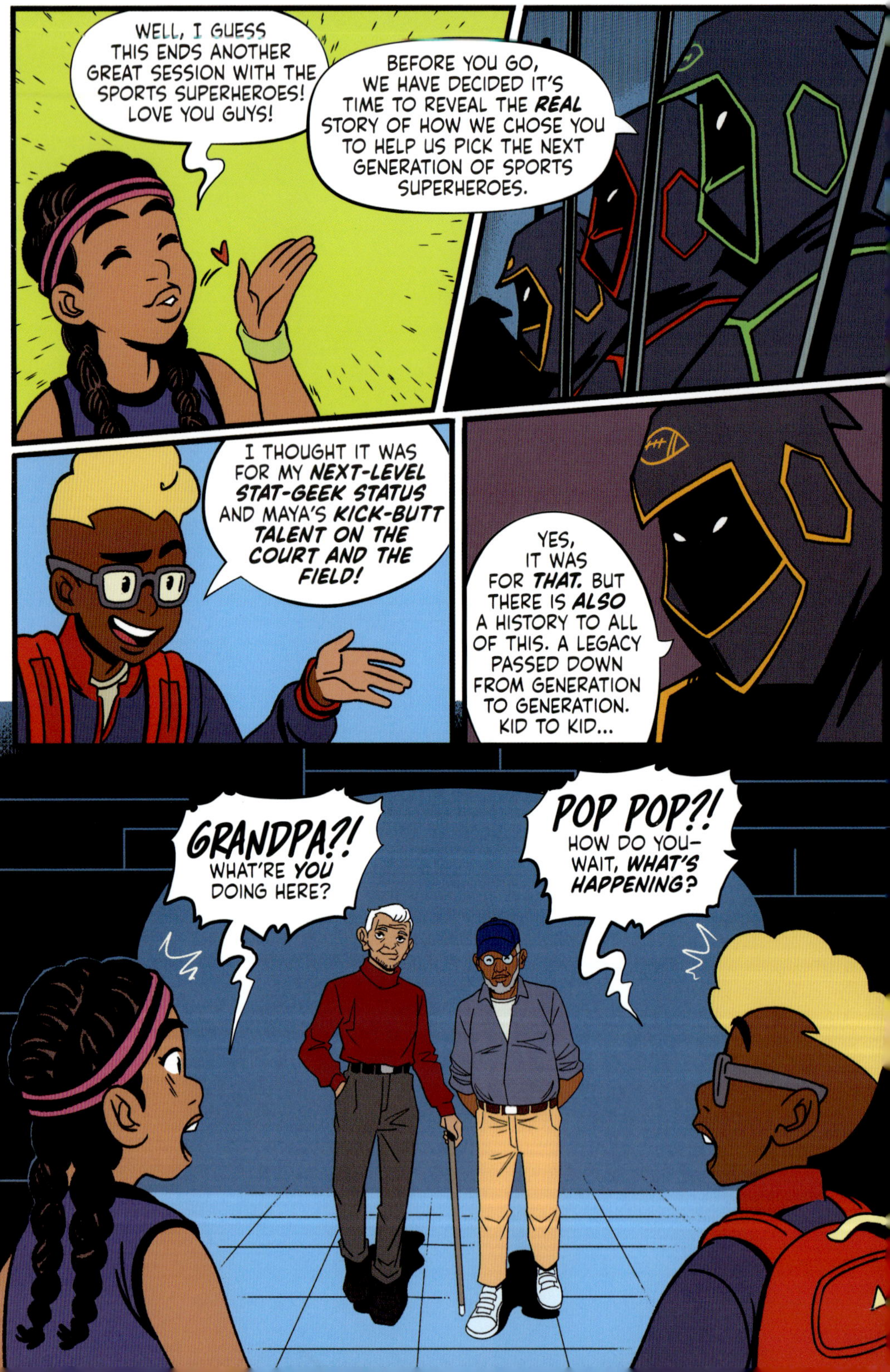
WELL, I GUESS THIS ENDS ANOTHER GREAT SESSION WITH THE SPORTS SUPERHEROES! LOVE YOU GUYS!
BEFORE YOU GO, WE HAVE DECIDED IT'S TIME TO REVEAL THE *REAL* STORY OF HOW WE CHOSE YOU TO HELP US PICK THE NEXT GENERATION OF SPORTS SUPERHEROES.
I THOUGHT IT WAS FOR MY ***NEXT-LEVEL STAT-GEEK STATUS*** AND MAYA'S ***KICK-BUTT TALENT ON THE COURT AND THE FIELD!***
YES, IT WAS FOR ***THAT.*** BUT THERE IS ***ALSO*** A HISTORY TO ALL OF THIS. A LEGACY PASSED DOWN FROM GENERATION TO GENERATION. KID TO KID...
GRANDPA?! WHAT'RE ***YOU*** DOING HERE?
POP POP?! HOW DO YOU— WAIT, ***WHAT'S HAPPENING?***

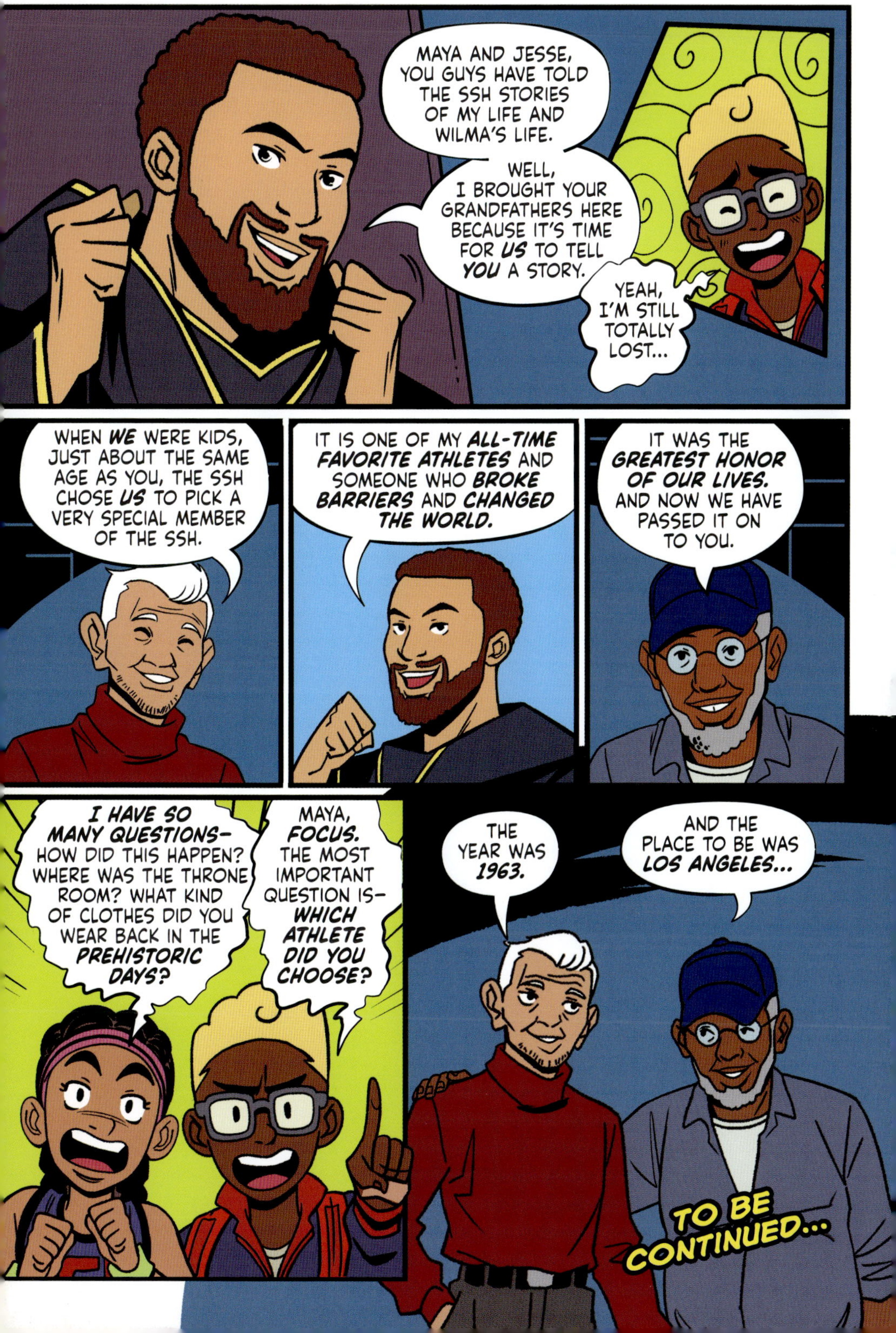
MAYA AND JESSE, YOU GUYS HAVE TOLD THE SSH STORIES OF MY LIFE AND WILMA'S LIFE.
WELL, I BROUGHT YOUR GRANDFATHERS HERE BECAUSE IT'S TIME FOR US TO TELL YOU A STORY.
YEAH, I'M STILL TOTALLY LOST...
WHEN WE WERE KIDS, JUST ABOUT THE SAME AGE AS YOU, THE SSH CHOSE US TO PICK A VERY SPECIAL MEMBER OF THE SSH.
IT IS ONE OF MY ALL-TIME FAVORITE ATHLETES AND SOMEONE WHO BROKE BARRIERS AND CHANGED THE WORLD.
IT WAS THE GREATEST HONOR OF OUR LIVES. AND NOW WE HAVE PASSED IT ON TO YOU.
I HAVE SO MANY QUESTIONS– HOW DID THIS HAPPEN? WHERE WAS THE THRONE ROOM? WHAT KIND OF CLOTHES DID YOU WEAR BACK IN THE PREHISTORIC DAYS?
MAYA, FOCUS. THE MOST IMPORTANT QUESTION IS– WHICH ATHLETE DID YOU CHOOSE?
THE YEAR WAS 1963.
AND THE PLACE TO BE WAS LOS ANGELES...
TO BE CONTINUED...

NEXT AT BAT...

STEPHEN CURRY PRESENTS!
SPORTS SUPERHEROES
VOL. #3
JACKIE ROBINSON

THE GRAPHIC NOVEL